IDEAS THAT ARE CHANGING THE WORLD

LEADING SOCIAL ENTREPRENEURS

2200 Wilson Blvd. Suite 102, Unit 313 Arlington, VA 22201 USA
Tel. (703) 527-8300 | Fax. (703) 527-8383
www.ashoka.org | www.changemakers.com

TABLE OF CONTENTS

ACKNOWLEDGMENTS & CREDITS

Many people contributed in many different ways to the completion of this year's LSE, and we are most grateful for their efforts.

- **Managing Editor:** Graham Everett
- **Campaigns Credit:** Michelle Moyes
- **Copy Editors:** Steve Kent, Karyn Kessler, Paul Rogers
- **Creative Director:** Edward Edilbi
- **Contributors:** Menno Moffit de Block, Avantika Jain Nadine Freeman, Maria Merola, Amy Clark, Leora Lihach, Celia Sanchez Valladares, Maria Cerdio, Constanza Astiarazan, Ovidiu Condurache, Santi Del Guidice, Dadisai Taderera, David Bonbright, Shruti Nair. Special Thanks: Cory Schutter.
- **Digital Content Manager (LSE Microsite):** Michelle Moyes and Mariana Sauna
- **Concept, Design, and Production:** The Creative Studio - Ashoka's In-house Creative Agency (Concept and design Edward Edilbi - Co-designers: Sima Nasr and Mariana Sauna - Account Manager Michelle Moyes)

ISBN-979-8-9873943-0-4; Leading Social Entrepreneurs, 2022 Edition.

This publication was printed by More Vang on a stock certified by the Forest Stewardship Council®.

FRONT COVER

Jagdeesh Rao Puppala

Ashoka Fellow from India
CEO, Foundation for Ecological Security

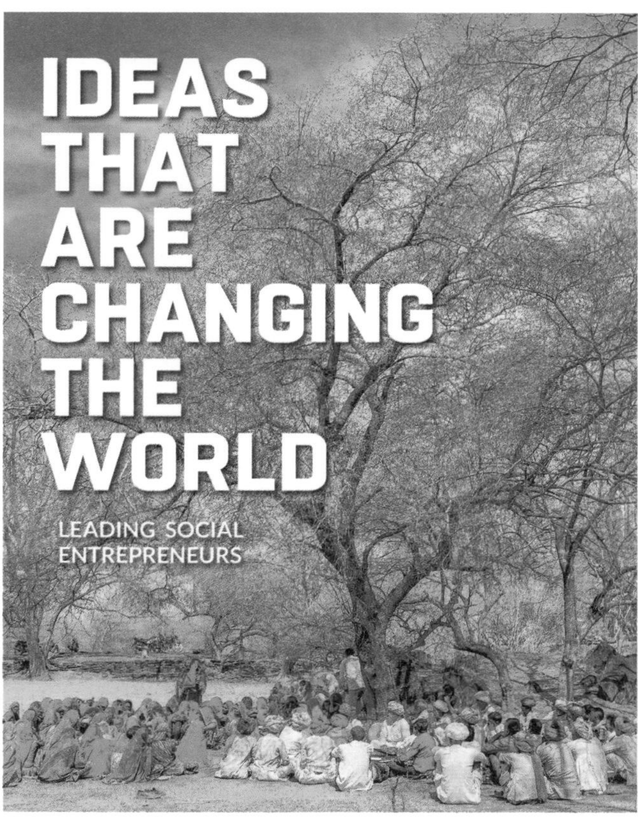

Photo Credit by: Jagdeesh Rao Puppala

TREES DON'T VOTE

Neither does groundwater or grazing lands.

In other words, if these dimensions of the environment are to survive, let alone prosper, people have to want this and act intelligently, with energy, and steadily long into the future. Only people vote.

Most critical are the millions of people who live in and/or depend on the forests, the groundwater, the grazing lands. Ashoka Fellows across the world understand this. Indeed, it is their entrepreneurial genius and relentless drive that is showing how to make this natural alliance work.

Local villagers don't have a global corporate staff that enables them to understand their changing circumstances and to create new options. The Fellows both create new opportunities where the interests of nature and humans are synergistic and help the people see these new possibilities, learn the science/technology/economics, and organize.

This book has two examples: Jagdeesh Rao Puppala (p. 108) of India and Carlos Nobre of Brazil (p. 120). This book's cover shows a village meeting where, helped by Jagdeesh's organization, the community is thinking through how best to manage the commons they now control.

Jagdeesh begins with full respect for the intelligence and local ecosystem knowledge of the villagers.

He helps them (1) gain legal control over the commons (e.g., local forest land); (2) gain access to the relevant science (e.g., soil types, ecological tipping points) rendered usable (including language); and (3) organize. Adapted to each cluster of villages, Jagdeesh has built all-India (and beyond) data sets, subject by subject information and training materials, and local colleges that strengthen community leaders. He has worked with 36,407 villages in ten eco-regions of India, restoring 11.38 million acres of common lands and enriching the lives of 22 million people. With the approach proven, backup structures working, and others ready to follow, these impacts now will multiply quickly.

One of Ashoka's special powers is that, in every key area of need, it has hundreds of Fellows whose entirely independent entrepreneurial creations are in fact hugely synergistic. Ashoka creates the network effect of collaboration. Carlos is creating a series of new classes of business for residents of Brazil's Amazon that both enrich their lives and make them value the forest more. A colleague has turned destructive illegal loggers into sustainable foresters managing huge areas across Indonesia. Imagine the power of these and many others Fellows in the area connecting. This is what gives trees real power.

OVERVIEW, MAP, AND INVITATION

Ashoka: *Everyone* a Changemaker catalyzes a global community that is leading the *Everyone* a Changemaker (EACH) movement. We now live in an everything-changing world. This fact requires everyone to be able to contribute to and adapt to change; i.e., to be a changemaker. This requires mastering four abilities: cognitive empathy-based living for the good of all; working in multiple, complex, and ever morphing networks; new leadership; and changemaking. There is a bidding war for those with these skills, certainly no job scarcity. However, the other forty percent who do not have these skills can't contribute in the new game. They face the grim reality of "go away, we don't need you; it's your fault; and your kids have no future." This leads to depression and straight on to permanent fury and then the "us versus them" politics that has swept across the world in barely eight years. This is "the new inequality." Allowing it to continue is unethical and hugely harmful. The Ashoka community, centrally including the Ashoka Fellows, is committed to "the right to give".

Ashoka uses a rigorous, highly-refined, five-step process to identify the most important emerging social change ideas and the entrepreneurs behind them who, together, will redefine their fields, be it human rights or the environment or any other area of human need. This process which finds the Ashoka Fellows focuses sharply on five key criteria:

- A big, pattern-setting new idea
- Creativity in both goal setting and problem solving
- Entrepreneurial quality
- The social impact of the new idea
- Ethical fiber

Once Fellows are elected, Ashoka makes sure that they have the support and full freedom—including the ability to work full-time—they need to launch their visions and succeed. This includes providing a launch stipend to the degree it is needed for an average of three years, organizing a wide range of high-leverage supports, and—most importantly—engaging them in a local-to-global collaborative community of their peers. This community, in addition to Fellows, includes equally carefully chosen (with parallel criteria) Ashoka Young Changemakers, E-2s, and staff.

Increasingly, the Ashoka community works through purpose teams. Its open source global/local search for the best big new visions and social entrepreneurs spots cross-cutting needs and therefore purposes. Its members' solutions lead quickly to solution patterns and then on to defining the new architecture that society needs. Then Ashoka helps the top quality mega-players (e.g., unions, companies, universities) change their core strategies to help those they serve see and navigate their need to transition to *Everyone* changemaking. The alliance between the Ashoka community and these "jujitsu" partners and organized metro areas is a methodological game changer that now allows the purpose teams to quickly and reliably get societies to jump to new frameworks and patterns.

The following pages will introduce some of the recently elected Ashoka Fellows in a diversity of fields and geographies. Each allows you to see, through a great entrepreneur's eyes, how the world will be different in five or so years. Three quarters of newly elected Ashoka Fellows change the patterns in their field at the national and/or international level five to ten years after their election. You will also find the ideas and stories of a few Senior Fellows. They are elected later in their careers, do not get financial support, but contribute to and benefit from Ashoka's Purpose Teams and community.

The book's final sections will introduce you to Ashoka Young Changemakers – and how they work with the mega jujitsu partners. Here you'll also find introductions to the endowments, opportunities to join, and insights into the organization and movement.

Ashoka invites you to join us to help co-lead in the "*everyone* a changemaker" movement. We are social entrepreneurs, young changemakers, and change leaders across sectors who have come together to bring this essential new framework to our communities, businesses, schools, and neighborhoods.

What could be more historic or satisfying?

WE ARE FINALLY ENTERING THE TURNING POINT YEARS

A Conversation with Bill Drayton, Author of "Changemaker" and "Social Entrepreneur"

What is your greatest power? It is that, in any situation you can recognize its problems and opportunities and envision how to fix problems and how to create something better. And you are practiced at taking that idea, building the necessary teams, and making it your worlds new, better reality. In other words, you are a changemaker. That's what allows you to be a giver, and that's what brings health, longevity, and happiness.

In our world, where change and interconnectedness are both accelerating faster and faster, your changemaking power is very fast becoming ever more essential.

Try to imagine (you'll have to stretch) what life is like now for the roughly forty percent of your fellow humans who don't have this power, who therefore more and more can't contribute, who increasingly feel they are failures. It's bitter. It's also unethical because we could easily help them (and their kids) master the lifegiving changemaking superpower.

Because we haven't committed to building an *everyone* a changemaker, everyone a giver society, the world is increasingly paralyzed by bitter rage and division.

> *Ashoka has...finally succeeded in winning over the critical one percent early adopters*

The first step is to see the problem. This requires us all to put on new eyeglasses, to see the world through a new framework.

Ashoka's central purpose, its core objective from its start four decades ago, has been and is to engineer precisely this framework change.

The work started with building and spreading the construct of "social entrepreneurship". That construct gives us all a new category of life possibility. Every Ashoka Fellow is a role model. And they spread their new ideas by recruiting local changemakers and helping them succeed.

The "*everyone* a changemaker" (EACH) movement that Ashoka has long been building has, over the last half dozen years, finally succeeded in winning over the critical one percent early adopters. (One indicator is the breakthrough use of the word "changemaker"—created by Ashoka in the spring of 1981 – over these few years.)

The world is now shifting gears and moving into the turning point years. This is when the next eighty percent, over probably five years plus or minus, change how they see the world and go to work to make the hundreds of changes they now must – in all aspects of their lives.

Recently, Ashoka founder Bill Drayton was interviewed by an Indian professional journal. Its questions and answers give both a succinct historical overview and practical insights that you can put to use in any organization about which you care. A copy of the conversation follows.

A CONVERSATION WITH BILL DRAYTON

In this freewheeling conversation, Bill Drayton emphasizes that everyone has the right, and ability, to be a giver. And in today's world where everything is changing, everybody can, and must, be a changemaker.

By Smarinita Shetty, Sneha Phili

Bill Drayton is a pioneering force in the field of social entrepreneurship. He's the founder and CEO of Ashoka: Innovators for the Public, which he launched in 1980 to find, nurture, and support social entrepreneurs. Over the last four decades, Ashoka's community of social entrepreneurs and changemakers has grown into a global network of individuals that strive to solve some of society's toughest challenges. Bill is a MacArthur Fellow and has received many awards for his contribution to social innovation and change.

Over the last 40 years, through your own work and that of Ashoka Fellows, you've had the privilege of seeing the world change. What is different about social entrepreneurship today versus when you set up Ashoka four decades ago?

Back when we got started in the 1980s, we had to invent words to describe the new world of social entrepreneurship whose birth we were helping. We were sitting at Nariman Point, in what was then called Bombay, and struggling with naming the idea. We first created the broader concept and name: changemaker. This was easy—just take the two strong verbs 'change' and 'make' and put them together. However, we needed a different phrase to describe the small number of changemakers who redefine or create society's big systems. After some trial and error, we ultimately settled on 'social entrepreneur'.

The word 'entrepreneur' tended to be synonymous with business, at least historically up to that point. However, around the late 1970s and early 1980s, the citizen sector was beginning to become entrepreneurial and competitive in the same way that business had been for several centuries. The citizen sector was also beginning to break free from being funded by, controlled by, and prohibited from being competitive by, the government. And India was one of the first places where a significant number of first-generation social entrepreneurs stood up and set out to change the world for good.

Today, the big difference is that the construct of social entrepreneur is part of everyday thinking and language. And just think about what that means. People can look at these entrepreneurs and think: If she can do this, and such work is practical, and she's being respected for it, then that's an opportunity for me; it could be an option for my life. So, the first step was to introduce the construct of social entrepreneurship everywhere in the world. Social entrepreneurs are people who can change major patterns or systems of thinking and acting. They have a vision, pull people together, multiply, and scale impact.

The second construct is what we are working on now: *everyone* a changemaker. You and I want everyone to have a good life. But one cannot have a good life if one cannot give. And to be able to give, one must be able to play in today's everything-changing and everything-connected new (and only) reality. So, the biggest change is that we understand that consciously.

Very few people are going to change society's big patterns. The difference between a social entrepreneur and a changemaker is that an entrepreneur changes major systems and/or frameworks of thinking on a large scale. But everybody can and has to be a changemaker. Change is need everywhere. Saying that out loud and actually working on it is the second big change for us at Ashoka. The Ashoka Fellows remain critical to this new thinking and this work.

So, we have an open-source system to find the best big pattern-change ideas for good in the hands of the best social entrepreneurs. Nothing has changed about that. But with that we are also able to spot where there's a whole group of new people and ideas coming up (recent examples are good tech and climate). In each such area, we then map and plan and then entrepreneur together to achieve maximum impact.

Both of the first major framework changes that we've been working on deal with livelihoods. Because if you can't contribute to change, in a world defined by everything changing (and yet connected), then you are not going to have a livelihood. This new reality is the complete opposite of the old world, where jobs were characterized by repetition. Those old jobs are dying. But if you are a changemaker, there is no job shortage; indeed, there is ever-burgeoning demand for you.

Societies everywhere are increasingly divided into the people who have the abilities that this explosively growing new world demands and those who do not. The demand for the former significantly exceeds supply, which is why the salaries and incomes of that group are going up. But then you have a large population that isn't able to play in this new game. Their jobs are in a precipitous death dive, as are their incomes and sense of belonging.

And we are at a stage of history where if you're not a changemaker, your livelihood, your satisfaction, your ability to contribute in any dimension of life are all in free fall. And, as a result, societies all over the world are divided and angry and therefore unable to deal with their problems. If you do not allow people to have the ability and power to give— which is the most fundamental right if you think about it—where are they in life? This power to give is linked to livelihoods, which is a far more accurate way to look at the field than mere jobs.

A lot that has changed as a result of the pandemic and the climate emergency and growing inequality. These are huge challenges. In India, we're seeing increasing unemployment as well. What needs to be

done differently to be able to solve the challenge of livelihoods in the context of all these other challenges that we face?

The areas your question talks about are several examples of a world where everything is changing faster and faster. For people like us change is the norm; it's comfortable, and we know what to do. We know how to put ourselves together with all sorts of combinations of people. We are part of not just one but many such teams. We help one another get better at it.

Now, imagine what it's like if you're not part of this team-of-teams world. Life is not going to go well for you. Those who already have the power to give must realize it is critical that they help everyone else be the best possible players, because otherwise neither their team nor society is going to do very well.

"

The right to give, to have the ability to give, is the most fundamental right.

The right to give, to have the ability to give, is the most fundamental right. The biggest gift is giving other people the gift of being able to give. And that's what every member of the team in a fast-changing, everyone-connected world requires. There is no ambiguity about this—it brings health, happiness, and longevity. And in all the great philosophic traditions, you can't practice love and respect in action if you don't have the abilities to give.

COVID-19, the climate crisis, and other changes are only going to get bigger, grow faster, and become more and more interconnected. Unable to play or contribute, you are a failure. Just think about that. We've got maybe 40 percent of the world's population that thinks they are failures. They know that there's less and less demand for them, and that things aren't going to be very good for their kids either.

I don't have the statistics for India, but in the US, when you compare the counties with little changemaking with those that are strong on changemaking, the low changemaking counties have lost four years of life expectancy in one generation. That's only one of the costs of not having the abilities to contribute.

Changemaking is the new literacy

How do you define counties that are changemaking versus those that are not? And what is the role of business in adopting this concept?

One simple measure is the proportion of the jobs that are repetitive. If you've got a significant proportion of repetitive jobs, your economy is going down fast, because those jobs are going away. Moreover, you've got a population that doesn't have the ability to play the new game, so no one brings the new jobs there because the people can't fill them. And so you have an accelerating downward spiral.

Now let's think about businesses for a moment. Your business is not going to succeed if you don't help all your workers become changemakers. The CEO of a large (5,000 employees), successful company in the US recently told me that his whole business system could be under threat from anyone. He therefore needs everybody in his organization to be looking for possibilities and threats all the time. He estimated that 10 or 15 of his people might spot such an environmental change, clearly not enough to survive in a rapidly changing world. He came to Ashoka for help because he knew he needed everyone in his company to be thinking like those 10 to 15 people. He is unusual in that he could see and articulate the problem. The answer to his—and other business leaders'—problem is that everyone needs to be a changemaker in their organizations. It's not just a matter of ethics, of being fair to your employees, but also of survival. Companies that are not everyone-a-changemaker organizations are in big trouble. And they're going to get into more trouble as the rate of change and interconnection keeps getting faster. Perhaps your company has been able to get by for a while because everyone else is behaving in the old way. But as that stops being the case, you are on thin ice.

If you want to move ahead, well, you should be able to see and understand this new everything-changing world. And you've got to have all your people be able to see it and play in it. You've got to organize as a fluid, open, integrated, purposive team of teams. And if you don't do that, changemakers won't work with you. Those two things go together.

WHAT GIVES YOU HOPE FOR THE NEXT GENERATION?

When you talk to anyone who has the gift of being able to give, they have a good life and they're helping other people have that gift. When you imagine what the world is going to be like when everyone is a giver, and everyone is helping others be ever more powerful givers, that is a completely coherent world. And it's very close to the traditional South Asian view of the purpose of life—it is about being one with the universe. That's the highest level of empathy.

Development has always been about how to help people be powerful. So, if we're all helping one another be the best possible changemakers, that is, givers, that's a pretty good world. Everyone has the ability. Everyone has that right. We just have to link arms and make sure that everyone does get that right. Because otherwise we're going to suffer a rapidly deepening 'new inequality'. That means society's divisions will get worse. As will our ability to deal with COVID-19, climate change, income inequality, and so on.

Changemaking is the new literacy. It is the new reality.

THE UNLONELY PLANET (2022):

HOW ASHOKA FELLOWS ACCELERATE AN EVERYONE A CHANGEMAKER WORLD.

This report presented an opportunity to deeply reflect on Ashoka's history, our evolution to our *everyone* a Changemaker vision, and how this vision meets the very moment we are in.

For forty years, Ashoka has been supporting social entrepreneurs, listening to their stories, and watching them drive social change. Our first theory of change held that there was no more powerful force for societal transformation than a system-changing idea in the hands of a social entrepreneur. While this theory of change still holds true; it has expanded.

Twenty years in, as we asked where social entrepreneurship was headed, we paid close attention to the way in which Fellows worked. We saw quite simply, but with profound effect, that they were helping many others to become changemakers. Their inclusive approach to changemaking not only hastens the pace at which Fellows can shift whole systems, but it creates the groundswell needed for societal transformation for the good of all: our *Everyone* A Changemaker theory of change and EACH movement.

This report is not about systems change nor is it about creating changemakers one at a time. It is about a shift in worldview. It is about a new reality that is unquestionably clear; namely, that the prosperity of society hinges on our ability to operate as a global community that builds better outcomes for all. The pandemic has forced us to reckon with the truth—our ability to survive and thrive as individuals is interconnected to others' ability to do the same. The future depends on our ability toprepare ourselves and one another to be changemakers in daily life.

This report presents 11 strategies Ashoka Fellows are using to build an *Everyone* a Changemaker world. Of course, these strategies are only a start, but we hope this report has provides compelling evidence that we can, and we are, building a world where everyone is a changemaker and therefore, a world where everyone can thrive.

Please share this people whom you believe will be inspired to join us.

As ever,

Diana Wells
President Emerita
Leadership Team Member

SCAN THE CODE
TO READ
THE UNLONELY PLANET
2022 REPORT

LETTER FROM ASHOKA

In the new edition of Leading Social Entrepreneurs, we are featuring the Ashoka Fellows that have recently been brought into the largest global network of social entrepreneurs. In the following pages, we present the newest innovations by some of these social entrepreneurs, ideas that are changing systems for the whole society all over the planet.

Ashoka believes that the most powerful force for change in the world is a new idea in the hands of a social entrepreneur. We pioneered the field of social entrepreneurship more than 40 years ago, and since then we have annually presented new social entrepreneurs with new ideas that benefit the whole of society.

Ashoka fellows, as we call the social entrepreneurs of Ashoka's global network, design and implement ideas that serve all of society, not just on a small, localized scale, but rather that are changing the reality of millions of people, including children and young adults, who are now part of the 'Everyone is a Changemaker' movement. Their impact depends on creating roles and engaging people to step up to lead societal change, and further spread solutions. The Ashoka Fellow Survey 2021 found that, over the last year alone, the work of Ashoka fellows has directly impacted more than 600 million people through their services and programs. Furthermore, because of their work, over 3 million changemakers were activated during this period.

Tasso Azevedo, an Ashoka senior fellow from Brazil, is tackling deforestation and climate change in tropical forest regions. He is doing so by creating a new architecture for sustainable forest management, as well as spearheading open data and multi-actor platforms that are essential in making the transition to a low carbon economy. Tasso has shown people in Brazil and the 9 countries in the Amazonian how to measure both greenhouse gas emissions and the state of ground cover by very skillfully engaging, and therefore educating, all relevant stakeholders in the Amazonian, from policy makers to indigenous populations to business community, in all the relevant areas of interest. These range from major companies to very poor Amazon Forest residents and communities. He has also become a deeply trusted interpreter for both the Brazilian population and the rest of the world in regards to what is truly happening to the climate and the direct impact this is having in the world.

In Trinidad and Tobago, Alpha Sennon is inspiring young people living in the Caribbean to value agriculture and explore opportunities in this sector, changing the mindset of a generation that sees little appeal in farming. Through WhyFarm, Alpha works at the intersection of education, communication, and entertainment to show this younger generation why they should care about agriculture in a way that is fun. Alpha is tapping into the power of pop culture to shift perceptions and make agriculture 'cool' for a new generation of farmers and "agripreneurs".

Concerned for sexually exploited children, at just 17 years old, Cheryl Perera went to Sri Lanka to learn more about the issue. Since then, Cheryl has been a committed, and creative, social entrepreneur. She designed a program, run by young people, that builds an understanding of sexual exploitation to help people affected and ultimately work towards solving the problem. The program was entirely student run for many years, during which it had a clear impact. Over 90 percent of the students involved felt that they would be able to spot a young person at risk, and over half felt they had learned enough to be able to act. Cheryl is now focusing on working at an increasingly larger scale, in fact, she has recently worked out an arrangement that will bring her work to 7th and 8th grade physical education classes. She also continues to invent steadily. As a result, her career now spans to 22 countries, where she has investigated the sexual exploitation of children in travel and tourism. In fact, she has lobbied across private, public, and civil society organizations to increase awareness of legislation that was put in place to combat the sexual exploitation of children in this industry.

Social entrepreneurs want to change the cultural narrative and influence decision makers, civil society, businesses, and governments to make positive changes. We all have work to do; and this starts by putting young people at the center of the narrative to allow them to become contributors of this progressive change. It is essential to do so if we want to everyone involved in creating a world that is 'good of all.'

Warm regards,

Anamaria Schindler
President Emerita

Anamaria Schindler

HEALTH

DIXON CHIBANDA
Zimbabwe

APARNA HEDGE
India

AYESHA VERA-YU
Philippines

DANIEL CORDARO
Indonesia

GREGOIRE AHONGBONON
Cote d'Ivoire

JIMMY WESTERHEIM
Norway

DIXON CHIBANDA

Founder and CEO, Friendship Benches

 www.friendshipbenchzimbabwe.org

Dixon brought mental health care to all with a single idea. Elderly women ("grannies") with several weeks' training welcome those suffering from depression and related mental health issues to join them on a "Friendship Bench". They listen to their guests and then help them begin problem-solving. Eighty-six percent of the half-million Zimbabweans who have come to the grannies see depression and ideas of suicide decline. Dixon's Friendship Benches have spread widely – – from New York to World Cup soccer.

SCAN THE CODE TO READ AND SHARE THIS ARTICLE ONLINE

NEW IDEA

Dixon Chibanda is shifting norms around mental well-being by bringing mental health services closer to the people. Through Friendship Bench, he is combating both lack of access and social stigma with an evidence-based model that trains and deploys lay health workers, particularly grandmothers (understood in the local context as elderly women regardless of familial relationship), in basic counseling techniques that take into consideration the cultural context.

Unlike many mental health professionals in Africa and elsewhere, Dixon has embraced local traditions and cultural norms and integrated them into Friendship Bench's approach, which is rooted in understanding and that addresses psychological distress in local languages and cultural contexts. Prospective patients who come to primary care facilities with a range of symptoms (both physical and psychological) are screened with a questionnaire in local languages. Individuals who score above a certain threshold for indicators of depression and anxiety are referred to sit with a grandmother on the Friendship Bench (a wooden bench just outside the health care centre) for up to six sessions. In this way Friendship Bench provides culturally appropriate and culturally sensitive mental health support.

> *Without the Friendship Bench, Zimbabweans would have virtually no mental health care, except for those who can afford the few private doctors.*

The New York Times

SCAN THE CODE
TO READ THE NYT ARTICLE ABOUT DIXON

Research shows that these services have a measurable impact on patients within the first one to two sessions. There is also a positive impact for the elderly lay health workers, for whom this work provides a strong sense of purpose and a way to contribute to society. Dixon's solution harnesses the power of community support and intergenerational relationships to build an ecosystem of care in a resource-strapped environment. Much of Friendship Bench's success arises from their lay health workers, particularly the grandmothers, who are rooted in local culture, are respected for their wisdom, and who create a familiar and safe environment far removed from the intimidating clinical atmosphere of a mental health facility. In the first iteration of Friendship Bench, it was called the mental health bench, and no one came, so it evolved to be Friendship Bench which was seen as a friendly place. To date over 500,000 clients have been seen on the bench and with an 86% reduction in depression and suicide ideation among people referred to the bench.

Photo credit: Friendship Benches.

THE PROBLEM

Zimbabwe has been seriously impacted by socioeconomic hardship. An estimated 70% of the population is living below the poverty line, and 34% are living in extreme poverty. Shortages in fuel, electricity, clean water, and climate related events have drastically impacted the agriculture sector and inflation rates in recent years. The economy has been in decline for several years and the health care system – which was once one of the most robust in the region – has suffered decreased government spending, high workforce emigration and epitomises this decline. In one high-profile case in 2018, a Zimbabwean businessperson had to provide stipends to nurses and other healthcare professionals to persuade them to stay on the job following months of protesting poor working conditions and what they described as "slave" wages (less than $200 per month). In 2021 alone Zimbabwe lost 2,000 healthcare professionals, according to state media.

> *[It is a] vehicle for promoting mental health, from park benches to football stadiums. The Friendship Benches project is a reminder of how the simple act of sitting down to talk can make a huge difference to mental health."*

Dr. Tedros Adhanom Ghebreyesus, WHO Director-General

This bleak economic outlook has had a devastating impact on mental well-being. Substance abuse is high and 45 percent of women report being victims of intimate partner violence according to Zimbabwe Demographic and Health Survey of 2015. This means the already overburdened public health infrastructure cannot cope with

Photo credit: Friendship Benches.

such a large burden of mental health and the authorities lack the monetary, staff and facility resources to tackle the challenge.

As a result, Zimbabwe has high suicide rates according to the World Health Organization data especially among young adults at tertiary institutions. An estimated 30% of primary care patients have common mental health disorders, yet even within primary care in Zimbabwe there is a lack of access to mental health care. There are only twelve certified psychiatrists in the country and very few psychologists serving a population of approximately 16 million.

The issue with such a large population with a pervasive presence of mental health issues is that clinical psychological methods simply cannot be scaled up to match the growing need, especially with the lack of professional training and knowledge. Moreover, many mental health treatment approaches are not compatible with local cultural practices as they are seen as Western while most mental illnesses are attributed to spiritual affliction, witchcraft, or vengeful spirits. As a result, there is stigma associated with mental health and treatment is often sought from traditional healers therefore reducing the success rates of clinical therapy or medication. When accessible, people are reluctant to use the formal health services for their mental health care, due to high rates of stigma (at a personal and societal level).

At a global level, the problem is equally pervasive. According to the organization United for Global Mental Health, mental ill health costs the world a staggering $2.5 trillion, but that figure could be cut down to a quarter of what it is today simply by making sure that everyone everywhere has someone to turn to. In the rest of Africa, the picture is not vastly different. Mental disorders are escalating amid the coronavirus pandemic lock downs that have slowed down economic growth leaving many unemployed and uncertain about the future. Investment in public health for mental illness is extremely low with most countries investing less than one percent of health budgets towards mental health. According to the World Economic Forum, an estimated 100 million people in Africa suffer from clinical depression, including 66 million women. The World Bank considers it "the greatest thief of productive economic life."

THE STRATEGY

The Friendship Bench model is built on the premise that with training, encouragement, development, and ongoing support, lay health workers, especially older women, can become the frontline health workers to deliver culturally appropriate mental health services transforming wellbeing in underserved communities. A key conceptual framework of Dixon and Friendship Bench is its focus on the cultural context and cultural beliefs around mental health, and especially the social determinants of mental health, such as housing, family relationships, illness, and socioeconomic hardship.

Friendship Bench's approach has attracted a significant amount of rigorous research documenting its success as an evidence-based solution for depression and anxiety. Dixon's background as a psychiatrist and a public health expert taught him the importance of clinical validation, and his networks have helped Friendship Bench gain access to skilled research and reviewers. The first publication to review the effectiveness of this model was the Journal of the American Medical Association. Dixon made the deliberate choice to focus on publication in a journal that does not solely focus on mental health, but health more broadly, to encourage primary care medical clinics to take up this solution, rather than limiting it to a mental health space. A study on the effectiveness of Friendship Bench was published in the *Journal of American Medical Association* in December 2016. The study found that patients with depression or anxiety who received problem-solving therapy through the Friendship Bench were more than three times less likely to have symptoms of depression after six months, compared to patients who received standard care. They were also four times less likely to have anxiety symptoms and five times less likely to have suicidal thoughts than the control group after follow-up.

Friendship Bench's reliance on elderly women (grannies) and other persons as lay counselors linked to primary health facilities addresses the crisis of chronic understaffing at government health facilities. These lay counselors engage in conversation with their clients, providing cognitive-behavioral therapy tools contextualized to local languages and norms, to individuals suffering from common mental health challenges such as depression and anxiety. Grannies are trusted messengers who share the cultural background of the people served by this solution and therefore lower the barrier for entry, making it easier for patients to take up new ideas. The emphasis of the interaction on the bench is less on the medical diagnosis but on providing a safe space for a patient to tell their story. Story telling in mental health helps people feel less alone, and it cultivates empathy and compassion.

The assessment tool used by primary care health clinics to determine who is referred to Friendship Bench is locally validated and designed for the communities it serves. Grannies (lay health workers or LHWs) who sit on the friendship bench and see patients are trained to provide six counselling sessions completed within four to six weeks. LHWs ask questions that encourage clients "kuvhura pfungwa" to open their minds, identify a problem, and proactively tackle it. Following problem identification and exploration, LHWs guide their clients on an action plan towards a feasible solution. Following the six sessions with the grannies, patients are invited to

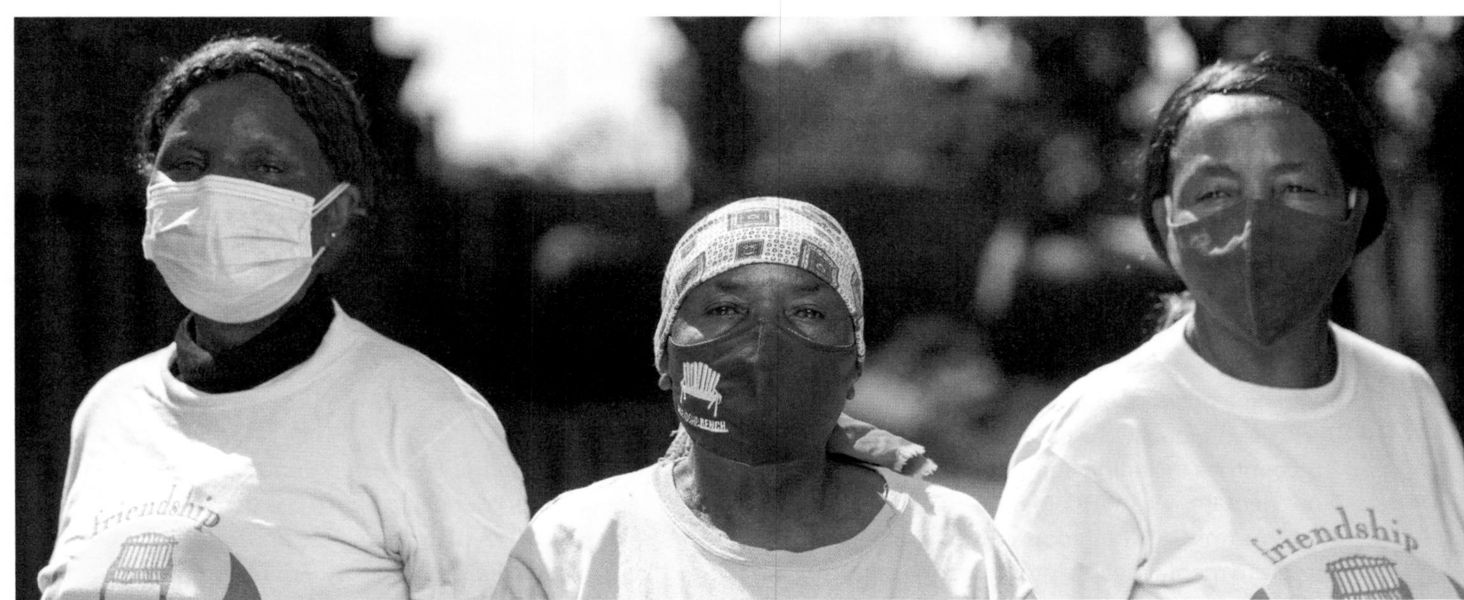

PHOTO CREDIT: *Friendship Benches – Friendship Bench has grown from a community of 14 grandmothers to over 700. The grandmothers feel a strong sense of purpose and pride in their work – and are deeply valued by their communities.*

an optional additional 6-session peer-led group support program.

The peer led support group are known as Circle Kubatana Tose (CKT), meaning 'holding hands together.' In these groups clients are connected to other Friendship Bench clients who received counselling sessions and became empowered to solve their own problems with others that they can relate to. Through the talk therapy clients have learnt about the benefit of empathic listening and can co-create a safe space to talk to and be heard by their peers.

These support groups contribute to clients' sense of belonging and reduce stigma surrounding mental health and sharing of personal issues. As an extension of problem-solving skills learnt on the bench, these groups are engaged in revenue generating opportunities, which is vital in a country with high levels of unemployment and poverty, factors that contribute to socio-economic distress. For instance, clients can participate in the creation and sale of large, colorful shoulder bags made from recycled plastic (known as "zee bags").

To date over 1,400 community health workers have been trained to provide psychosocial support to people in need in their communities. Friendship Bench has seen over 150,000 patients served and according to results of a randomized clinical trial published in the Journal of Medicine, clients seen on the Friendship Bench demonstrated a 60% improvement in quality of life and 80% reduction in depression and suicidal ideation. As a result of its demonstrated effectiveness, it has been adopted by the government as part of the national mental health strategy. Scaling its implementation across all primary health care facilities in Zimbabwe is a priority for Friendship Bench.

Simultaneous to the roll-out of Friendship Bench throughout Zimbabwe, Dixon and his team have been undertaking pilots globally. Drawing on his affiliations with the London School of Hygiene and Tropical Medicine and the African Mental Health Research Initiative (AMARI), Friendship Bench is tapping into a network of professionals undertaking core research for its expansion and building a network of adopters of the model throughout Africa and globally. To date, the initiative has spread to six countries including Kenya, Malawi, Tanzania, the U.S., and Vietnam. The WHO Mental Health Gap Action Programme (mhGAP) has adopted it as a blueprint of how to integrate mental health into primary health care. Friendship Bench has developed a five-phase implementation model they use to establish suitability of the model for potential partners and develop a roll out plan. Within each phase exists various stages which get worked in collaboration with potential partners; every delivery will be unique to each community. The phases are as follows:

1. Establishing Suitability
2. Theory of Change Workshop
3. Partner Preparation
4. Training of Trainers and Training of CHW
5. Monitoring & Evaluation and Tech & Online Support

This makes it easier to scale the Friendship Bench into other countries. The strategy for growth involves providing technical assistance to other organizations and health ministries that would like to implement the Friendship Bench model.

> ***'Friendship Bench' is a novel way of providing free mental health support to poor compatriots by enlisting the help of older health workers. The Zimbabwean project is temporarily setting up shop at the FIFA World Cup in Qatar late this month to highlight the importance of health therapy.***

SCAN THE CODE
TO WATCH THE AFP FILM OF DIXON'S WORK

In addition to the Friendship Benches at primary health care centers, Friendship Bench has developed peer counselling services at universities, and offers online counselling services delivered by Friendship Bench trained mental health supporters. Online sessions are held on WhatsApp call or chat. They include screening for depression and anxiety as well as problem-solving talk therapy-based support. Sessions last 30-60 minutes (the first session is usually the longest). This is designed for people struggling with mild-moderate depression, anxiety, as well as substance misuse, suicide ideation, emotional distress, relationship difficulties, or people who have poor quality of life due to the emotional distress brought on by chronic medical illnesses such as cancer, diabetes, or HIV/AIDS. The online platform has made it gender inclusive in that men and woman have differences in health seeking behaviours and preliminary data shows more men are active on the online platform than women.

Dixon's ability to spread the Friendship Bench model is significantly helped by his professional ties to leading universities and research institutions in Zimbabwe, all of Africa, and the U.K. This brings in research on the science and the efficacy of the approach – and therefore credibility and connection. Dixon has deliberately used Friendship Bench to nest PhD students to carry out rigorous research on its work and later to spread the idea. This also helps him recruit new staff. The current research lead, for instance, is a former PhD student, and the Youth-Friendship Bench lead is another former student. Dixon's university and research ties also provide an opportunity for the wider team to interact with other researchers including international collaborating partners and develop an interest in mental health among medical doctors and researchers.

THE PERSON

Dixon Chibanda was born in Zimbabwe during the liberation struggle for independence. Part of his early years were spent in Zambia as his parents were in exile. For the most part he had a normal childhood, but two traumatic events would unconsciously shape his path to working in mental health. The first was his parents' divorce when he was 12 years old which he took very badly. The second was finding himself being the only boy of colour in an elite boy's school in Harare, Zimbabwe shortly after independence from colonial rule. The racism he faced from the teachers and the students was unimaginable. According to Dixon no one wanted to stand next to him or speak to him and when his father complained things only become worse and eventually, he was transferred to a more diverse school. He went to Comenius University in Bratislava, Slovakia and again the racism was rife, which strongly impacted him.

Dixon always knew he wanted to become a doctor, but dermatology and pediatrics were his original interests. While in medical school in the Czech Republic, however, one of his classmates died by suicide and this tragedy had a profound impact on him, which led him to choosing psychiatry.

Another seminal moment influenced Dixon to understand the nexus between culture and medicine. Between 2003 and 2005 Dixon spent time in Ouidah, Benin as a Junior Consultant for the World Health Organization trying to formulate policies around the rights of people with mental health issues. Outside their compound was a Voodoo priestess and after many nights hearing the drumming from the compound Dixon's curiosity led him to the compound to observe what was going on. As a psychiatrist he could see that many of the people brought to the priestess had clear mental health challenges and that the way the priestess related to the clients and understood the deep cultural idioms of mental distress helped to calm clients and make them feel understood, and thus more open to treatment. He also observed a deep disconnect between science and the culture of people living with mental illness. Unsure how he would use this knowledge he returned to Zimbabwe.

In 2005, back in Zimbabwe, two tragic events occurred that led Dixon on a path to urgently find solutions to bridge the treatment gap of mental wellbeing. One of his patients died by suicide in a rural village because the family did not have money for bus fare to bring her for treatment in the city. The second was the mass displacement of the urban poor in Harare following a brutal government led campaign, Operation Murambatsvina ("remove the filth"), which saw the destruction of informal settlements around the capital city leaving 700,000 people homeless and in deep mental distress. Dixon was the only psychiatrist working in the public sector at the time. He began studying public health to understand better the social determinants of mental health and to look for solutions to address access to mental health in the poorly resourced public sector. Informed by the lessons in Ouidah of embracing cultural wisdom he started training grandmothers to provide psychosocial support and thus the Friendship Bench was born.

Dixon completed his medical studies in 1993 at Comenius University in Bratislava, Czech Republic. He also holds master's degrees in Psychiatry and Epidemiology from the University of Zimbabwe and a PhD in Psychiatry from the University of Cape Town. After graduating from the University of Zimbabwe, he worked as a consultant for the World Health Organization.

APARNA HEGDE

Founder, ARMMAN

 www.armman.org

Aparna Hedge conceived and scaled up the world's largest system of mobile phone networks for maternal and neonatal medical information and health-care training. The networks help tens of millions of women access timely, targeted information and care, thereby saving lives, improving maternal and child health, and changing the experience of pregnancy and childbirth from one of fear and trauma to one of hope and empowerment.

SCAN THE CODE TO READ AND SHARE THIS ARTICLE ONLINE

THE NEW IDEA

Maternal and infant mortality in India are frighteningly high, yet millions of mothers lack access to the necessary information and healthcare that could prevent it. To change that, Aparna and her organization built Kilkari, the largest maternal mobile voice messaging program in the world.

The service, which is free, delivers targeted, preventative care information to mothers in their vernacular language during pregnancy and early childhood, from the second trimester of pregnancy until the child is a year and a half, the period in which most deaths occur. Mobile phones are ubiquitous in India, and Kilkari effectively connects with some 25 million women and counting across the country, regardless of where they live or their literacy or educational attainment.

Aparna and her organization also created Mobile Academy, the world's largest mobile-based training program for frontline health workers. It uses mobile phone networks to deliver refresher trainings and certification in maternal and child healthcare for government frontline healthcare workers, reaching over 235,000 workers in 16 Indian states and union territories.

These "tech plus touch" innovations are evidence-based, cost-effective, replicable, and growing on a national scale. They're combining to close system-wide gaps in health service delivery in India, and promote proactive health-seeking behavior among mothers, with dramatic improvements in outcomes. For example, one study of rural villages of Maharashtra state found that among the mothers who received preventative care information through mobile voice messaging and home-based consultation and referral services, incidence of complications from pregnancy fell from 38% to 9%.

Photo credit: Credit: Dr. Aparna Hedge – Aparna's program empowers local women by training them to provide basic prenatal and infancy care to their communities. This work not only expands health-care delivery to hard-to-reach areas, but creates a new class of health entrepreneurs.

THE PROBLEM

There are 30 million pregnancies a year in India, and one woman dies in childbirth every 15 minutes. For each of those deaths, 20 others suffer with lifelong disabilities from childbirth. Two Indian children under the age of five die each minute. HIV transmission from mother to baby contributes significantly to child mortality. Four out of ten Indian children's growth is stunted from chronic malnutrition, which has lifelong consequences.

But it doesn't have to be this way, and Aparna refused to accept it. "Pregnancy is not a disease," she says. "Childhood is not an ailment. Dying due to a natural event is not acceptable." 90% of these deaths and many of the other bad outcomes are preventable with the right interventions. Yet millions of Indian women can't access them through normal healthcare delivery channels.

Aparna describes what she calls "the three delays" that can lead to lifelong disabilities and deaths from pregnancy complications. The first is lack of access to necessary preventative care information. The second is inability to physically get to a place to receive care. The third is lack of trained staff, equipment, and supplies. Most deaths and disabilities could be prevented if it weren't for these chronic problems.

46% of maternal deaths and 40% of neonatal deaths happen during labor or within the first 24 hours of birth, most often from such causes as birth asphyxia, infections, or prematurity. The mortality risk correlates to some degree with the mother's income, level of education, and the rural-urban divide. But the larger factor determining survival and health outcomes is the ability or inability to access prenatal and postpartum information and care, proper nutrition, sanitation, and hygiene. For example, there are interventions that can prevent HIV transmission from mother to baby, but if mothers can't access them, the risk is as high as 45%.

The Indian government offers free monthly healthcare visits during pregnancy, but most women can't take advantage of them, especially in rural areas, because they can't give up a day's earnings to travel to a distant healthcare facility. In Bihar, for example, just 3.3% of pregnant women reported fully accessing government prenatal care, despite it being free. Instead, mothers often rely on informal care from people who aren't medically trained.

India's government and civil society organizations have been working to address these systemic design and resource issues, but problems persist. Historically their programs often relied on expensive pilots and/or access to hospitals and professionals, which made them difficult to scale. Most were narrowly focused on childbirth, but, as Aparna understood, protecting mothers and children requires a more holistic approach including antenatal care during pregnancy, specialized care during childbirth, and ongoing support in the weeks and months after birth.

THE STRATEGY

Through her incisive understanding of service gaps, and her remarkable ability to leverage partnerships to fill them in innovative, large-scale ways, Aparna has succeeded where government and CSO programs often failed, supplying the basic care and information that long eluded many millions of Indian women, cutting across regional and societal divides, preventing maternal and child deaths and disability on a continental scale.

Aparna started by creating an online platform for real-time data on the availability of ICU beds and blood types at hospitals across India. But she soon had the fundamental insight that reaching more women required shifting from hospital-based care to preventive care. Working with healthcare facilities, technology companies, CSOs, the Indian government, and local communities, she focused attention on early identification, referral, and treatment of risk factors in pregnant women and children which could keep them out of the hospital. That was a structural shift that ended up bridging service gaps and improving many elements of India's primary health care and referral systems.

> *Hegde met plenty of skeptics—it took five years to get external funding—but today, her nonprofit, which partners with the Indian government and dozens of NGOs in 17 states across the country, represents one of the largest mobile health programs in the world and a lifeline for women in India.*

Forbes

Working with partners, Aparna conducts "community needs assessment" research to inform her organization's program designs, and uses the high penetration of mobile phones across India to scale those programs up cost-effectively without loss of impact.

One of Aparna's early successes was her mMitra program, which uses mobile voice messaging to deliver free preventive healthcare information to mothers during pregnancy and infancy. The program cost less than five dollars per recipient to run and reached women in rural as well as urban areas. After a few years of operation, by 2016 the program had enrolled a million women in 15 states. Compared to the general population, enrolled women had 25% higher rates of adequate iron and folic acid supplementation, and 17% more of their babies tripled their birth weight at the end of their first year.

Building on the achievements of mMitra, Aparna partnered with India's Ministry of Health and Family Welfare to create Kilkari, the world's largest mobile messaging network for maternal and neonatal care information, available in five languages. It reaches some 25 million women and counting with life-changing and life-saving health information.

In rural and tribal areas that lack cell service or have low mobile phone penetration, the information is recorded on mobile devices, and female health workers trained by Aparna's organization play it for mothers during home visits.

Aparna also built Mobile Academy, the world's largest mobile-based training program for frontline government healthcare workers, created in partnership with the Ministry of Health and Family Welfare. Mobile Academy reaches over 235,000 workers and counting in 16 Indian states and union territories. The trainings refresh workers' knowledge of life-saving preventative care measures, and effective ways of connecting with mothers and families. The trainings are available in four languages and are expanding India's capacity to manage pregnancies ranging from routine to high-risk.

One of the keys to the scale and impact of Aparna's programs is that they don't just disseminate expert information or provide continuing education for healthcare professionals; they also empower women in the community to take an active role in improving maternal and neonatal health.

> *...available in five languages, it reaches some 25 million women*

For example, Arpana designed a program which trains local women to provide basic home-based antenatal and infancy care, for which they get paid a small fee. A mobile tablet application helps these local women identify high-risk signs and symptoms, alerts them when referrals for treatment are needed, and provides resources for counseling. These women help expand healthcare delivery to hard-to-reach areas.

Working to connect with women in need wherever they are, Aparna's organization enrolls women in its programs through what Aparna calls "two verticals" – – a hospital vertical where health care workers register women during their first check-up visit, and a community vertical where partner CSOs on the ground register women in poor communities. Community health workers also enroll women in early stages of pregnancy and get a small incentive for signing those women up.

These strategies are creating a new class of health entrepreneurs, empowering women in the community to improve health outcomes and get paid for it, and extending the reach of Aparna's programs far beyond the former limitations of the healthcare system. As of 2020, the various programs from Aparna and her organization benefitted some 20 million pregnant women, mothers, and children, and 1.7 million healthcare workers across India.

As the reach of Aparna's programs has grown, she has continually demonstrated her ability to adapt to changing healthcare needs. For example, when the pandemic hit, India's hospitals converted to COVID centers, so Aparna launched a virtual clinic to fill the resulting gap in antenatal and pediatric care. Its mobile network and virtual training platform were also impactful tools for educating women and health workers about COVID-19 and vaccination.

THE PERSON

Aparna was born into a lower-middle-class family in Mumbai, India. Her family had to work hard to make ends meet, but Aparna understood that she was lucky, since growing up in Mumbai afforded her opportunities for education and pursuing her dream of becoming a doctor.

Mindful of her privilege, as a young person she empathized with those who weren't so lucky and was attracted to causes on their behalf. Aparna worked with the Akanksha Foundation, helping develop small clusters of model schools which were designed to be replicated across the education system. She also felt strongly about animal safety and rights and worked for the welfare of stray dogs in Mumbai.

After medical school, Aparna did her residency near the Nallasopara slums of Mumbai. One day, while working in the clinic, a woman from one of the slums arrived in labor, convulsed with hypertension, and died from the condition. When Aparna opened her records, she was stunned to recognize her own handwriting. Aparna had seen the woman before, during the third month of her pregnancy, but she hadn't come back to the clinic after that. Aparna was stricken with guilt. She wondered, "Had the overcrowding in the clinic meant that I had not counseled her enough to watch for signs of trouble, or to seek regular care?" Aparna saw cases like this every day: preventable deaths of women and children that could have been averted by a little information or some routine care at the right time, if only health workers were trained to provide it, and if only the women could access it before it was too late. The preventable death of her one-time patient galvanized Aparna, and set her on the path to becoming the highly impactful social entrepreneur she is today. "It instilled the spark in me, that now we try to instill in the millions of women and children we serve," she said.

PHOTO CREDIT: *Dr. Aparna Hedge – In India, one woman dies in childbirth every 15 minutes. Aparna is fighting to make sure pregnancy and childbirth are seen and treated as natural life events rather than as fatal ones.*

From the beginning of her career Aparna was committed to using her specialized knowledge and skills (she holds three medical degrees, a master's degree in biological sciences from Stanford University and an International Fellowship in Urogynecology and Pelvic Reconstruction Surgery) to benefit people who lack access to specialist care, especially women and children from lower socio-economic backgrounds. For example, Aparna worked closely with Ashoka Fellow Armida Fernandez as Armida was launching her first venture to deliver quality maternal and neonatal health care to low-income families. That experience helped Aparna recognize the potential of technology to transcend the limits of the existing healthcare systems to deliver the care and information mothers and infants need.

Today, through her firsthand insights into service gaps in India's healthcare system, her serial innovations to fill them, and her talent for building strategic partnerships to extend their reach, Aparna is fundamentally changing how and by whom healthcare is delivered, empowering more women to deliver it as well as receive it. As a result, Aparna is saving and improving millions of lives.

AYESHA VERA YU

Co-Founder, Advancement For Rural Kids (ARK)

 www.ruralkids.org

Through neighborhood barter markets and other self-organizing patterns, Ayesha Vera Yu helps poor rural Filipinos quickly banish hunger and take charge.

SCAN THE CODE TO READ AND SHARE THIS ARTICLE ONLINE

THE NEW IDEA

Ayesha, who left a successful career in banking to take on rural hunger in the Philippines, inspires hungry, discouraged rural communities to adopt new patterns of growing and sharing food, which leads to their taking charge far more broadly.

Rural food producers in the developing world often go hungry themselves. In the Philippines, over a third of rural residents, most of them fisherfolk and farmers, live in poverty and struggle to feed their own families. Their children often go to school hungry, suffer malnourishment, and risk dropping out.

Ayesha's many ideas changed that. Her first innovation was a co-investment approach that partners with schools and parents, starting in 16 Filipino rural communities, to create a nourishing school lunch program by leveraging the communities' own resources. It sparks parents to plant organic vegetable gardens in their backyards and schools to plant their own gardens.

Her next innovation was Feed Back, a simple but powerful model that helps rural residents grow and exchange their own food through backyard farming and self-organized exchanges that feed the entire community.

After four weeks of growing, community leaders organize a weekly collective barter market, a celebratory event that turns out the whole village. In this way, community members end hunger and malnutrition in just five weeks. Soon after, they are producing surplus food they can sell to neighboring villages, creating a new income stream and a new sense of self-determination.

Feed Back has been implemented by 35 communities across six provinces of the Philippines, securing 100% of at-risk families in these areas, strengthening those communities a whole, and enhancing food security in other towns. The program will expand to over 200 rural communities in 2023, reaching 250,000 people. Ayesha and her team are working with government and private partners to reach a million in the next three years.

PHOTO CREDIT: *ARK – Backyard farming has become a community activity. Those who decided to join danced Zumba on basketball courts and held vegetable costume contests to kick off the planting cycle.*

THE PROBLEM

Two billion people around the world suffer from chronic hunger. In the Philippines, half the population has gone hungry, which especially harms children. Over a third of rural Filipinos live in poverty. The majority are farmers and fisherfolk—the lowest income earners and the most vulnerable to food insecurity.

Filipino farmers typically don't own their land. Two-thirds of agricultural land holdings in the Philippines are rented to tenant farmers who contract with landowners, mostly growing rice and corn for private companies. But chemical-intensive farming techniques and climate and supply disruptions make this an increasingly risky, disempowering proposition. Terms are dictated by landowners and middlemen. Farmers are dependent on commercial seeds, pesticides, and fertilizers, and often must borrow at high, e.g., 20%, interest to buy seeds and chemicals.

"When the Spanish colonized the Philippines, they gave out big land grants," said Ayesha. "When Americans came, they kept the same feudal system intact, and it hasn't changed. What gets produced on the farms of big landowners is for export. The rest of the country is fed by smallholders. It used to be that small farmers always turned a profit because they produced all the inputs, they needed themselves. But chemical farming has created deep poverty. Smallholder farmers have to borrow to get the inputs, and if a storm wipes out their cash crop, they can never repay."

Focused on their cash crop, these farmers have turned away from the traditional practice of raising other produce and animals for subsistence alongside cash crops, so they have to buy food for their families instead of growing it. This often means borrowing more money, especially during the rainy season when farmers have to buy inputs for planting, which also coincides with the start of school. This is the leanest time for them, when their children are more likely to go to school hungry and malnourished, leading many to drop out and seek work.

The problem is a global one. Farmers in many developing countries struggle to feed their families, and a quarter of a billion children worldwide aren't in school.

This year, Russia's invasion of Ukraine disrupted the global supply chain, making matters worse. Food and fertilizer costs tripled, resulting in a hunger crisis in the Philippines and elsewhere. Add climate disruptions, typhoons, and the pandemic, and rural farming and fishing communities can end up feeling helpless and hopeless.

Many have at least some access to food aid (though some rural communities have none). But external aid is not a comprehensive solution and does not build lasting food security. Government and philanthropic programs depend on scarce funding, and can only help until money runs out. Citizen organizations offer food augmentation programs that send vegetable packs from farmers to

PHOTO CREDIT: *ARK – At just pennies per head per meal, the ARK program has been able to provide a million meals comprising locally sourced vegetables and protein.*

beneficiary families, but the relief they provide is temporary. One important Philippine government program fed at-risk kids in public schools during 2018-2019, but only a portion of hungry or malnourished children qualified.

"Relief packs and handouts are good in an emergency, but they don't solve chronic hunger," says Ayesha. "Community pantries that require outside food aren't sustainable. If there is no path for the community to grow the food it needs, they fail in the long term."

At the root of rural hunger, malnutrition, and poverty is the loss of agency of rural people and their dependence on commercial inputs and volatile markets for monoculture cash crops. Treating them as passive aid recipients fails to address those problems.

As Ayesha recognized, rural farmers and fisherfolk are the key resources for solving their own food security problems. They are more than capable of feeding themselves and even creating surpluses once they step outside of a system that has failed them. So, she partnered with them to build a new system to step into.

THE STRATEGY

In 2009, Ayesha founded Advancement for Rural Kids (ARK), to find new structures, including co-investments that empower at-risk communities to solve their own hunger and malnutrition challenges. Community members lead and own the solutions. They have the ball, not outside forces.

Parents and teachers create backyard and schoolyard gardens, raising vegetables and livestock to feed the children. And they inspire others in the community to do likewise. Pooling what they produce yields lunches with full, balanced nutrition for every child who attends school, every day that school is open.

The lunches aren't free, but because the community is providing almost all the inputs, they cost less than 5 cents a day. Parents in poor rural communities can afford to pay that themselves, so they buy into the program from the beginning as co-investors, rather than relying on outside aid.

Each parent makes substantial in-kind investments, taking time off from work to come to school and make the lunches, learning to use Excel to track every dollar and impact. ARK helps them integrate and take over the program entirely within three years, so the system becomes fully self-sustaining, owned and operated by the community, with no outside input or funding needed. In time, as families learn to increase their yields, they produce surpluses they can sell, giving them an additional income stream.

ARK Lunch has delivered one million lunches and counting. In many schools, it reduced prior malnutrition rates from 30% or more to zero, and raised school attendance to 100%.

In 2019, the program was poised to scale up nationally. But when the covid-19 pandemic hit, schools closed. Many villages, including the entire island of Luzon, went into lockdown. Mobility and business activity were severely restricted. Many fisherfolk were prohibited from fishing, and/or from selling fish. Rural families were again at risk.

> *Advancement for Rural Kids creates a path for rural communities to solve hunger, get kids back to school, and be self-sustaining starting with 5-cent school lunches.*
>
> TECHINASIA

So, ARK pivoted. Ayesha created a new co-investment program called Feed Back that applies the same basic principles as ARK Lunch to feeding the whole community, pooling food grown by community members, and delivering it through village market exchanges instead of schools.

Like ARK lunch, Feed Back is 100% community-led and –owned. It starts with recruiting local community leaders who go door to door, asking residents to plant organic gardens with at least three kinds of vegetables, and providing advice and support. After gardens have been growing for four weeks, the community organizes a weekly collective barter market in a central village space. Families bring three kinds of produce to exchange and take home a nutritious array of 20 different kinds. Hunger and malnutrition are gone by the time of the first market, just five weeks into the program.

The markets are much more than a food exchange; they're communal, festive affairs (known as "Fiesta Feed Back") that engage the whole village and knit it together. Everyone's contribution is valued, all produce is weighed,

Credit: ARK – The answer to previously rampant hunger

PHOTO CREDIT: *ARK – Ayesha Vera-Yu of Advancement for Rural Kids catalyzes villages to organize and grow organic food to provide school lunches and cut family hunger.*

tracked, and accounted for. Small incentives sweeten the pot and strengthen participation. For example, for every $1 worth of vegetables a family brings to the weekly market, they get a raffle ticket for a prize.

It's not a line to receive outside aid; it's a joyful celebration of what the community is doing for itself. Instead of a disempowered relationship with landowners and cash crop markets stacked against them, families get to invest in themselves and rely on each other, building a stronger, more unified, resilient community.

"To solve hunger and create food security, you have to dismantle the existing inequitable structure," Ayesha said. "Aid organizations are sincere, but they have this idea that they know better. It's a holdover from colonialism, the notion that they can solve it for you. There is an underlying level of racism and classism. Those with access to capital and influence over policy tend not to embrace the idea that people have the solutions. But that's the key to solving big, structural problems."

The markets continue, especially, getting families through the hazards of the rainy season. Ayesha's program is even more helpful when a community is hit by a typhoon (some participating communities were hit by successive ones) or other unforeseen disruptions.

After a disaster, Feed Back communities are able to rebuild their food systems and local economies quickly.

The benefits are lasting and self-sustaining. For almost all Feed Back "graduates," the shift in behavior is permanent. Many become entrepreneurs, producing food and organic fertilizer beyond what they need for their own use, and selling it for extra income.

For example, in the rural village of Traciano, which was hit by Super Typhoon Odette in 2021, 94% of residents are still harvesting from their backyards a year after graduating from the Feed Back program. Not only don't they go hungry, two thirds of them derive 25% of their income from selling the surplus.

In the past two years Feed Back has taken root in 35 communities across six provinces of the Philippines, securing 100% of at-risk families in these areas. About 325,000 kilos of food have been exchanged so far.

The program is posed to roll out nationwide to over 200 at-risk communities, reaching 250,000 people by 2023. ARK continues to work with Feed Back "graduate" communities to further build their skills and connect them to wider markets for their surplus, helping fight hunger in other parts of the Philippines.

Ayesha and her team are in high-level dialog with the Philippine government on how to leverage Feed Back to end hunger and malnutrition nationwide. In the previous administration, Feed Back became the only sustainable food security solution endorsed by Pilipinas Kontra Gutom (Philippines Against Hunger), a major consortium of government agencies, corporations, and foundations. ARK is now attracting wide support, ranging from the Rotary Clubs in the Philippines to major idea hubs including Google and Facebook.

Those relationships are a conscious effort to "positively influence how corporations, foundations, and governments partner to create truly sustainable solutions and systems," Ayesha says. She wants them to embrace new models in which beneficiaries are "trusted and treated as true partners, solutions come from within, communities implement and fund them on their own."

From once being seen as extra work, backyard farming has become a community activity. Those who decided to join [the ARK program] danced Zumba on basketball courts and held vegetable costume contests to kick off the planting cycle. And families make a day out of going to market.

To scale up further, Ayesha is working on a "play book" communities can use to replicate the Feed Back model themselves, as opposed to working directly with ARK trainers. That lowers costs and can extend the program's reach. Ayesha's current goal is for Feed Back to reach 1 million people in the next three years, and from there to keep scaling globally, so farmers and fisherfolk never go hungry again.

THE PERSON

During the Marcos regime, the Philippines was under martial law from 1972 to 1981. Ayesha's parents decided to emigrate and moved the family to the U.S., settling first in Oakland, California, then in New York. Ayesha attended private schools, and was accepted to a top New York charter school, but she was told she would need to repeat a grade. Already frustrated by the covert discrimination she encountered as a Filipino-American, Ayesha left in defiance, and opted to attend public school for the first time.

There she encountered more racial and ethnic diversity and felt a desire to connect with her Filipino roots. She participated in Filipino-American activities in high school and at Mount Holyoke College, where she studied biochemistry and the politics of the developing world. She took an executive MBA degree from Columbia University and went on to a successful career in finance, becoming the youngest director at BNP Paribas, handling billion-dollar leveraged buyouts and mergers and acquisitions.

Her family had kept their farm in Capiz on Panay Island in the Philippines, and in 2006, Ayesha's mom asked if she would invest. She agreed on the condition that the farm would become fully organic and sustainable. She began spending time in Capiz, using her biochemistry knowledge to help the farm transition. It became the first farm in Capiz to go back to organic and regenerative methods, emulating the way it had been run by her grandparents.

Recruited by a local teacher to help support the schools in Capiz, in 2008 she met with parents to ask them what they needed. She was surprised to learn the help they wanted most wasn't with infrastructure or school supplies, it was to address student hunger. When Ayesha asked how that could be done, a parent answered, "the same way we fixed the roof – we partner!"

That was the germ of ARK. She quit her full-time job to focus on ending rural hunger and malnutrition by working with communities as full partners and leaders of the solution. She drew on her experience in finance to create new co-investment structures that provided the support rural communities would need to buy in and get started, and a pathway for their ventures to become self-sustaining quickly.

DANIEL CORDARO

Founder and CEO, The Contentment Foundation

 www.contentment.org

Daniel Cordaro is very systematically changing schools into fulfilling spaces for students, teachers, and everyone involved where they learn and live with empathy, emotional self-awareness, and resilience.

SCAN THE CODE TO READ AND SHARE THIS ARTICLE ONLINE

THE NEW IDEA

Daniel imagines a world where schools are psychologically safe spaces, where every student is connected to one another and has a deep sense of love, trust, and connection within their community. Daniel believes that a culture of social-emotional well-being can be built from a very young age and can be effectively embedded throughout school ecosystems, so that everyone involved (teachers, students, parents, counselors, administrators, support staff, security personnel, etc.) can access practical tools to develop and manage their well-being.

Daniel, a former Yale professor of Psychology, and his organization the Contentment Foundation, have designed a comprehensive program that measurably improves the well-being of everyone in the school ecosystem. Increased wellbeing invariably then contributes to improved learning. Their program – the Four Pillars of Well-Being, integrates ancient traditions of human wisdom with contemporary science on wellbeing in ways that easily adapt into local cultures and school curricula around the world, and they include:

- Mindfulness: ability to recognize and channel emotions
- Community: ability to build empathy and trust with peers, teachers, family, community
- Self-curiosity: eagerness to explore emotional responses to situations
- Contentment: skill to recognize and heal old reactive patters and develop gratitude

To augment the curriculum, and increase efficacy of implementation, Daniel also developed a data-driven platform that measures progress along 48 critical aspects of school health, wellness, and safety at an individual, group, and whole-school levels. The easy-to-digest visual reports allow the school to consciously step back and analyze the emotional well-being of staff and students in real time. Partner schools and communities also receive access to a curated, extensive library of materials covering a wide range of mental health and well-being topics.

In a three year-long study[1], published by the American Psychological Association, their Four Pillars program was implemented and designed in a K-8 school in Florida. The results showed that it enhanced students' vocabulary to recognize and express emotions. There was an overall reduction in stress and an increase in the emotional state most conducive for focused learning, attention, and reflection. Bullying went down, as did stress indicators.

By building this multi-layered infrastructure in a school system, the program provided measurable, evidence-based safety and mental resilience practices to every stakeholder of the school's ecosystem. It also enabled the teachers to be more compassionate and feel far more content. It also significantly improved their teaching efficacy.

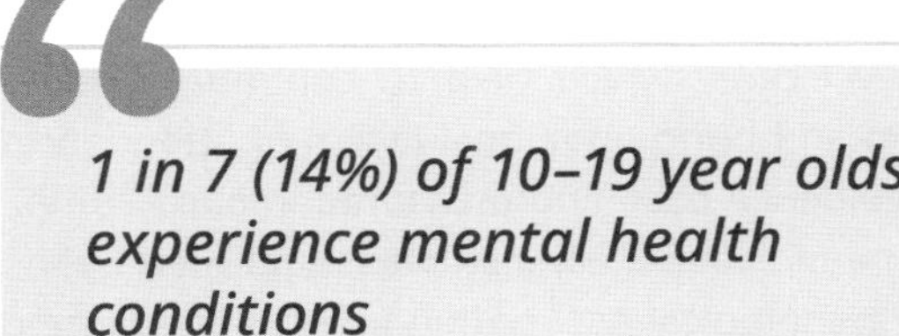

1 in 7 (14%) of 10–19 year olds experience mental health conditions

At the core of the model is a rigorously researched curriculum that Daniel wrote in collaboration with a team of domain expert educators, developmental psychologists, teachers, neuroscientists, and philosophers from around the world. Daniel, based on decades of empirical evidence, believes that wellbeing is a skill that one can learn with practice. His system is activity based, age appropriate, and provides the space for students to understand their own emotions and be more empathetic with their peers, teachers, family, and community.

Success in implementing the Four Pillars model begins with the adults in the system making personal commitments to the well-being practices. Training in these practices is available to these adults (including families) through a 24/7 digital platform. Understanding and implementing the program, as co-learners with their students, makes teachers more emotionally balanced. This has a positive impact on their personal lives as well and in their roles as caregivers with their family and friends. The positive change in the personal sphere then reinforces their role-modeling of the mindful behavioral patterns in their classroom activities. You're a better teacher when you are a better parent and a better person overall.

Daniel believes that in a decade's time, we will reach a tipping point when the vast majority of countries will have policies and programs to support well-being in every school within their borders. Collecting well-being data will be the norm, just as it is with students' physical health and academic achievement, and scientifically based well-being programs will be the standard and an expected part of pedagogy.

THE PROBLEM

The Global Health Data Exchange , estimates that 1 in 7 (14%) of 10–19year olds experience mental health conditions like anxiety, depression, ADHD, and eating disorders. With a growing population of young people, especially in the Global South, and more children joining schools every year, there exists a serious need to institutionalize preventive measures and provide scaffolding for individuals to better manage their mental health from an early age. Moreover, it is imperative to not look at mental healthcare purely from the Euro-centric lens and to learn from older and indigenous wisdom across cultures. This will help develop newer community-based models of caregiving that enable every individual to practice empathy and act as both preventors and as early responders to mental health challenges.

Though many countries have declared mental health as a priority in their educational institutes, there remain two critical problems — there simply are not enough trained individuals to guide students on this journey, and, without systematic measurement of such programs, they fall by the wayside. Moreover, today there is little to no grasp of the need and therefore support for schools to cultivate a culture of wellbeing that counteracts mental health risk factors like bullying and academic stress. Usually, mental health takes a backseat to academic results, which are carefully measured – and define success. And what doesn't get measured, often doesn't get done.

THE STRATEGY

Daniel has shifted the responsibility of mental health from school counselors to everyone in the school. This shift, which catalyzes a cultural shift in the entire school

---

1 Bradley, C., Cordaro, D. T., Zhu, F., Vildostegui, M., Han, R. J., Brackett, M., & Jones, J. (2018). Supporting improvements in classroom climate for students and teachers with the four pillars of wellbeing curriculum. Translational Issues in Psychological Science, 4(3), 245–264. https://doi.org/10.1037/tps0000162

Daniel has built a community of 250 schools across the USA, the UK, New Zealand, Singapore, Indonesia, and Bhutan.

environment, is achieved by training the teachers, providing an evidence-based curriculum, personalized support for implementation, building the requisite digital infrastructure, and measuring progress in real-time. This gives opportunity to students, teachers, parents, and the school administration to have a finger on the pulse of their own wellbeing and that of their whole school. In addition, Daniel has applied medical-grade approaches — from positive psychology — through a combination of personalized human support along with digitally accessible dashboards, activities, and learning journeys.

Daniel's first step is to build a well-being team in a school. The well-being team is a group of 3-10 of the most enthusiastic champions in the school's ecosystem. After several coaching sessions, the well-being team creates a localized strategy to implement various pieces of the Four Pillar program.

Daniel is shifting the role of teachers from instructors to that of role-models who practice positively reinforcing skills of empathy and wellbeing in action. They model the well-being practices and behaviors and act as guides both in helping students to take ownership of their own well-being and in supporting their journey toward practicing it as a skill. This emphasis provides a deep return on investment for the partner schools, as teachers report greater job satisfaction, less stress, and reduced burnout.

Teachers also play a significant role in capturing and reporting data on individual student learning, levels of stress, academic performance, rates of bullying, as well as student engagement, interaction, collaboration, and leadership All of which helps provide the whole school with a data-informed picture of students' progress, needs, and successes.

Rigorous research studies accompany this collection of school-level data, which help to continually refine the program and bring additional layers of attention to program's evidence base and measured impact. For example, in one of Daniel's early studies, published by the American Psychological Association in 2018, they found that three years into one partner school's implementation of the Four Pillars, teachers showed schoolwide increases in contentment, self-compassion, and efficacy as well as decreases in burnout compared to the Year 1 baseline assessments. In addition, the amount of time spent teaching and personally practicing the well-being lessons correlated with the teachers' subjective well-being and self-compassion. The more time teachers spent practicing the program's lessons on their own, the farther with those teachers' levels of stress fell. And, at the end of the rollout, students were also exhibiting better well-being in multiple ways, including the use of a more varied, rich emotional vocabulary, significant improvements in self-awareness, and more frequent experiences of positive emotional states.

The Contentment Foundation has now set out to build the largest dataset on the well-being of children, teachers, and school staff internationally. Given the digital components of the model that offers continuous and comprehensive evaluation, this dataset builds depth and usefulness over time as more and more schools across the world join the program. The dataset will help the model evolve, strengthen, an build confidence. It also allows more players to contribute to the movement with data-driven ideas and practices.

In service of Daniel's goal to build a system applicable globally across schools set in different cultural contexts, he has built a community of 250 schools across the USA, the UK, New Zealand, Singapore, Indonesia, and Bhutan. Now, the Contentment Foundation is partnering with large education networks—such as Pearson Education (100k schools worldwide), Communities in Schools Foundation (2500 schools in the USA), and Eton House (200 schools across Southeast Asia)—in pursuit of the vision to transform schools around the world. Additionally, Daniel is building collaborations with the governments of Bhutan, New Zealand, and several states in the United States to continue to spread the well-being program within public education systems.

To facilitate the spread and scale of the Four Pillars platform and model, Daniel utilizes a "Robinhood" model that uses grants and income from wealthier schools to offset the cost for schools who cannot pay to participate. To scale internationally, Daniel and his team comply with eligibility and cultural norms for each country, which ensures that this team can fully interact within the larger legal, funding, and political structures and systems. Additionally, positioning themselves in culturally responsive ways helps local partners participate in the scaling their work, and ensuring them that as long as they align themselves with the values, protocols, and implementation model, they are completely in control of the work.

THE PERSON

Daniel's early life was focused on school, and he spent much of his time in academia, including six years of undergraduate and graduate study in chemistry. But the stress and anxiety associated with his studies left Daniel feeling burned out, isolated, and increasingly empty inside. So, after experiencing a personal well-being crisis, he made a radical change—he committed to learning about human well-being from a psychological perspective and he began deep-diving into the study of human emotions. He also began to travel and learn from ancient and indigenous traditions of well-being, and started to become clearer, more grounded, and increasingly more capable of managing life's most intense situations, including the loss of most of his family due to severe mental illness.

Daniel went on to earn a PhD in psychology and led three of the largest cross-cultural studies on human emotion ever conducted in the field. He has spent the last decade studying what it means to live a flourishing life, and then sharing the findings with schools around the world. Daniel's research teams have studied over a dozen cultures around the globe, including making first contact with an isolated community in remote Eastern Bhutan.

In July 2014, the National Bureau of Economic Research published a paper that made a huge impact on Daniel's life direction. The study quantified the psychological well-being of every city and region in the United States, listing those cities and regions in order from best to worst in access to mental health resources and highest rates of mental illness. As Daniel read through the data, his entire childhood and unusual career track came into focus for him in a single instant. At the very bottom of this list of hundreds of places was his hometown of Scranton, Pennsylvania. This listing rang true to Daniel's experience as he and most of the people he knew growing up had deep experiences with addiction, abuse, and suicide at home. It was a turning point in Daniel's life and career—he decided to dedicate his research to establishing the foundation of an organization that would make well-being accessible to everyone.

Daniel spent two years as the Director of Wellbeing at the Yale Center for Emotional Intelligence. While there, he and his team inaugurated a new area of research on contentment, publishing some of the first original research on what it means to cultivate unconditional acceptance of the present moment. Daniel's goal is to significantly improve the lives of 1 billion children and 1 billion adults—25 percent of earth's population—within his lifetime.

"Dr. Daniel Cordaro (1985) is one of the top scientific researchers in the fields of emotion psychology and human wellbeing... [who] as founder and CEO of The Contentment Foundation, helps schools, families, companies, and entire nations cultivate sustainable wellbeing by using scientifically-evidenced practices" – Ivo Valkenburg for the New Financial Magazine

GRÉGOIRE AHONGBONON

Founder, Saint-Camille-de-Lellis Association

 www.amis-st-camille.org/en/

In West Africa, in most communities, as it is around the world, mental illness is still very much misunderstood. It is often attributed to a curse or being tormented by evil spirits. The situation is worsened by the critical shortage of qualified mental health practitioners. Seeing the impact and suffering of those living with a mental disability, Gregoire invented and spread a new system of grassroots outreach, care and full reintegration.

SCAN THE CODE TO READ AND SHARE THIS ARTICLE ONLINE

THE NEW IDEA

For over 30 years, Grégoire Ahongbonon, a former mechanic from Benin, has developed a now broad-spread system that spots, helps and re-integrates the ten percent of the population suffering from a mental illness. From being stigmatized and isolated, they can recover their dignity and reclaim their lives. Rejected and forgotten, many people with treatable illnesses like epilepsy, bipolar disorder, schizophrenia and even depression end up chained to trees or in their homes, or are left to wander the streets, without proper clothes, searching for food in the trash.

Grégoire, and his organization, La Saint Camille Association, have created a model, high impact, highly economic system of care that is needed widely across the continents. It transforms the lives of people suffering from mental illness and has contributed to changing public understanding. It points to where all health care must go.

As Grégoire and his team travel across West Africa, they are on alert for reports of mentally ill people who are shackled or mistreated in remote villages. When they find such individuals they offer to take them to one of the reception centers they have established, where they receive food, shelter, a diagnosis from a psychiatrist, and access to treatment and medication. At these centers they are surrounded by caregivers who ensure they receive medical care, affection, and help in reestablishing their self-esteem. Based on the patient's personal progress, and after some months, many individuals are directed to training centers in the community to learn an occupation and begin reintegration into normal social life. A network of drop-in centers and relay centers help to ensure that medication and medical follow-up continues. Family members are often a part of these processes, and they become advocates as they see the results and become educated on the facts regarding mental illness.

Through Grégoire's unwavering tenacity, more than 100,000 patients have been released, cured and rehabilitated through the more than 20 Centers he has established across Ivory Coast, Benin, and Burkina Faso. La Saint Camille continues to expand into new territory, and to build its capacity to provide an alternative for people with mental illness. Many staff members (cooks, managers, nursing assistants, and nurses) are former patients who have themselves benefited from care provided at La Saint Camille. Several of the centers are now even directed by former patients.

Grégoire has proven that people with mental illness can live normal productive lives with proper treatment. The success of his approach has led family and community members to eagerly share the results they have witnessed with others across West Africa. This recognition has spread to the extent that it has almost eliminated demand for alternative centers, where one might previously have found as many as 150 individuals with mental health issues chained to trees.

With facilities also in Ivory Coast and Togo, St. Camille fills a gap across West Africa in mental healthcare provision, left by the state and even the humanitarian sector, said Dr. Jibril Abdulmalik. [Founder and CEO of Asido Foundation/ consultant psychiatrist at the University of Ibadan in Nigeria

THE PROBLEM

The Société Africaine de Santé Mental (SASM) has estimated that 10% of the African population has some kind of mental disorder. When it comes to health care, the highest priority is given to diseases like AIDS and malaria. The World Health Organization (WHO) noted that while in Europe there is one psychiatrist per 1,000 inhabitants, in Africa, the ratio is one psychiatrist per 5 million. The entire country of Benin (population 12.45 million) has one psychiatric hospital, while the Ivory Coast (population 27.5 million) has two. Patients and families must pay to be treated in these facilities. For the poor there are no psychiatrists, no facilities, no treatment, and no medicine. Instead there are only traditional remedies, fear, stigma, taboos, and widespread misunderstandings associated with mental illness. According to SASM, in 43% of such cases across Africa, family members consider that such illnesses have a mystical origin, with only 12% of cases finding their way to trained therapists.

THE STRATEGY

Grounded in his own life experience, Grégoire came to a realization of how fragile human mental health can be, and how in the absence of support, devastation could easily follow. In 1990, he became deeply concerned for the fate of the mentally ill people he saw wandering abandoned and alone. He decided to confront his own fears and to begin approaching them. Every night he would walk to observe their condition and to see where they were sleeping and what they were eating. Together with his wife, they bought a freezer to keep food and fresh water, which they began distributing in the evening to the mentally ill people, creating a bond of friendship.

Gregoire soon realized that they also needed a place to sleep soundly, and so he met with the Director of Bouaké Hospital, who agreed to give him a small abandoned space in the hospital to gather the first patients for treatment and provide them with necessary medication. Quickly, many of these patients began to improve. It was the first time in Côte d'Ivoire, that a general hospital had treated mentally ill patients.

The hospital director, intrigued by Grégoire's actions, took advantage of a visit by the Minister of Health to the hospital of Bouake to share the experience and build ministerial-level support for widening the scope and impact of Gregoire's work. Over the next few years, Gregoire then developed a tiered system of centers – (1) Relay Centers to identify mental health patients and negotiate their

PHOTO CREDIT: *Saint-Camille – Grégoire's human-centered model has helped more than 100,00 patients lead normal productive lives.*

consent or safe transportation to (2) Care Centers for treatment, and (3) Training/Reintegration Centers where the patients learn skills that allow them to be financially independent, build relationships and reintegrate into their communities.

Grégoire has also set up relay centers (mental health care clinics), which are led by nuns. Each Care Center houses around 200 patients. The nursing staff is primarily composed of former patients, thanks to nursing courses that are paid for and arranged by La Saint Camille. A mobile nursing team conducts a quarterly tour of each center with the supervision of local and foreign psychiatrists associated with Saint Camille who prescribe medicines and provide clinical review of new or challenging cases. While public systems do not have capacity to treat mentally ill patients, Saint Camille has built a voluntary system of care that serves the local population for free or in some cases for a small fee.

Former patients have become ambassadors in the fight against the rejection of people suffering from mental disorders. Grégoire has also conducted national and international conferences on mental health. His relentless approach has helped him develop vital partnerships with church and state leaders, and has earned him a dynamic group of friends at Saint Camille composed of volunteers including visiting psychiatrists who help train the nurses and others who carry out awareness campaigns and fundraising activities to provide human, material and financial support.

Thus far, Grégoire has opened 8 reception and care centers, 28 relay centers and 13 training centers in Côte d'Ivoire, Benin, and Burkina Faso. Grégoire and his organization are currently interested in expanding to Togo where the first reception center is already under construction, and plans are in the works to expand to Nigeria.

> *"Grégoire Ahongbonon is a truly remarkable individual and just the kind of leader that the Chester M. Pierce Human Rights Award was designed to honor," said APA President Vivian B. Pender, MD, in a news release. "Guided by his own fierce humanity and his personal experience with mental illness, he has made compassionate care for individuals with mental illness a reality throughout West Africa*

Psychiatric Times

THE PERSON

Although he did not study medicine, Grégoire Ahongbonon has become an important figure in the delivery of mental health services in West Africa. Originally from Benin, he emigrated to Ivory Coast and opened a tire repair business. His business became prosperous but then suddenly declined, leaving him bankrupt. Debt-ridden, this father of six children sank into a great depression, and found himself deeply troubled with suicidal thoughts.

With the support of a Catholic priest, Grégoire went on a pilgrimage to the Holy Land where he rediscovered his faith and regained equilibrium in his mental state. Grounded in his faith, he set out on a mission to help people like himself, who were struggling with mental health issues, be healed. He began visiting patients in hospitals offering what assistance he could and visiting prisons to talk with the prisoners to bring comfort.

With the unwavering support of his wife, he founded the association Saint Camille, and made the promise to end the suffering of people with a mental illness and restore their dignity. Guided by his faith and by an absolute commitment to the mission of Saint Camille, he traversed the streets to unchain and tend to people with untreated mental illnesses. For Grégoire, it is unacceptable, in the 21st century, to find people shackled to trees due to a mental affliction. "As long as there is one man in chains, it is humanity who is chained. Because when I see a man or woman tied to wood or in chains, I see my own image and the image of each and every one of us."

> *For almost 30 years, Gregoire Ahongbonon, a former mechanic from Benin, has helped thousands of West Africans affected by mental illnesses, caring for them in residential centres run by his charity, the Saint Camille association. Above all else, he is determined to stop the practice of keeping mentally ill people in chains*
>
> BBC NEWS

PHOTO CREDIT: *Gregoire Ahongbonon – Grégoire has proven that people with mental illness can live normal productive lives with proper treatment. The success of his approach has led family and community members to eagerly share the results they have witnessed with others across West Africa.*

JIMMY WESTERHEIM

Founder and CEO, The Human Aspect

 www.thehumanaspect.com

In a world where trained mental health professionals can hardly begin to reach all those in need, the world has long needed a peer-to-peer alternative model that meets the gap in provision and shores up formal systems. Jimmy makes recorded stories of people like you, who have been through a mental health challenge like yours easily available to all.

SCAN THE CODE TO READ AND SHARE THIS ARTICLE ONLINE

THE NEW IDEA

Imagine that you are struggling emotionally and mentally, and you don't know how to think or talk about it, don't have access to professional help (or even know how to find it), and are reluctant to talk to family and friends, who, in any case, would have little idea what to do.

Jimmy has discovered a unique new form of help for you. Jimmy's organization, The Human Aspect, skillfully interviews people like you, people who have experienced similar challenges, struggled. They are also different from you, and like you will be soon – they have returned to health. Jimmy has discovered that by watching these profoundly relatable video interviews you only understand that so many others have experienced the same difficulties. And more than that you develop your own capacity successfully to regain your own mental health. Jimmy makes these stories easily and broadly accessible – through the media, online, as a part of the regular high school and college experience, and even increasingly as a tool that psychologists use to reach patients more effectively.

This approach is showing such promise that it being touted as the most effective innovation in how society deals with its growing mental health problem. According to the UN, over 10 percent of the world's population is affected.

By making clear that wrestling with mental health issues is common, in fact "normal", and that people like you regularly struggle and succeed, Jimmy's approach replaces despair, fear, and shame with connection, determination, and self-efficacy.

By flipping the mental health resource pyramid on its head, Jimmy is enabling people with limited access to professional care to share their experiences and learn from peers. Furthermore, Jimmy's model helps us all

PHOTO CREDIT: *Matias Hagen – Jimmy has partnered with social media giants like Facebook to share The Human Aspect's clips in nearly every country*

support those struggling with mental health – classmates, friends, neighbors, and family – to better understand the nature of these adversities and to grasp how they can help.

Jimmy's model is spreading virally around the world, spurred on by Jimmy's entrepreneurial creativity and drive. The interview recordings are free and easily accessed from the 'Life Experience Library', which operates from multiple online platforms. Proactive positioning aims for high-need areas, such as refugee reception centers. The library currently holds over 750 interviews, which have been viewed more than 1.6 million times across 190 countries. The interviews profile both everyday people and well-known influencers, deliberately underlining the message that mental anguish can cripple anyone, anywhere. Users can select by themes like depression, anxiety, addiction, grief, poverty, dyslexia, and traumas resulting from conflict and displacement.

A relentless innovator, Jimmy's most recent addition is podcasts. The Norwegian-language podcast has just surpassed 650,000 downloads in a country of 5.3 million. The English-language podcast will re-launch this year. Governments are beginning to build Jimmy's work into public health systems. In particular, the UK's National Health Service is exploring how to integrate Jimmy's videos into their online mental healthcare programs.

THE PROBLEM

In Norway, Jimmy's home government has pledged to prioritize mental health, yet stigma remains around the topic, especially for the young people who are most at risk. Depression and anxiety have become the third and fourth most common causes of non-fatal illness in the country. The World Health Organization reports similarly dismal patterns across the world. Those affected often don't know how to seek treatment, and, even if they do, finding a therapist can be extremely difficult due to long queues of patients. In Norway, the availability gap in mental health services is so severe that the OECD has explicitly advised the government to address it proactively. In addition, recent studies from universities across Norway indicate that the proportion of students with debilitating mental challenges, such as anxiety or depression, has increased roughly 7 percent for men and women from 2010 to 2021.

Although mental health challenges are commonplace, conversations about them remain rare. Schools and workplaces rarely address these challenges, and people afflicted with poor mental health often feel broken or alone. Due to bureaucracy, limited resources, and increasing demand worldwide, professional care has become harder to find and more expensive. The global mental health crisis continues to grow.

> *It's really hard to relate to a therapist or doctor who hasn't got anything in common with you who is trying to help you. How about you listen to someone of a similar age, same gender, with the same experiences and they will tell you how they overcame that experience. You have someone you can connect to and feel understands you.*

MAXIE EARLE, Volunteer with The Human Aspect

The World Health Organization reported a widening gap between the number of trained mental healthcare professionals and the number of people needing their services. On average, developed countries need 40 to 60 percent more trained professionals to meet the estimated demand. The need for providers in developing countries like India is many, many times higher. Additionally, funding for public health agencies to engage in effective interventions remains chronically insufficient. Although public health officials run information campaigns, their impact is limited. Groups with information about how to manage one's mental health are difficult to access and are too few in comparison to the growing number of people in need.

The existing mental health resource pyramid is not capable of meeting the population's needs. Those at the bottom of society suffer most yet again. Increasing natural (and man-made) disasters and refugee flows further increase the imbalance between need and what the traditional professional dependent system can provide.

THE STRATEGY

Jimmy's model works by destigmatizing conversations about mental health struggles and turns those conversations into a new language that anyone can use to heal themselves.

To realize the model, Jimmy employs a highly original four-step approach. First, using a large volunteer base, The Human Aspect records high-quality first-person stories of overcoming mental health challenges.

Second, he teams up with social media platforms to ensure that his Life Experience Library profiles are freely accessible everywhere. He uses the data gathered to inform future programming to reach more people and better arrive at the needs of communities.

Third, Jimmy partners with schools in Oslo and around the world to engage them in conversations related to changing the way young people learn about and understand mental health.

Fourth, he enriches current mental healthcare provision across Norway and other countries such as Poland, Latvia, the UK, and Nepal by sharing Life Experience Library videos with therapists and professionals, as well as developing additional resources specifically for powerful delivery vectors like public health systems.

To ensure that as many people as possible can access the Life Experience Library, Jimmy and his team create abbreviated versions of each interview. This allows a wide audience to engage with their social media platforms, which over time have garnered a broad global distribution. These videos are designed to engage viewers who are suffering in silence, showing how they are not alone, how others have managed to deal with similar struggles, and that they can do the same. The library is also designed to increase the general knowledge of common mental health illnesses, conditions, and struggles, so people who want to help someone in their own social circles are empowered. For example, three-minute teasers are posted to The Human Aspect's Facebook page, which currently has more than 150,000 followers. Jimmy has coined a new term '*spending positive time on Facebook*' as part of his efforts to transform the way people use social media and how they perceive mental health. Links to the full-length interviews are also included in the posts. A partnership with Facebook, which considers Jimmy's digital platform and no-cost access particularly compelling, has ensured that The Human Aspect can share its abbreviated clips and Library links to users in nearly every country. On top of this, Google's robust platform, including its geo-location service, allows Jimmy to know where videos are viewed most frequently. This drives decisions about whom to interview and what languages to target in the future.

Furthermore, much of The Human Aspect's impact to date is measured qualitatively rather than in numbers alone. Feedback from users across six continents points to the deep impact that the lived experience videos have had on the way people address their mental health. Each interview is categorized, so users can quickly conduct searches based on their specific needs or interests. People from 95 countries appear in the Life Experience Library videos, and while the primary language used is English, interviews are also conducted in Arabic, Somali, Turkish, Tigrinya, Norwegian, Icelandic, Swedish, Danish, French and German.

Jimmy also caters for the many who have limited (or no) access to high-speed Internet and are therefore unable to watch Life Experience videos. To tackle this reality, he is now developing audio-only versions and investigating video compression technology, so the most vulnerable or marginalized can access the site's resources. The Human Aspect has also started a Norwegian-language podcast (www.hverdagspsyken.no) to ensure that its message about mental health reaches as many people as possible. The podcast just surpassed more than 650,000 downloads in a country of 5.3 million. The podcast hosts both mental healthcare professionals and those affected by poor mental health. Recent topics include social anxiety, burnout, animals as therapeutic tools, men and mental health, and the effects of being dyslexic. A new episode is released every Monday. Their English-language podcast is also re-launching this year.

Jimmy also partners with Oslo schools and universities to ensure that young people have access to real-life examples of people living with mental health struggles and vivid examples of how others have overcome them. Use of The Life Experience videos in classrooms ensures

PHOTO CREDIT: *Jimmy Westerheim*

that more students grow up knowing that mental health challenges are common and that they can be comfortable talking about their own struggles. To accommodate the national curriculum's new 'Life Mastery' course for all high school students, Jimmy launched a companion digital educational platform in the summer of 2021. Jimmy is introducing the platform in several schools and conducting research to measure its impact on students. Teachers are also using the platform to find slide decks created by The Human Aspect team that match specific objectives with relevant Life Experience videos. This variety of courses has improved teachers' and students' understanding of mental health.

> *While the primary language used is English, interviews are also conducted in Arabic, Somali, Turkish, Tigrinya, Norwegian, Icelandic, Swedish, Danish, French and German."*

Additionally, Human Aspects also collaborates with professors at Oslo University, Oslo Metropolitan University, and other institutions to introduce the Life Experience Library in curricula. The Oslo-based higher education institution Høyskolen Kristiania has included The Human Aspect's interviews into curricula for three different psychology degrees to help bridge the gap between academic case studies and real-life stories. Together, they are conducting qualitative studies on student learning experiences. Furthermore, academic institutions in the UK, Ukraine, Sierra Leone, Nepal, and elsewhere have now begun supplementing coursework with the Life Experience videos.

The Human Aspect brings a profoundly different approach to mental health, and clinics of professional psychologists, psychiatrists, and therapists in Norway are using the Life Experience videos as tools to help their patients feel less alone and ashamed. In November 2021, more than 3,000 mental health professionals at Schizofrenidagene, Scandinavia's largest conference for mental health professionals, were introduced to interview excerpts provided by The Human Aspect. This reach amongst professionals continues to grow. Jimmy, along with several professional partners, is now testing how different therapy sessions across the country perform when employing his model. Additionally, he is in discussions with both local and regional governments, as well as Norway's National Health Department and the Norwegian Digital Health Directorate, to determine the best method to use the Life Experience Library as a tool for primary and specialized health care workers. The UK's National Health Service, as well as healthcare providers in Warsaw and Rotterdam, are exploring how to integrate the videos into their online mental healthcare programs.

To complement the videos' impact, Jimmy and his team have launched Norway's first Help Resource Page (www.hjelpesiden.no), which lists all the helplines and digital mental health resource links in an accessible and user-friendly way. The team has also started initial work identifying resources to launch similar pages in other countries, including Greece, the UK, and Nepal. On top of this, Jimmy is partnering with the World Health Organization to verify information on resources for mental health around the world.

Jimmy's next steps include making it possible for users to download interviews from anywhere – while at an Internet café for example – and watch them offline – similar to how people use Netflix and Spotify. Jimmy and his team have created a user guide for Life Experience Library viewers, so they can effectively manage their own challenges through the strategic use of interview learnings.

In order to secure new funding streams, Jimmy's organization is launching a paid membership portion of The Human Aspect website for mental health professionals. The baseline resources for this website will be downloadable user-guides for Human Resource managers, psychologists, prison professionals, and professional descriptions of Life Experience interviews.

THE PERSON

Jimmy grew up in a town of around 500 people where he says boys were expected to push through difficult feelings and experiences rather than draw attention by asking for help. In his case, he had to keep inside his feelings arising from an absent, abusive dad and chronically ill mum affected. Despite these travails, or perhaps because of them, at a young age he found his gift for recognizing his peers' talents and leveraging their individual abilities by fostering collaboration. For example, during recess time at school, Jimmy noticed who was better at foraging and who was more design minded. He recalls that he would use that information to build teams where everyone could contribute. In this way, he spread a sense of fairness and belonging. As he got older, Jimmy became a coach at a local summer camp and used these skills to foster a supportive team environment in which everyone felt committed and valued.

Despite assuming leadership roles, Jimmy realized his own biggest obstacle to improving his mental health was himself. Believing this ironic flaw was common if not universal, he named his social venture, 'The Human Aspect'. Jimmy believes mental health struggles and challenges are something all humans experience and should, therefore, be seen as a simple reality for all of humanity rather than a failure or source of shame.

Jimmy's first positive role model was his grandmother. He remembers her practicing empathy with humility. She brought joy and warmth to people's lives through her commitment to helping others. It wasn't until after Jimmy's grandmother died, however, did he hear from her neighbors and friends just how much of a difference she made in their lives. He strives to be just as impactful.

> *The Norwegian-language podcast has just surpassed 650,000 downloads in a country of 5.3 million.*

Following a life-changing sporting accident at the age of 27, Jimmy left his job in shipping and joined a leading international citizen group. He was posted to Afghanistan and Greece and soon realized that no one was talking about the stressful situations affecting his colleagues. For many, alcohol and drug-use became essential for coping, and a few sought support by opening up with each other. Having witnessed these mental health challenges accompanied by poor management, Jimmy returned home to Oslo and started to ask people on sidewalks and public squares whether they had faced mental health challenges and, if so, how they had managed them. After filming around 20 of these interviews, Jimmy realized that everyone had struggles, regardless of their backgrounds. This fact confirmed his earlier instinct about the commonality of mental health issues even though no one ever talked with him about it. He couldn't understand why people didn't talk about their situations or ask each other for help despite facing similar experiences with mental health. It was then that Jimmy when mental anguish was reunderstand as 'normal' and 'ordinary', people could start to talk freely about it and enable others to support their healing. Inspired with his vision of what he came to think of as "the human aspect" of being human, Jimmy next set out to find a digital company to help him build the Life Experience Library, and, with the help of the Oslo municipal government, his organization, The Human Aspect, became a reality.

PHOTO CREDIT: *Jimmy Westerheim*

FULL ECONOMIC CITIZENSHIP

MOUSSA CAMARA
France

TIM LAMPKIN
United States

MOUSSA CAMARA

Founder, Les Déterminés

 www.lesdetermines.fr/en/

Moussa Camara advances social and economic justice in France's ghettoized suburbs and other segregated, underserved communities through democratizing entrepreneurship. By lowering the barriers to entry for out-of-school, out-of-work immigrant youth, he's not only setting them on the path to starting their own businesses and developing their communities, he's also changing the way they and their communities are viewed, breaking through stereotypes and cycles of neglect that have kept them disadvantaged.

SCAN THE CODE TO READ AND SHARE THIS ARTICLE ONLINE

THE NEW IDEA

Moussa Camara combats discrimination and chronic unemployment – especially youth unemployment – – in the ghettoized suburbs and other underserved communities in France by lowering the barriers to entrepreneurship. His programs help thousands of people who would otherwise be jobless, disaffected, and alienated crack the code, learn their way around the entrepreneurial ecosystem, and forge their own place in the French economy and society. Moussa's work transforms longstanding barriers that have effectively excluded these people into new opportunities for them to learn skills, start their own businesses, and become employers themselves.

His organization Les Déterminés ("the determined ones") exposes people in marginalized immigrant and rural communities in France to entrepreneurship. It's the only free support program that combines all the keys that participants need to unlock entrepreneurship: Training, mentoring, networking, and incubators. Requiring no prior background or qualifications, Les Déterminés helps participants learn to see themselves as entrepreneurial and enables them to develop their ideas and skills to launch and grow their businesses.

Like entrepreneurs everywhere, participants in Moussa's programs self-select. Given where they are from, they would normally face many subtle and not-so-subtle walls. But unlike the way many other entrepreneurs get started, Les Déterminés has no barriers to entry and no prerequisites other than the desire to learn about

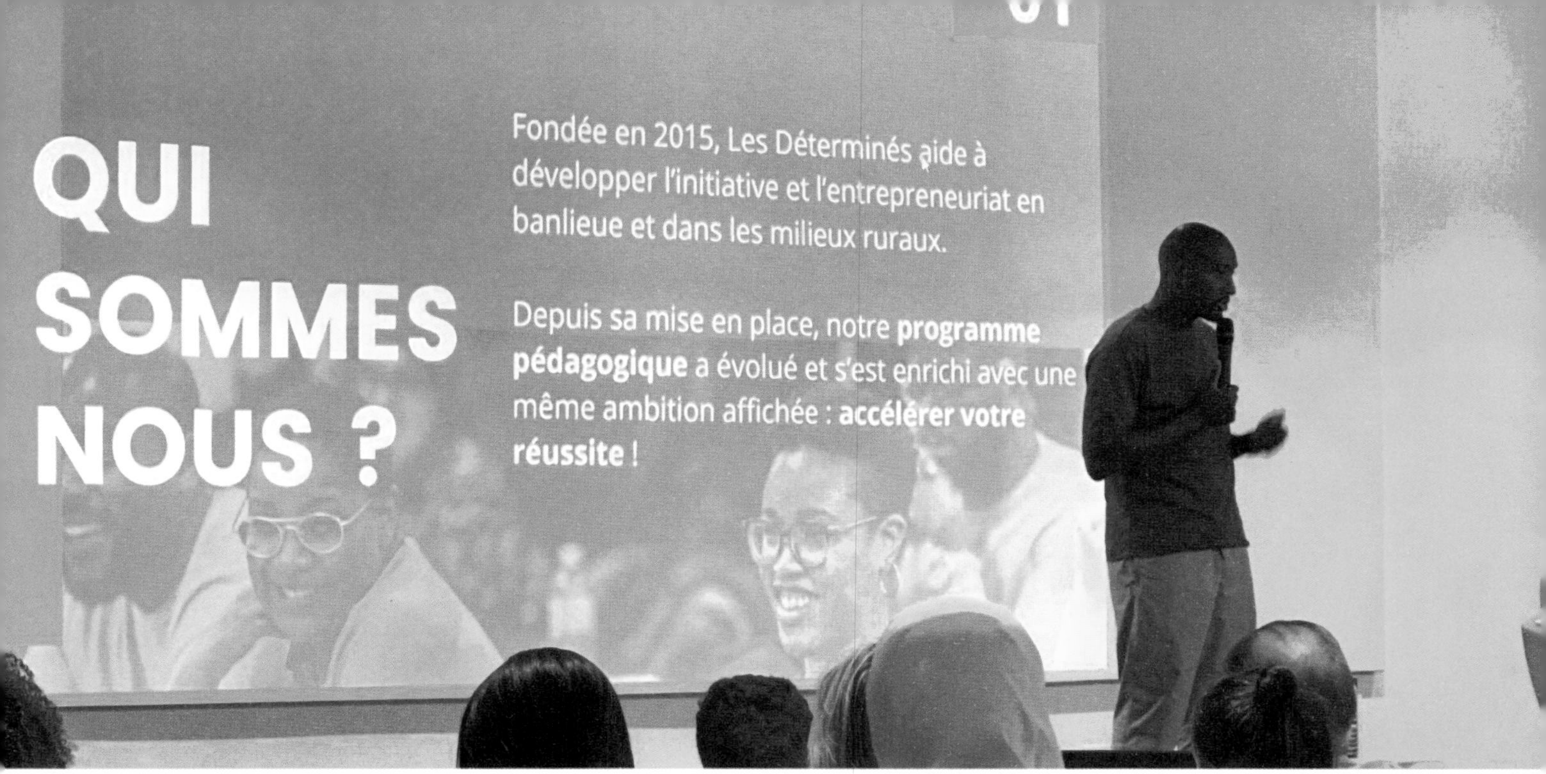

PHOTO CREDIT: *Les Determines – There are no prerequisites to join Les Determines except the desire to learn, making entry into the entrepreneurial world more accessible to young people from underserved communities*

entrepreneurship. Race, class, culture, social status, connections, or educational attainment have no bearing on candidates accessing the program. Diversity, equity, and inclusion are fundamental. Anyone from any background can and does apply. Success is determined by motivation, commitment, teamwork, and aptitude. Over 60% of trainees are women (double the percentage of business creation by women nationally), and 64% are under 25. Three-quarters of them go on to found their own ventures, many of which employ others.

Participants' high success rate not only helps them and their employees, it also helps shift social attitudes, replacing the negative mindsets and narratives about these youth—that these out-of-school, unemployed, disadvantaged immigrants and children of immigrants are a lost cause—with actual evidence that they are in fact self-motivated, proactive, innovative, and determined and able to succeed. That shift itself has broad social and economic implications.

Founded in 2015, Les Déterminés has grown rapidly into a national network, with programs in 17 cities. Moussa has built a vibrant, influential community of entrepreneurs across France, in which alumni of his programs connect with one another and with other business leaders and mentors. Moussa himself has gained wide recognition and credibility as a successful entrepreneur and next-generation leader from France's working-class suburbs, positioning him as an effective advocate for changing policies that have long left these communities segregated and disadvantaged.

> *From Cergy-Pontoise (Val-d'Oise), where the entrepreneur grew up, to Marseille, via Paris, Nancy, Lyon, Roubaix, Rouen, Toulouse, and Montpellier, Moussa Camara and his team work on democratization of entrepreneurship. The only selection criteria for the program are the candidate's determination and motivation to complete his or her project.*

75% of those who have taken Les Determines' trainings have started their own businesses.

THE PROBLEM

The French word *banlieue* refers primarily to France's working-class suburbs. It's a contraction of the words ban ("to forbid") and lieue ("league," a unit measure of about four miles). It originally referred to territory beyond the edge of urban tax collection zones, but today it connotes a sense of enforced removal or exile outside a city center.

The banlieues were built on the outskirts of French cities from the end of World War II though the 1970s. Their original purpose was to help house those left homeless by the War. They were designed as mixed-income neighborhoods with huge housing complexes, intended to maximize interaction among different social classes and encourage solidarity.

That was the theory, but in practice, over time, middle-class families moved out, and immigrants from former French colonies moved in. In the 1980s, a major recession hit, sparking high unemployment. It left many more immigrants jobless and stranded in the *banlieues*, and generated debate and tension over the presence of immigrants in France. The *banlieues* increasingly became low-income, predominantly Black and Brown, satellites segregated from their wealthier, whiter urban centers, spatially as well as culturally and socially. As poverty and crime rose in these communities, public health, education, transportation, and other public services declined. *Banlieue* residents – largely Muslim immigrants of color – found themselves out of school, out of work, and feeling abandoned.

It's a deep, intractable social and economic rift. Today *banlieue* residents comprise 8% of France's population. 40% of them live below the poverty line. Their unemployment rates are three times the national average, with youth unemployment rates hovering around 40%.

Despite decades of work to address the inequities of the *banlieues* with policy, and through the citizen sector's social policies, as well as more than 40 years of considerable efforts from citizen and social sectors, high crime, poor public health, failing schools, and other deep problems persist.

Government and social sector programs intended to ameliorate these problems generally haven't worked. They are typically siloed and exogenous, looking at the *banlieues* from the outside, treating its residents as passive recipients of ineffective aid. Not surprisingly, many in the banlieues, especially youth, are disaffected and alienated, unlikely to become or even imagine becoming stakeholders in the larger French economy and society.

THE STRATEGY

Moussa's organization, *Les Déterminés*, lowers the barriers to the entrepreneurial world by recruiting candidates from the *banlieues* and other underserved communities, including rural communities. And the organization raises its success rate by putting these candidates through a rigorous selection process, finding and honing the strengths of those who have a desire to succeed and can benefit from the program most. Community leaders and local associations help identify local young people whom they feel would be strong candidates. Applicants are interviewed in front of a jury and undergo three days of workshops prior to selection.

Successful candidates participate in a free, six-month training and mentoring program. It starts with a three-week intensive course to develop and differentiate these participants' ideas and hone their entrepreneurial skills. After that, the trainings continue two days a week for another five months. Participants learn how to identify their value proposition, conduct market research, write a business plan, attract investment, and be effective at marketing and communications. From inspiring successful business leaders who participate in the trainings, these participants learn about what it is like to build a business and become a business leader. They are also connected to a network of professionals in the field of their chosen venture, continuing to meet with these professionals one-on-one for mentoring when the formal trainings end.

In addition to looking outward and learning about the entrepreneurial world, an important dimension of the training involves looking inward, doing personal development work, learning from one another in a supportive peer environment, and discovering how to function as a strong team.

Demand for Moussa's programs more than tripled in 2020 due to the pandemic ("During lockdown, many people discovered their passion or just realized a life of wage labor was not for them," he said) and continues to grow. To date, thousands have taken the *Les Déterminés* trainings, 75% of whom started their own businesses, and some 80% are still in business four years later. Notably, the entrepreneurs behind four hundred of these businesses are women.

PHOTO CREDIT: *Les Determines*

> *"Moussa Camara founded Les Déterminés in 2015 to bring out talented entrepreneurs in working-class neighborhoods.... Coming from a modest family in Cergy-Pontoise, he needed extraordinary tenacity to carry out this project from scratch. By focusing on his mission, he has given a leg up to 700, now thousands of young entrepreneurs. 80% of the companies they created are still active four years later."*

PHOTO CREDIT: *Les Determines – Opening partnership spaces in the banlieues helps keep the economic benefits of the entrepreneurial ventures in the community, while helping change the negative perceptions toward the banlieue.*

Many of the ventures are located in the heart of the banlieues and other underserved communities, replacing the stereotype of endemic joblessness and empty storefronts with bustling entrepreneurial activity. To make sure the activity is highly visible, Moussa works with social housing organizations to obtain ground-floor spaces and set them up for Les Déterminés graduates to use as co-working spaces for the first six to 12 months after launch and as incubators, such as food laboratories for catering ventures. With Erigère, a social housing organization in the Paris region, Moussa is working to open a dozen such partnership spaces in the banlieues and is starting new housing collaborations with the federal ministry for the Paris region. Locating these entrepreneurial ventures in the heart of the banlieue keeps in the community the economic benefits these ventures generate and keeping these ventures visible creates a tangible symbol of banlieue entrepreneurship that surprises some and inspires others – – a powerful way to change mindsets and attitudes toward the banlieue.

Les Déterminés alumni who start their own businesses can join a group of other Les Déterminés entrepreneurs in their region, supporting each other and sharing problems, ideas, and best practices as their ventures develop, and accessing workshops and networking events specially designed for them.

A significant minority of Les Déterminés trainees seek jobs rather than start their own businesses, using the skills they learned to become intrapreneurs within their organizations. That outcome has led Moussa to pilot short-term employability programs for out-of-school or unemployed banlieue youth, designed in collaboration with companies which are experiencing talent shortages and are eager to recruit new workers. Trainees work with business leaders and entrepreneurs to develop business skills, and the partner companies commit to hiring a certain number of them. So far, five companies have taken part in the program. 62% of participants have found work upon completion, while others have decided to obtain more training. As a result of the pilot's success, Moussa is advising France's National Employment Agency on how to reach unemployed banlieue youth and help them find jobs.

Government officials have recognized Moussa as a powerful next-generation leader and have even suggested that he is a candidate for political office. Moussa is starting to effect policy change, for example convincing the Parisian authorities to identify and map key community-based organizations they can work with to remediate underrecognized problems. Moussa has attracted dozens of corporate partners to Les Déterminés, such as the auditing and consulting firm, Mazars; the software manufacturer, SAP; and the bank, BNP Paribas.

[Moussa Camara] set out to convince university professors, business leaders, chartered accountants and all types of stakeholders to train women and men who feel they are under the radar. He also won over public and private funders, including BPI France, Mazars, BNP Paribas and Engie. Les Déterminés offers over 400 hours of free training over a six-month period, divided into discreet modules dealing with financial, marketing, or sales issues. Since its creation, the group has helped 700, now thousands of people, found some 450 companies

LE FIGARO

THE PERSON

One of eight children, Moussa grew up in a diverse, densely populated Croix-Petit district of Cergy-Pontoise, a *banlieue* outside Paris. There, he forged friendships with kids of different nationalities and learned the values of solidarity, sharing, and community engagement. From the age of six, he and his siblings participated in neighborhood clean-ups and political demonstrations.

Moussa's parents emigrated from Mali and were illiterate, but always pushed him to succeed at school. Many of his friends dropped out by age 16 or earlier, but Moussa stayed and took a professional baccalaureate degree. To earn money, he invented informal jobs for himself. For example, at age 15 he earned 50 euros a week by convincing the owner of the local supermarket to let him find and return shopping carts from across the neighborhood.

In 2006, when Moussa was 20, an urban renewal project threatened to decimate his neighborhood and destroy the local soccer stadium. That motivated Moussa to organize his friends and found the citizen sector organization, *Agir pour Réussir* ("Act to Succeed"), which pushed back against the demolition plans. It rallied the community with civic and sports events, and facilitated dialog between *banlieue* residents and public authorities, bridging two normally separate worlds.

The next year, riots broke out in Cergy after a police officer shot a local youth. "We felt injustice on a daily basis," Moussa says. "A young man is shot in the shoulder and nearly dies. After the strong tensions that ensued, we said to ourselves that we had to come up with another solution." To counter the riots and protest the shooting, Moussa and *Agir pour Réussir* organized peaceful demonstrations in which *banlieue* youth registered to vote en masse to show their determination to engage civic life and demand their say. The demonstration was well publicized and served as a sharp, intentional contrast to the rioting that had dominated French media coverage.

When Moussa finished school at 21, he sought work at a telecom company as a technician, and was told the company wasn't hiring, only working with independent contractors. So, he decided to become one. He took a technical training course and launched his own business, and even hired a few employees from the neighborhood. The company failed after five years, but in the process, Moussa learned firsthand the barriers banlieue youth encounter to cracking the codes of entrepreneurship, including lack of knowledge, connections, role models, and access to support programs and funding.

In 2011, Moussa attended a conference at the University of Cergy-Pontoise where he met Thione Niang. Born in Senegal, Niang was an entrepreneur former leader of the Young Democrats of America. Impressed by Moussa's accomplishments and leadership potential, Niang invited him to Washington, DC, to join a two-month mentoring program for emerging next-generation leaders.

That proved to be a turning point in Moussa's career. *Agir pour Réussir* addressed social issues, but Moussa came to understand that economic empowerment was key to social change in the banlieue. "In the United States I learned two things," he said. "The importance of communication and the importance of business. If you want to do more socially, you have to do more business. For there to be social justice, you first need economic justice." Upon returning to France, he developed his idea for empowering banlieue residents through entrepreneurship and launched *Les Déterminés.*

TIM LAMPKIN

Founder and CEO, Higher Purpose Co.

 http://www.timlampkin.com

Tim unlocks opportunities for wealth creation for Black, rural entrepreneurs by shifting everything from their sense of what is possible through mutual support to finances.

SCAN THE CODE TO READ AND SHARE THIS ARTICLE ONLINE

THE NEW IDEA

Tim recognizes that the current economic system is not working for everyone, and that rural Black potential entrepreneurs are often unable to start businesses and generate family and community wealth because of barriers such as lack of capital and collateral. Through his organization, Higher Purpose Co., he is creating a statewide community of Black entrepreneurs, artists, and farmers who support one another as a "new generation of local economy practitioners." He strategically links this community with an engaged and transformed network of the full range of financial institutions and funders that collaborate and coordinate in new ways to build community wealth. Through these efforts Tim is creating rural economic development for Black Americans to collectively build political, cultural, and financial capital and break the cycle of generations of economic injustice that have dominated the South.

Tim's insights and new approach are rooted in his experience in Clarksdale, Mississippi, a city of 15,000 in the heart of the Mississippi Delta. But the entrepreneurs he supports are scattered around the state. The funding network includes institutions from coast to coast. And demand for his novel approach is already international. Tim has created a model that can spread to other rural communities where economic opportunities that generate wealth, employment, and prosperity are missing and desperately needed. Leaving past patterns behind that do not address underlying systemic inequities, Tim and his work point us towards a world of collaboration with neighbors across sectors, leading to community knowledge and strength and broad, inclusive prosperity. This in turn points to economic, social, and political change and revival across rural America.

THE PROBLEM

The development of personal wealth and capital in the U.S. is mostly driven by business and home and land ownership, all of which have been historically limited for Black communities in America (and federally subsidized for middle class white communities). In 2020, The Washington Post reported that the home ownership gap between Black and white Americans is larger today that it was in 1934, when the Federal Housing Administration was established. This legacy of wealth disparities has been compounded by a lack of investment in rural and Black, Indigenous and people of color (BIPOC) communities, resulting in neighborhoods that are underfunded and overlooked.

Both (1) Jim Crow and (2) a finance system that has systematically undervalued Black neighborhoods and therefore properties have terrible, deep consequences. The power of mutual help and a deeply changed financial system are needed to reverse course.

This work of bringing a community together and then helping it unite to drive towards a big, bold, and collective vision takes talent and time. There is an urgent need for organizations that have long-standing, rooted, and locally committed teams with social capital and knowledge of how their community operates. And yet local teams with years of experience, energy, and support to maintain momentum and morale are exceedingly rare in the rural economic development sector. In fact, this underperforming sector has a way of repelling energized, entrepreneurial talent (who generally conclude that they can do better venturing out on their own and starting businesses, rather than helping other aspiring entrepreneurs make a go of it).

Tim experiences all these challenges in his life and work in the Mississippi Delta. And yet he's not about to jump ship, either by going solo or moving away. This is where Tim was raised, and where he realized an idea for how to help lead his community towards collective wealth and prosperity.

THE STRATEGY

Tim has developed a comprehensive model for economic transformation that builds on the strengths of potential local changemakers, gets funders unstuck, and leverages the untapped assets of changemakers and funders alike to create better systems that work towards the goal of shared prosperity. Notably absent from Tim's model is dependence on prior wealth or access to capital as a measure of someone's promises, trustworthiness, or creditworthiness.

Tim's core belief is that Black entrepreneurs need access to opportunities and capital in order to thrive. Higher Purpose Co.'s (HPC) clear focus here has allowed it to successfully serve 1,500 Black entrepreneurs, farmers, and artists to date, many of them Black women. They statistically have earnings far behind white men and women in the U.S. HPC's new membership work currently serves 200 Black entrepreneurs and aims to increase this number to 300 this year.

And yet, unlike traditional business accelerators or incubators, HPC isn't fixed on the number of individual businesses, or on a few individual break-out success stories. In addition to providing more traditional resources for emerging entrepreneurs, Tim believes that community-based knowledge and encompassing cultural and

PHOTO CREDIT: *Trent Calvin Photography – Tim's 'wealth creation' model is breaking the cycle of intergenerational poverty in Black rural communities*

PHOTO CREDIT: *Ivory Cancer, Higher Purpose Co. – HPC's coordinated and supportive network of entrepreneurs helps contribute to community knowlegde and inclusive prosperity*

historical contexts are crucial to building collective success and a collective economy.

The programming that Tim and HPC provide benefits individual entrepreneurs while also reinforcing the overall regional business community. The Higher Purpose Business Fellowship is the first organization for Black entrepreneurs in Mississippi. It begins with a six-month program for emergent Black entrepreneurs. Cohorts can learn about entrepreneurship through community building and partnership investments. Immersion trips to cities like Jackson, MS; Montgomery, AL; and Selma, AL, have resulted in community-based research and policy education for Black Southern residents. These programs serve as a launchpad for creating local businesses and relationships. They also provide a space for community reflection around the systemic policies and structural barriers that have limited collective prosperity in the Black community for so long, and how to collectively build communities that thrive. And that's exactly what happens next.

The work of spotting new business opportunities, making connections, doing business with peer organizations, and weaving all this together is central to the success of HPC and its members. For example, an HPC business member with a successful juice bar business in Jackson helped another entrepreneur within the membership set up their own store in Greenville (2 hours north and outside their target market). Entrepreneurs working as midwives, childcare providers, educators, photographers, chefs, nurse practitioners and more share resources through membership meetings. They also signal to the network where gaps – like mental health support — might be filled by HPC up-and-coming entrepreneurs.

An intelligent connected and coordinated network stands a far better chance of interfacing and influencing the current system than individuals.

This collective intelligence and peer support de-risks the individual enterprises. This value is not lost on funders — another obvious stakeholder in asset building programming who have long been disconnected from rural Black communities.

HPC is building a vetted and engaged network of funders (the "Funding Network") who are eager to do business with previously overlooked (they might say "untapped") community members. HPC provides services like capital matchmaking, application packaging, and customized business growth support to help funders and local entrepreneurs alike get acquainted. HPC then helps their members navigate the full 'capital stack' of grants, small zero interest loans, low interest loans, and venture capital that the Funding Network brings to the table. This allows HPC – or any other organization adopting this approach – to act as a status-quo-shifting intermediary, creating capital blueprints for businesses that acknowledge and meet the entrepreneurs' and funders' changing needs over time, with fewer unknowns, less friction, and support throughout.

In addition to linking their entrepreneurs with banks and funders, HPC has also been successful in raising funds from national impact investors and philanthropic investors. They offer loan guarantees, helping funding

Network members overcome the hurdles of pre-existing capital or collateral. HPC can also facilitate zero interest loans through their partnership with Kiva, as the region's first Kiva Hub. And HPC's own fundraising has allowed them to deploy over $1 million in affordable capital to date to Black entrepreneurs across Mississippi. Paired with the fact that Tim has been able to effectively collateralize peer support and collective intelligence, HPC's ability to fundraise flexible capital further contributes to a guarantee system that ensures even risk averse funders can do more business with HPC's community entrepreneurs.

The experience of funders has been so positive that Tim and team have found they can apply even more leverage, asking for better terms or at least more accessible processes, like common applications and tweaks that streamline application processes (limiting the number of in-person meetings, printing, and scanning) in a way that acknowledges the experience of their entrepreneurs, like farmers and hourly workers for whom the current system is too inflexible.

The HPC idea is also catching on and being replicated in other rural communities, such as Little Rock and Bentonville, both in Arkansas. Tim has also spoken to colleagues in Canada about replicating the model there, ensuring that this concept of "wealth creation" is beginning to be reimagined in communities across the North American continent. Non-profit community-based economic justice organizations will be a key component of Tim's spread strategy, and he's finding that they have many of the ingredients necessary to adopt and deploy this much fuller and now proven model. It may only require a few tweaks to center collective wealth and coordinated business practices in these groups, and then they too can build funding networks, capital blueprints, loan guarantee funds, and unlock economic opportunities. While it requires time and effort, the outsized value that supporting organizations operating in this way significantly de-risks investments and can translate into more options for funding, even without existing capital or collateral. Through this approach, Tim is helping communities crack open the current wealth-creation system so that it finally works for those who need it most.

Tim and his team are committed long-term to the work of interrupting inter-generational poverty. To stay the course, they prioritize team wellbeing, professional development, and tenure. And as Tim starts to formally share and spread the model far and wide, he and his core team are setting down roots in the Delta by developing a large downtown Clarksdale hub for a range of uses, from HPC operations and programming to mixed-use venues for their up-and-coming entrepreneurs

THE PERSON

Tim's family history has deep roots in Mississippi and the Delta region. While he was born in Chicago, he was still in grade school when his family moved back to the region. Tim decided to stay close to home and attended Mississippi Valley State University, which helped him to understand the significant role of African Americans in the world. Following college, Tim had hoped to find his footing in the private sector in Alabama. Yet, after talking to family and a close mentor, Tim was inspired to move back to Mississippi where he felt he could have the most impact.

Once he returned, Tim began a consulting company and contracted work that had him directly engaging with the Mississippi public. In this role, Tim was able to work with Delta State University on a USDA grant, where he assisted business owners across five counties in the Mississippi Delta. This experience of "apprenticing with the problem" and learning all about the barriers and systemic flaws motivated him to apply for a development role at a local community development financial institute. During his time working at a local CDFI, Tim and his team distributed over one million dollars in funding for community-based projects related to tourism, housing, youth engagement, public safety, and arts/culture. After talking to community members and hearing stories from his fellow neighbors, Tim was inspired to create a small business program. While the CDFI (currently a HPC partner) did not initially see how this would be possible, Tim's idea then became the blueprint for Higher Purpose Co. that would transform community wealth within the region.

Tim is inspired by and honored to serve Black entrepreneurs, farmers, and artists in the pursuit of economic justice, reparations, and building community wealth for current and future generations of rural residents. Tim has a deep contextual understanding of the Delta's histories, people, and potential. Rather than abandoning it, he is determined to see it flourish. In a time when so many are told to leave for the city and coasts, Tim is opening a door for future generations to develop rural communities through the deep knowledge and power that they hold as residents.

CIVIC ENGAGEMENT

REV. HEBER BROWN III

United States

MARIA TERESA RONDEROS

Columbia

MEENA PALANIAPPAN

Indonesia

REV. DR. HEBER BROWN III

Community-Inspired Food Ecosystems

 www.heberbrown.com

By engaging the most resilient of Black institutions – the Black Church – Heber Brown III is building a national network of Black-led food ecosystems that bring wealth, health, and power to Black communities across the United States.

SCAN THE CODE TO READ AND SHARE THIS ARTICLE ONLINE

THE NEW IDEA

To address disenfranchisement and food insecurity in the Black community, Heber is creating a new, alternative, Black-led food ecosystem anchored by the Black Church. From his base in Baltimore, MD, he has modeled a set of practical interventions that Black Churches around the country are now taking up, from hosting community gardens and farmers' markets to coordinating wholesale purchasing and food distribution. The more that Black Churches and communities can rely on their own systems of nourishment, the less they have to depend on government, charity, and industrial food production – key enablers of our broken food system.

Over the last five years, more than 170 churches have heeded Heber's invigorating call and have committed funds, land, kitchens, classrooms, and organized congregations in historically red-lined communities as key assets that can be utilized in the creation of Black-led food ecosystems. Now Heber is weaving together a national network of the most robust local nodes and creating "Black foodways" and other lines of support, thus complimenting bottom-up power with national infrastructure and scale. Networked Black churches can then do something that individual churches alone cannot: they can contract with increasing numbers of Black farmers who aspire to grow larger than direct-to-consumer market gardens.

Looking ahead, Heber wants the image of a pastor driving a refrigerated produce truck on a Saturday to be as vivid as the image of a reverend preaching a Sunday sermon. He wants to see Black churches serving up physical as well as spiritual nourishment, and Black farmers looking to the future with optimism... and, together, Black communities around the country stewarding vibrant, locally owned food systems that nourish bodies, respect the earth, and build self-determination, resilience, pride, and joy.

PHOTO Credit: The Black Church Food Security Network – With $500 grants, BCFSN helps churches start their own garden program

THE PROBLEM

According to some estimates, ten million Black Americans experience food insecurity – over three times the rate for white Americans. One reason for this is that Black communities consistently face "crisis level" poverty and a situation Heber and a growing number of social innovators describe as "food apartheid," a term that underscores the racially discriminatory political structures that affect control of the food system and food access and help make sense of the resulting inequities in health, wealth, and power along racial lines.

Were someone to tally the policy decisions that have negatively affected Black communities' food access and control just in the last century and a half, the list would be long and all-encompassing, including the broken promises of land for Black soldiers who fought in the American Civil War, the 1933 Home Owners Loan Corporation that introduced "redlining maps" and notions that Black communities weren't credit-worthy, and our industrial food system that prioritizes profits over all else. And while the agriculture economy has grown in the U.S., the number of Black-owned farms has declined – from 14% of the nation's farms a century ago to just 2% today.

Many organizations address the negative impacts of food apartheid through delivering services and meeting material needs. But, as Heber points out, "one of the weaknesses of the 'service provider approach,' is that it can replace people's dependency on the corporate food system with dependency on benevolent nonprofits and NGOs" that, with the best of intentions, do not address the root problem.

THE STRATEGY

Despite legacies of loss and inequality, Heber focuses on the many assets of the Black community, with the Black Church at the top of the list. Heber is a third-generation pastor who led the Pleasant Hope Baptist Church in Baltimore, MD for fourteen years. Early in Heber's tenure, as the youngest reverend there, he watched many in his congregation end up in the hospital because of diet-related problems, and he yearned to do something beyond praying with them for their comfort. So, he and his congregation tilled up the front lawn of the church, put in garden beds, and planted fruits and vegetables. Indeed, this experience aligned with Heber's understanding of the Black Church as the place, throughout American history, where Black communities have had the most agency and autonomy, where Black people have been "freest to speak, share, sing, cry, put resources together, and to support each other."

PHOTO Credit: The Black Church Food Security Network – Local control over the means of food production is key to eliminate food apartheid.

Heber took his work to another level in the spring of 2015, a time now referred to by many as the "Baltimore Uprising" due to widespread unrest in the wake of the death of Freddie Gray, a Black resident, in police custody. Heber watched city services and non-profits retreat during the month of protests and demonstrations. Public transportation stopped. When the public schools closed, 80,000 Black children lost access to free breakfast and lunch. "Support that we needed was just not there," Heber observed. "Charity had failed us; it was time for us to do something for ourselves." And a few raised garden beds in front of one church wasn't nearly enough. Heber called his farmer friends and his pastor friends. Churches became community kitchens and parishioners delivered meals. Pastors hosted farmers' markets at church on Saturdays while preaching on Sunday about self-care and food sovereignty. The Black Church Food Security Network, an organization that Heber now leads full-time, was born.

By the next growing season, ten more Baltimore congregations had committed resources, established community gardens, and joined the Black Church Food Security Network (BCFSN). By 2018, Heber had formally organized and launched a national appeal to other churches and farmers to join the network. Depending on a church's capacity and needs, BCFSN offers $500 grants to start a garden program, advice on how to host a successful farmers' market, strategic growing plans based on a particular church's USDA growing zone, and support in starting food preservation classes or small-scale food businesses. Heber hopes to offer $50,000 grants to churches that are ready to invest in transportation and cold storage, for example, and serve as nodes in the growing national network.

To ensure these efforts are sustainable, Heber invites churches to align their financial practices with their values by directly funding this work. After payroll and facilities, food is often a church's biggest expense. Rather than spend that at Walmart or Costco, BCFSN can help churches put funds to work in the community. And rather than send money around the world on missions, churches can support food sovereignty right at home. Five churches already commit annual support in their budgets to BCFSN.

Heber is adamant that the work grows beyond church gardens. The antidote to food apartheid isn't a garden patch; it's local control over the means of producing and distributing healthy food. It's a food system where all involved are working in a coordinated way towards a shared purpose. And it's a national network of support coordinating extra efforts to link and lift those local systems. The effort isn't just matchmaking between farmers and churches. As Heber puts it, "we're working hard to influence Black farmers to prioritize Black churches and see these anchor institutions as viable options for strategic and transformative partnership."

> *As of early May, [Rev. Dr. Heber Brown III] expanded his ministry beyond Baltimore, bringing 125 churches across the country into the network"*
>
> Baltimore MAGAZINE

As for fellow pastors, Heber invites them to extend their idea of mission. His appeal starts, "similar to the biblical story of Noah, we believe that God has called us to help build the infrastructure needed to withstand the ramifications of climate change, food scarcity, and white supremacy by organizing Black churches to serve as food hubs, food distributors, and economic engines for more just and locally managed supply chains." Heber might also remind church leaders that at various times during the continuous Black Freedom Struggle, congregations have often made their assets and resources available for social justice.

Heber is now focused on stitching together geographically strategic chapters in the BCFSN into a truly national infrastructure. His current budget includes line items like refrigerated trucks and sprinter vans for local deliveries as well as national operations managers. This is critical as the next phase of his model will see him refining these inter-state, node-to-node operations and logistics to bring scale to all these efforts. For example, Heber and the BCFSN will work to enable mid-sized farmers to access bigger markets, like the sweet potato farmer who may be too small to sell to big grocery store chains, but big enough that he shouldn't have to sell potatoes by the pound at his farm gate. Enter the BCFSN and this farmer can have one contract at the beginning of the season,

PHOTO Credit: The Black Church Food Security Network

one sale at harvest time, and then the buyer, the BCFSN, can take on the transportation, storage, distribution, and sales of his crop. The truck that arrives in Baltimore with sweet potatoes can then return to the Carolinas, for example, filled with fresh crabs from the Chesapeake Bay.

That is how local food systems will come together as a "foodway," the first of which will stretch along the East Coast's Interstate-95 corridor, from Florida up through Baltimore, New York, and Boston. Heber estimates that a Black-led food supply chain will be capable of transporting at least 100,000 pounds of produce and value-added food items to communities through BCFSN member churches per year.

Looking ahead, Heber expects the number of Black Churches in the network to reach 250 in 2023. Ten years out, or sooner, he envisions Black food ecosystems across the northeast, southeast, and parts of the Midwest anchored by African American churches in partnership with Black farmers. On top of that, any church, mosque, synagogue, or community group can tap the network. Through all this, Heber draws on the resilience, ingenuity, and pride of the Black Church to help everyone – from Black farmers to farmers' market shoppers to all people in need – not just to critique current systems but, as Heber puts it, to "create what should be."

PHOTO Credit: The Black Church Food Security Network

> *In the city of Baltimore, The Reverend Dr. Heber Brown, III is a fixture in the fight for environmental justice for his community. As Pleasant Hope Baptist Church pastor, Dr. Brown has been an environmental warrior for over two decades, raising the systemic issues of land conservation and food insecurity in Baltimore and beyond.*

THE PERSON

Heber grew up in Baltimore and in the Church. While he saw many family members struggle with poverty and addiction, he feels fortunate that his parents and grandparents helped him view his surroundings – including his relatives – through a lens of health inequity rather than personal failure. This early understanding that powerful actors and systems had failed the people he loved ignited in young Heber a "righteous indignation against every force responsible for robbing people of their opportunity to reach their highest potential."

Shortly after graduating from Morgan State University in Baltimore, Heber began working for a youth violence prevention program and mentoring initiative at Johns Hopkins University. "I loved working with the young people because I was from the same neighborhood and, in many ways, they reminded me of myself. However, I was not able to engage and connect with them the way I wanted to because of the dictates of my supervisors who were not African American and did not live in the same neighborhood as the children. There was a cultural disconnect and I felt like my voice was muted. The power dynamics in that experience were very difficult for me and helped to hone my resolve to find a better way to serve my community."

> *The senior pastor of Pleasant Hope Baptist Church in Baltimore grew up picking string beans and tomatoes from his grandparents' backyard... Today he carries that legacy forward as founder of the Black Church Food Security Network, an organization that connects churches with farmers in numerous states. His goal? To create alternative food systems that address systemic issues such as racism and climate change.*

bon appétit

Heber sought out other roles serving local families and young people, traveled to West Africa, and attended seminary. He launched a freedom school in Baltimore to increase racial self-esteem through a blend of African culture, civil rights history, and non-denominational "Sunday school" values. And Heber also established an organization of his own focused on consulting, training, and speaking engagements. Later, he organized Young Clergy for Social Change, a group that brought together youth ministers from Baltimore to address social injustices and urgent community needs.

At age 28, Heber was elected by the Pleasant Hope Baptist Church community to be its youngest-ever senior pastor. Fourteen years later, in May 2022, he preached his last sermon at Pleasant Hope to focus full-time on leading BCFSN. Leaving this role has been bittersweet. He has attended funerals of elders who took a chance on him early on, and many births and marriages of people who he has watched set down roots and blossom in the community. But Heber says, "it's an 'all-in' moment for me professionally and personally. It was a leap of faith to leave my vocation at my church, but it's something that I felt I had to do right now."

MEENA PALANIAPPAN

Technologist, Founder & CEO, Atmaconnect

 www.atmaconnect.org

While some social media can deplete social capital and cohesion, Meena Palaniappan created a trusted peer-to-peer social network that builds them up, amplifying local voices and agency. Her digital platform AtmaGo connects and empowers millions of people in vulnerable communities in Indonesia and elsewhere to be changemakers. Community members use it to help each other anticipate and respond to emergencies, share real-time information and solutions for community needs, advocate for better government services, and build community resilience from within.

SCAN THE CODE TO READ AND SHARE THIS ARTICLE ONLINE

THE NEW IDEA

What outsiders may think of as "vulnerable," "marginalized," or "disaster prone" communities in need of humanitarian relief actually have their own inherent powers of resourcefulness, confidence, resilience, and changemaking, which Meena's digital peer-to-peer platform AtmaGo unlocks.

It takes advantage of increasing mobile phone penetration in previously underserved communities across Indonesia and elsewhere. It also draws on the Indonesian cultural value of gotong royong ("mutual support" or "people helping people"). Shaped by user-generated posts, the platform connects and empowers community members to help each other anticipate and respond to emergencies, solve local problems, and become effective change agents.

AtmaGo provides an early warning system for emergencies proven to save lives and property, and to result in accurate, efficient decision-making when disaster strikes. Users share information on evacuation routes, where to find food, water, and healthcare after a disaster, and much else.

Beyond disaster relief and recovery, AtmaGo serves as a user-driven platform for solving local problems, rewarding and aggregating the positive social and environmental impacts users create themselves. It also helps service

AtmaGo improves users' disaster preparedness. It allows users to spread local solutions and make informed decisions quickly.

providers be more effective. Posting complaints or flagging needs on AtmaGo prompts local government officials and NGOs to act fast to resolve them.

> *I look at AtmaGo weekly to see what challenges I need to address. Atma Go is building the movement of mutual support, a pillar of democracy.*
>
> **Alamsyah Saragin,** *Ombudsman of Republic of Indonesia*

Atma also has a face-to-face community empowerment dimension. It organizes in-person trainings in digital literacy and citizen journalism skills which connect and amplify previously unheard voices, and it identifies and supports emerging local leaders. For example, women have been speaking up in the citizen journalism trainings to share their knowledge—one of the most unique results of this community empowerment dimension. 54% of the application's users are now women, who are up to 14 times likelier than men to die in a disaster.

> *AtmaGo gives users early warnings for fires, flood and crime, so they have time to prepare and take shelter, while also offering advice and solutions about jobs, education and health. Besides giving notices, AtmaGo also provides advice on what people should prepare to anticipate a disaster, such as clothing, basic food and healthcare supplies and clean water. Users' posts will also be responded to by local government and NGOs.*
>
> **TheJakartaPost**

Meena founded AtmaConnect as part of her lifelong mission to give voice to the voiceless and make the invisible

PHOTO CREDIT: Meena Palaniappan – Meena's projects have benefited over 9 million people in over 100 communities so far.

visible. But AtmaGo and Atma community empowerment programs are more than a megaphone. They're a smart changemaker toolkit that keeps evolving as users engage it, tapping and honing communities' ability not only to survive and recover from disasters, but to make and lead positive change. For example, Pak Abdul Razaq, a 49-year-old community leader in Yogyakarta City, realized that the poverty in his neighborhood was the root behind his community's poor health and was worsening any number of other social problems. As a local speaking to the people's interests, one of Razaq's posts about the local women's farmer group drew visitors to the village to learn. Razaq explains,

"I believe my posts have been inspiring others to improve their own neighborhood conditions, encouraging my people to do more good things, providing transparency on the local governance and serving as village documentation for better knowledge management."

THE PROBLEM

Natural disasters have increased tenfold globally since the 1960s, and their pace and scale is accelerating with climate change. This is true everywhere, though worse in some countries than others. Indonesia is especially subject to increasing floods, droughts, landslides, and tsunamis, as well as non-climate-related disasters such as earthquakes and volcanic eruptions. The need for better emergency preparedness is acute and growing along with the risks.

When disasters strike, people need emergency notifications and timely information from trusted sources. As mobile phones and internet service become widely available, technology is an increasingly important resource for managing disasters and improving outcomes. Digital emergency warning systems can save lives and protect property.

> *"After a 7.5 magnitude earthquake and tsunami hit in Sulawesi, Indonesia on September 28, 2018 causing more than 1,700 deaths and displacing over 700,000 people from their homes, local residents turned to their mobile phones and AtmaGo to alert and support friends, family and neighbors. Thousands saw posts on how to get food, water and healthcare."*
>
> **Forbes**

But in Indonesia as in other countries, technology's spread isn't always positive or equitable. Digital emergency warning systems are less accessible to those who need them most: underserved communities and vulnerable populations – – women, children, people with disabilities, the elderly, and some ethnic minorities. Indonesia's increasing mobile phone penetration and internet connectivity are often exploited by developers in untrustworthy ways – – extracting and selling user data, flooding social media with advertisements and negative content. Online hoaxes abound. When Indonesia's 2019 election results sparked rioting, fake news was rampant, and the Indonesian government restricted social media access. Globally, online misinformation and disinformation pose threats to democracy and human progress.

Disaster survival and recovery rates are higher where social cohesion is stronger, and neighbors work together. Digital tools have the potential to enhance social cohesion. But systems users can't access equitably and online content they can't trust alienates them.

THE STRATEGY

Meena uses technology to amplify social connection rather than social division. She built a trusted, pro-social, human-centered platform which offers an antidote to existing social media, and weaves and strengthens the social fabric of vulnerable communities, making them less vulnerable.

AtmaGo is a free, low-bandwidth, mobile-friendly website and mobile app for Android phones that sends users emergency alerts to help them prepare for disasters, and real-time information that helps them recover effectively. Last year, it sent out 338 flood alerts and 365 earthquake alerts.

An independent research study found that people took early action in response to AtmaGo warnings—evacuating, moving valuables, warning others, etc. These actions save lives and health and avoid property loss. Aggregated per million users, the study estimated each year AtmaGo can reduce mortality and morbidity by 6,000 years of healthy life, cut healthcare costs by up to $4.6 million, and avoid property losses of over $100 million.

67 percent of users surveyed said AtmaGo helped them improve their disaster preparedness, with the greatest impacts reported in more disaster-prone areas (Palu, Lombok, and Yogyakarta). The study showed it helped affected communities make decisions accurately and efficiently when disasters hit, enabling them to take collective action and spread local solutions to their neighborhoods quickly. During 2015 flooding in Jakarta, people used the app to share safe routes through the city, locate government shelters, and to point out signs of waterborne diseases to watch for in children. After the 2018 earthquake and tsunami in Sulawesi, residents used AtmaGo to find food, water, and healthcare.Government also uses the platform to anticipate local needs after a disaster.

"AtmaGo helps me know what issues people are facing, and what will be soon reported to my office," said Alamsyah Saragih, Ombudsman of the Republic of Indonesia.

When the pandemic hit, AtmaGo launched a new microsite sharing verified COVID-19 information, raising awareness, assessing community needs, locating resources like vaccination sites, offering free mental health telecounseling, and promoting behavioral changes like social distancing. 85% of the site's users reported shifting their behavior.

> “
> ***AtmaConnect is a non-profit organization that focuses on community development through the use of IT.***

In March 2020, as Covid-19 entered Indonesia, Atma developed covid19.atmago.com, an AtmaGo derivative platform that functions as an integrated Beyond emergency response and recovery, AtmaGo enables users to generate and share posts reporting local problems, discussing home-grown solutions, announcing events, and finding jobs (some 4000 job listings were posted to the app last year). Users can comment on the posts and flag them, and vote them up or down. These posts are hyper-locally targeted, organized by city, district, and neighborhood, so when they log on users see posts from their neighbors which concern them directly.

79 percent of those surveyed say AtmaGo helped them connect with their community. The app holds contests and uses profiles of local leaders, success stories, and gamification to engage more users and reward positive social and environmental impacts they create. Through its ruang komunitas ("community rooms") feature, users document, share, and aggregate their impacts, for example collecting garbage, empowering local women

PHOTO CREDIT: *AtmaConnect – AtmaConnect empowers local women through digital literacy trainings and citizen journalism workshops.*

to build small businesses, or organizing the planting of mangrove trees to prevent flooding from sea level rise.

"What we have heard from community leaders is that they need a way to document their impact, inspire and learn from others, and get more support from their own community, the government, and the resources to grow their work," explains Meena.

> *In March 2020, as Covid-19 entered Indonesia, Atma developed covid19.atmago.com, an AtmaGo derivative platform that functions as an integrated information and service platform related for Covid-19, which also provides support for secondary economic and mental health impact recovery.*

TIMES INDONESIA™
BUILDING · INSPIRING · POSITIVE THINKING

With the "community rooms" feature, users can form or join a community in which they can then conduct discussions and share activities. The feature also enables users to develop a community portfolio, with which they can recruit volunteers, set measurable goals, and document actions.

Further development looks towards enabling communities to monitor their work through data and analytics, to measure their achievement against a goal, and to interconnect between Indonesia and Puerto Rico, transforming 18,940 kilometers into an immediate connection.

In addition to the AtmaGo digital platform, AtmaConnect offers non-virtual community empowerment programs, including in-person trainings in digital literacy and citizen journalism. These are skills which connect and amplify previously unheard voices, and women make up the majority of trainees. Atma identifies, networks, and supports emerging local leaders known as Resilience Ambassadors, who volunteer to run their own workshops and events and monitor platform postings in their area for commercial ads, hoaxes, and other non-beneficial content.

Founded in Indonesia in 2015 and launched in Puerto Rico in 2019, AtmaGo has reached and benefited 9 million people in over 100 communities so far. Meena is working to scale it up globally with funders and collaborators to further develop and scale the platform, including Red Cross, Mercy Corps, Qualcomm Wireless Reach, Cisco Foundation, Vodafone Americas Foundation, and Hilton Foundation.

For Meena, scaling up is part of a conscious strategy to build a global changemaker movement. As the pace of change accelerates everywhere, changemaking is a critical skill for everyone in the 21st century, including in communities considered vulnerable or marginalized. Working to scale AtmaGo "supports the agility and creativity of citizens and reinforces the value of gotong royong [people helping people]," says Meena, "to build a citizen movement to help residents prepare to face and bounce back from disasters, and rebuild their communities." Her goal is to expand AtmaGo over the next five years, from millions of users to billions globally, as a way to build changemaking capacity in vulnerable communities everywhere, so they are strong, resilient, and able to thrive in an everyone-a-changemaker world.

> *Atma is just the beginning of protecting vulnerable communities through a fundamentally different approach. AtmaGo allows users to read, write, and comment on posts in four categories: Reporting problems, discussing solutions, finding jobs, and sharing events.*

THE PERSON

Meena was born and raised in India before moving to the United States. As a girl, she felt motivated to champion and amplify those whose voices weren't being heard. She saw how environmental impacts disproportionately affected vulnerable populations, and witnessed the suffering of farm animals. In high school, she started an environmental club and an animal rights club, and recruited her friends and teachers to take part.

Growing up she was keenly aware of children and adults in India dying from poor water quality. When she attended Northwestern University, she chose to study environmental engineering to find solutions. The field was male dominated; she was often the only woman in her classes, which fueled her determination to empower women and amplify unheard voices.

She went on to take a Master of Science degree in Energy and Resources from the University of California at Berkley. She taught in underserved communities through Teach for America, and worked for more than a decade on environmental justice issues and sustainable community development with major CSOs.

For the Environmental Defense Fund, she co-authored EDF's Environmental Sustainability Kit, which gives citizen environmentalists advice on how to start projects, engage diverse stakeholders, and advocate for policy change.

For the Pacific Institute, she worked on water and sanitation issues in Africa, India, and Indonesia. She initiated the Water SMS program in Indonesia, which used mobile phones to track and improve urban water services. It enabled transparent digital communications between residential water users, local governments, and water utilities and the informal water sector, empowering users, especially poor urban residents, to advocate for better service.

That experience demonstrated the potential of digital technology to empower and amplify unheard voices to make change, and led Meena to found AtmaConnect. The first iteration of her platform let users share information about water prices in Jakarta with neighbors to create transparency. It quickly evolved to share information on chronic flooding and other emergencies in and around Jakarta. From there, Meena and her team worked to understand social problems in vulnerable communities, and iterated the platform using a human-centered design approach to enable community members to solve them.

PHOTO CREDIT: *AtmaConnect – AtmaConnect empowers local women through , e.g., digital literacy, job access, practicing organizing and journalism workshops.*

MARIA TERESA RONDEROS

Author, Journalist; Co-Founder and Director, Latin American Center For Investigative Journalism

www.elclip.org

María Teresa Ronderos, herself a top investigative journalist, is empowering journalists across Latin America to collaborate beyond borders—allowing them to break bigger stories and more effectively hold large, transnational powers to account.

SCAN THE CODE TO READ AND SHARE THIS ARTICLE ONLINE

THE NEW IDEA

Aiming to identify, connect, and coordinate journalists to jointly report on transnational stories, María Teresa Ronderos founded the Latin American Center for Investigative Journalism (*Centro Latinoamericano de Investigación Periodística*, or CLIP) in 2019. Cross-border collaboration is crucial for investigative journalists, in a time and place where the most important stories require seeing the driving forces and incentives at work on a continental level. Powerful actors, such as drug cartels and corrupt politicians and corporations, often operate across borders, but journalists in Latin America traditionally have not. CLIP breaks down these national barriers by initiating and coordinating transnational investigations throughout the continent. In addition, it supports journalists in their own investigations, by providing safe access to collaborative tools and relevant and sensitive information.

As a secondary objective, CLIP aims to serve as a platform for broader community collaboration. As journalism is slowly losing its legitimacy in many parts of society, María Teresa recognizes the critical importance of engaging the audience as active participants, rather than looking at them as passive recipients. With its digital platform, CLIP aims to build a network of at least 10,000 strong community voices who contribute their skills, know-how, and information to investigations across the continent. Currently, this digital community has around 1,000 active members.

CLIP's methodology, leaving old organizational limitations behind, is rapidly setting a new standard for investigative journalism in Latin America. The collaboration and sharing enables reduced investigation costs and personal risk. In an increasingly authoritarian environment, where journalists and other critical voices—in Latin America more than in most of the world—are being threatened, silenced, and even murdered by authoritarian regimes and criminal organizations, working through CLIP provides some level of safety and support to individual journalists.

Since 2019, CLIP has forged collaborations with over 80 outlets in almost every country in Latin America and published more than 200 significant articles and other pieces of media. It has provided a platform for sensitive stories that couldn't be published locally—such as the murder case of Mexican journalist Miroslava Breach—and shed light on previously unknown or underreported stories, like the systematic disappearance of public funds meant to fight Covid-19. CLIP's investigations have inspired political action in multiple countries, including Colombia, Mexico, Panama, and Peru, and are serving to strengthen and corroborate the work of civil society organizations across the continent.

> *At a time when internet technology should be allowing journalism to flourish, independent journalism is embattled on almost all fronts. María Teresa Ronderos knows those battles first-hand. She has devoted her career to fearless reporting, while working to protect and nurture the independence of her colleagues worldwide."*

OPEN SOCIETY FOUNDATIONS

THE PROBLEM

Corruption, organized crime, human rights violations, and environmental deterioration are some of the most urgent challenges that every Latin American society is facing in modern times. Moreover, many of these challenges are far more pronounced in Latin America than elsewhere in the world. Nearly all countries on the continent (except Chile, Uruguay, and Costa Rica) rank in the bottom half of Transparency International's Corruption Perceptions Index, cartels vying to control the transportation of drugs to the United States are responsible for tens of thousands of deaths across the continent each year, while South America, home to the world's largest forest, is losing millions of hectares of trees every year, recently at record rates.

Well-organized and independent investigative journalism is one of the few, and one of the most powerful, tools available to uncover these large-scale issues and hold the influential organizations and individuals behind them to account. As such, investigative journalists play a key role in supporting and upholding democracy, by informing the public and compelling lawmakers to take action. For example, when one of CLIP's stories uncovered the systemic failures of Colombia's carbon market—intended to be an innovative solution against deforestation—it was discussed extensively in a debate in the Colombian Congress on October 26, 2021, leading the then-Minister of Environment to announce plans for greater transparency.

However, Latin American journalists' ability to report on these larger problems has been limited, due to their geographical limitations. Many of these crucial issues have a transnational nature. They are driven by actors that operate on an international level and have implications in multiple countries. By contrast, investigative journalism in Latin America has traditionally had a strong local focus. Journalists do report on these larger phenomena, but only from the lens of what happens within the borders of their own country.

The problem with this limited approach can be seen in the corruption scandal around Brazilian construction giant Odebrecht, which led to the sentencing of the company's top executives and a score of politicians across the region, including multiple (former) heads of state. For over a decade, Odebrecht paid hundreds of millions of dollars in bribes to public officials and political parties in at least 12 Latin American countries. In return, the company received billions of dollars' worth of public contracts, inflated prices, and ignored environmental safeguards.

Crucially, it wasn't investigative journalists who first uncovered this story in 2014, but rather the Brazilian police, who stumbled upon Odebrecht's practices while conducting a different investigation. For many years, the absence of an organization like CLIP meant that when local journalists received leads on Odebrecht's bribes, their investigations didn't look beyond their own country's borders. As a result, they didn't realize that these were not isolated incidents, and they never uncovered the extent of Odebrecht's corruption machine. By the time the Brazilian police finally did, many more public resources had been lost.

CLIP's existence has fundamentally changed this. Its impact is clear in the case of another multinational construction company: Costa Rican firm Meco. Even though Meco and its owner have been under judicial investigation for bribery in Costa Rica since 2019, the company has continued to win public contracts in other countries, including Panama and Colombia. CLIP's reporting on this story—a collaboration by journalists from all three countries—has led to a significant shift in public opinion, forcing Meco to remove its owner from the board of directors and to cede $300 million worth of contracts in Colombia.

THE STRATEGY

CLIP initiates, coordinates, and supports collaborative, cross-border investigations throughout Latin America. Most of its investigations focus on corruption, environmental deterioration, and human rights abuses by governments, criminal organizations, and religious institutions. In addition, CLIP supports local outlets and journalists with strategic guidance and sometimes funding, offers several online tools that facilitate collaboration, and serves as a publication outlet for sensitive stories. Through these efforts, CLIP provides journalists with safety, helps reduce their research costs, enables them to conduct larger investigations, helps maximize their impact on public opinion and legislative action, and engages the public as active participants.

Working through CLIP provides individual journalists with safety, both because collectives are harder to target than individuals and because CLIP offers the possibility to publish sensitive stories anonymously. One of these stories was the "Miroslava Project," in which Mexican journalists spent almost two years to investigate the judicial operation of the murder case of journalist Miroslava Breach in 2017. Because publication in local media would have been highly dangerous for the investigators, CLIP gave them the opportunity to publish anonymously, with María Teresa acting as the media spokesperson for the project. In response to this publication, almost the entire Mexican press ended up covering the story, informing a much wider audience and likely influencing the sentence of one of the murderers.

The Miroslava Project illustrates CLIP's role as a publication platform, but also how the strategic guidance and operational assistance it provides to journalists and local outlets serves to catalyze their impact. CLIP helped the original journalists with the final stretch of their investigation and with creating and editing individual stories. This support, as well as María Teresa's role as a spokesperson, enabled the story's widespread coverage and amplified its effect on public opinion.

CLIP has developed several online tools that are crucial in facilitating cross-border collaboration. Its private database, NINA, enables journalists across Latin America to access information on campaign financing, public procurement, and public sanctions. In addition, CLIP created an encrypted platform called "La Vecindad," *"The Neighborhood*," which is used for all collective investigations. It enables journalists and other contributors to share and access all documentation related to an investigation, including data, images, interviews, and others.

> ***"[Her] eagerness to offer readers clear, comprehensive, and profound information became her personal seal, and it has given results.***
>
> **Semana**

These tools drastically reduce investigation cost and time and allow journalists to conduct larger investigations with significantly more parties involved. The largest of these projects, "Migrants from Another World," which was initiated by María Teresa herself, involved 30 journalists from 14 different countries. The project covered the harrowing stories of the thousands of Asian and African migrants who land in Latin America each year, with the objective of reaching the United States or Canada. Having paid a fortune to traffickers, these people embark on an arduous overland journey, often starting in South America, only to end up in detention camps in Mexico or before. Along the way, many lose their own lives, or those of their family members, to the jungles they must cross. Of those that make it to the overcrowded detention camps, where they receive little food and no medical care, many get deported back to their country of origin. Only a handful reach their destination.

The Migrants from Another World project yielded a large collection of stories, an interactive website, and a book that was published by Penguin Random House in August 2021. Its publication bolstered human rights organizations across the region in their work, was presented in a Panamanian court to compel the government to better

PHOTO CREDIT: *Maria Teresa Ronderos – CLIP's online tools like "La Vecinidad" allow journalists to share and access documentation easily, reducing cost, time, and geographic limitations when conducting collective investigations.*

protect immigrants' rights, and likely influenced the Mexican government's decision to remodel some of its overcrowded detention facilities.

In addition to enabling cross-border collaboration, CLIP's online tools also facilitate María Teresa's vision for engaging the public as active participants. CLIP offers individuals and organizations a way to safely share information, expertise, and evidence that can help initiate or strengthen an investigation. CLIP provides not just the opportunity to contribute safely and anonymously—sensitive evidence is shared through encrypted emails—but also the reliable promise that shared leads and information will be in good hands and taken seriously. For example, in its reporting on Colombia's carbon market, CLIP relied heavily on the alerts, expertise, and online collaboration provided by multiple carbon bond experts.

Beyond achieving these main objectives, María Teresa is also working hard on making CLIP more financially sustainable and independent. CLIP's primary financial objective is to expand and diversify its donor base, in order to decrease its dependence on individual donors. The goal is to have its largest donor contribute at most 10-12% of the annual budget (this figure is currently 24%). In addition, CLIP has started generating revenue worth roughly 10% of its budget, through services offered to large media outlets, civil society organizations, and other clients across the region. These include data services, such as support with mining and processing data or creating algorithms, as well as high-level training on topics like specialized data visualization. CLIP is also piloting a tailored service that helps clients identify what information they should want to obtain from public records on a recurring basis, and then write the necessary algorithms.

In addition to expanding its donor base, service offerings, and media products like books and podcasts, CLIP's aim is to continue improving access to information and collaborative partners for journalists across the region. Eventually, María Teresa wants to expand CLIP's network and investigations to all countries in Latin America and the Caribbean, as well as the Latin American communities living in the United States.

THE PERSON

María Teresa founded CLIP on the back of a long, international career as a prolific investigative journalist and a committed defender and innovator of her profession. Her international exposure began even before her professional career. Born in 1959 in Colombia's capital, Bogotá, she was raised by her father, who was a serial entrepreneur in construction, banking, and hospitality, and her mother, who was an artist. They sent María Teresa to attend a year of boarding school in Scotland when she was 16. After her undergraduate studies in Colombia, she studied at Florida International University, and she holds a master's degree in Political Science from Syracuse University.

> *In 1983 [María Teresa Ronderos] started as a reporter in Buenos Aires [...] and in all these years she has maintained her balance while walking the tightrope of a threatened profession. [With CLIP], she once again demonstrates her ability to innovate and renew the sector.*

María Teresa quickly developed a passion for journalism and serving the public good. As a student at the University of the Andes, she became the leader of the university newspaper, where she reported on how the armed forces were using the country's State of Emergency—meant to combat guerillas—to arbitrarily arrest students and other youth who were not guerilla fighters. In her first job, she spent five years in Argentina, covering the country's transition to democracy and the trials of the former military dictators.

María Teresa perfected her craft as a journalist back in Colombia. She wrote and directed an investigative 60 Minutes-style TV show and became the first female political editor of the newspaper El Tiempo, where she reported on drug terrorism in Colombia. She worked as a reporter, editor, and columnist with several other outlets, before joining Colombia's leading news magazine, Semana. Starting in 2000, she spent 14 years with the magazine, as a reporter, website editor, and managing editor.

Her cutting-edge investigative reporting earned María Teresa wide-spread recognition. As early as 1996, she won the King of Spain Award, Latin America's most

PHOTO CREDIT: *Maria Teresa Ronderos – Maria Teresa received the King of Spain Award in 1996, Latin America's most prestigious journalism award.*

prestigious journalism award, for her examination of Colombia's media coverage of corruption scandals and the ties between politicians and drug lords. The difficult and risky investigation—which she conducted together with a journalist from a competing newspaper—not only showed María Teresa's initiative and courage, but also her instinct to collaborate. María Teresa's impact grew to extend far beyond her own research and publications, and beyond her own country. She became acutely aware of the dangers and pressures investigative journalists are exposed to in Latin America and the rest of the world. This understanding, and her commitment to the importance of high-quality investigative reporting, drove her to devote a significant and growing part of her career to promoting and protecting the overall field of journalism. She worked towards this goal with the Open Society Foundations, where she led the Independent Journalism Program from 2014 to 2018. There, she supported over 130 media and freedom of expression organizations around the world. In addition, she has held several board positions, including on the international Committee to Protect Journalists, and worked to protect the lives of journalists in danger as the president ad honorem of the Colombian Foundation for Press Freedom.

Beyond taking up these types of positions, María Teresa has gradually learned how to fortify and innovate the field of journalism, by building websites that both facilitate collaborations and fundamentally transform the relationship between journalists and the public. Her experience began with LaNota.com, a website with information, analysis, and opinions about business in Colombia, which she co-founded in the early days of the internet. In the early 2000s, María Teresa developed VoteBien.com ("Vote Well"). Uniting media and civil society organizations, this website provided independent coverage of Colombian elections at all levels for about 10 years and offered an interactive test to help voters identify which candidate aligned most with their views. In 2008, María Teresa founded VerdadAbierta.com ("Open Truth"), where she served as the editor-in-chief until 2014. This specialized, interactive website continues to cover serious human rights violations, transitional justice, and the consolidation of peace during the internal armed conflict in Colombia.

With CLIP, María Teresa is able to bring together her different passions: Creating investigative reporting of the highest quality, collaborating across borders and with the region's best investigative journalists, and teaching, mentoring, and building capacity with younger journalists around the continent. In addition to her work with CLIP, María Teresa plans to continue to devote a significant part of her life to promoting freedom of expression through her pro bono board memberships.

Beyond that, working in journalism in Latin America has taught María Teresa that making plans is often futile. Instead, she intends to remain flexible to changing circumstances, and deeply committed to her vision: Bringing investigative journalists together, making journalism more transparent, and "ending the era of *us* journalists versus *them* audience."

GROWING UP

ALPHA SENNON
Trinidad & Tobago

CHERYL PERERA
Canada

IARINA TABAN
Romania

ARUNDHUTI GUPTA
india

ALPHA SENNON

Agripreneur, Founder and Executive Director, WhyFarm (We Help Youth Farm)

 www.whyfarmit.com

By shifting negative narratives around farming that discourage young people from entering the field, Alpha is reframing and marketing farming as an exciting, impactful career that embraces STEM, innovation, and creativity. His "agri-edutainment" programs inspire kids from pre-school up about farming, while his "agripreneurship" programs mentor young people up to age 30. Young agripreneurs going into farming makes the career more sustainable, efficient, and attractive to more young people.

SCAN THE CODE TO READ AND SHARE THIS ARTICLE ONLINE

THE NEW IDEA

Alpha Sennon, the first and only Ashoka Fellow from Trinidad and Tobago to date, founded WhyFarm (We Help You-th Farm) to confront a slow-motion, global food security crisis that is already underway: Aging populations will need food that today's youth do not have the skills, knowledge, or interest to grow.

Based in T&T, with programs elsewhere in the Caribbean, Latin America, and Africa, WhyFarm reframes farming in fun, engaging ways that spark young people's curiosity about farming and show them why they should consider it as a career. Its agripreneurship education and mentoring programs show older youth up to age 30 how to become farmers and market and grow their operations. In place of an old-fashioned, stigmatized image of rural farmers scratching a marginal living from the land, WhyFarm promotes an updated view of farming as "agripreneurship," an exciting, creative, innovative, respected profession that saves and improves lives.

Alpha believes that youth are the key to innovating agriculture and feeding the world sustainably. "We need young people to become agripreneurs," Alpha says. "They are technologically savvy, creative, and open to new approaches in ways that older folks aren't. We need to engage them to ensure we'll have farmers to feed people in the future. It involves a lot of heavy marketing to make it attractive – we call it 'agriKOOLture' – – showing young people they can find their future in the food value chain."

“

WhyFarm (We Help Youth Farm) [is] a Trinidad-based non-profit that pioneers agricultural educational entertainment, promoting sustainable agriculture among the youth— founded by Alpha Sennon, one of the region's preeminent voices in food security.

Forbes

As part of what he calls “agri-edutainment,” Alpha created a comic book series following the exploits of Agriman, the world's first farming superhero, who heroically solves agricultural problems and fights food insecurity. WhyFarm puts on live shows at schools and community events using the Agriman character to tell real-life stories of adventures in agriculture.

Agriman engages younger kids, but WhyFarm offers what Alpha calls “agripreneurship” programs with how-to trainings, curricula, and mentorship all the way through university and graduate school and beyond. The curricula have been adopted internationally.

In addition to Trinidad and Tobago, WhyFarm identifies and mentors next-generation agripreneurs in Zambia, Haiti, Brazil, and Cameroon. They act as ambassadors for the profession, putting on their own school programs, setting up school produce gardens, and promoting agriculture as an exciting, essential career to students. For young adults who have already decided to become new farmers, WhyFarm provides technical support, entrees to markets, and ongoing professional development.

Farmer and social entrepreneur Alpha Sennon is sparking some serious youth engagement in agriculture around the world through his creative approach on food, health and climate. The AgriMan character is the first food and nutrition superhero.

THE PROBLEM

The global population is both growing and aging. By 2050, there will be 9.7 billion people on the planet, whose median age will be 16% higher than today.

The United Nations Food and Agriculture Organization (FAO) estimates the world will need to increase food production by 60% to feed them. Yet it's unclear where that increased output will come from.

Today, most of the world's food is produced by aging smallholder farmers in developing countries, many of whom are poorly educated. The global average age of farmers is about 60. Older farmers will soon age out, and meanwhile they are less likely to introduce innovative techniques that can raise yields in sustainable ways. Without younger people entering the field, by mid-century there will be a shortage of farmers, and therefore of food.

Youth must be the future of food security. Our ability to feed the world in 2050 hinges on the life paths of children who are just 10 years old today. Yet few young people are taking up farming.

***PHOTO CREDIT:** Alpha Sennon – Alpha is reframing young people's views on farming from its being perceived as backbreaking and boring into a challenging, available, and innovative career path.*

A report by the Inter-American Institute for Cooperation on Agriculture showed that Trinidadian youth don't want to go into farming because they associate it with back-breaking labor and poverty. A U.S. Government report on agricultural development noted the stigma of servitude that taints agricultural work in the Caribbean, connected to the region's legacy of slavery.

> *Agripreneur and WhyFarm founder and executive director Alpha Sennon is motivated by helping the youth of Trinidad and Tobago learn more about agriculture, food, and nutrition and how they can contribute to TT's food security. WhyFarm is dedicated to helping change negative stereotypes surrounding agriculture and helping young people see it as a viable career option.*

TRINIDAD and TOBAGO
NEWSDAY

A study by FAO found that young people in developing countries see low-productivity agriculture as drudgery and a marginal way to earn a living, so they often migrate instead to cities in search of better paying jobs. By 2030, 60% of the world's population is projected to live in cities. The urbanization trend not only drives more young people away from farming, it places an untenable burden on fewer and fewer food producers to feed larger and larger urban populations.

Yet convincing young people to try farming is "an uphill battle," according to Wayne Ganpat, Dean of the Faculty of Food and Agriculture at the University of the West Indies. Agriculture is stigmatized and not seen as a viable career path. The Trinidadian economy still places greater emphasis on producing fossil fuels than food. But those priorities are the polar opposite of the transformation the world needs for a viable future – it needs to phase out fossil fuels and ramp up sustainable food production.

Credit: Alpha Sennon

"Agriculture has not been marketed as a professional career," says Alpha, an omission he's working hard to remedy. Technical training is also lacking, especially in sustainable agriculture methods. Conventional farming practices in the Caribbean are chemical-intensive and cause environmental damage. In Trinidad and Tobago, farming is mainly subsistence-based with sparse financial and technical backing, so there is little possibility to invest in improvements and adopt more sustainable practices. Development organizations, such as the International Fund for Agricultural Development and the Inter-American Institute for Cooperation on Agriculture, have called for improved training and more engagement, but big gaps remain.

THE STRATEGY

Alpha seeks to impart both the "why" and the "how" of farming to young people across the developing world. He has created programs geared towards youth of all ages, from pre-school age to 30. He uses entertainment

PHOTO CREDIT: *Alpha Sennon – Alpha's has partnered with the UN Food and Agriculture Organization (FAO), United Nations Development Programme (UNDP), and Trinidad and Tobago's Ministry of Health to help alleviate food insecurity.*

to capture the attention of young audiences and explain why they should want to grow up to be farmers, then builds on that captured attention with educational programs that explain how they can enter the field, innovate it, and succeed.

On the entertainment side, Alpha began by creating Agriman, the world's first farming superhero. Agriman and his squad of agriculture-themed sidekicks fight food insecurity. They are the protagonists of a multimedia communications empire that markets farming as a desirable profession to young people. This marketing includes a comic book series, a YouTube video series, social media campaigns, original songs, and branded food products that emphasize local production. Alpha is in negotiations on an Agriman video cartoon series and a movie. Agriman also makes in-person visits to primary schools, career fairs, conferences, and community events.

The comic book series is available online and in print, with thousands of copies circulating. It has been translated into several languages, including Portuguese. Local artists and advocates in Brazil ran with the character, created their own version of Agriman, and took him on a school tour, reaching 40,000 students across ten Brazilian states.

On the education side, Alpha designed STEM Agriculture, a 10-week curriculum that schools use to integrate agriculture and climate change into their existing science and math courses.

"For example, a favorite vegetable here is pimento, and we work with students to do the calculation of how much it costs to plant pimento trees, the investments necessary before harvest, the average market price, and the profit margin," says Alpha. "It's a whole, real-life math class. We teach them about the soil inputs, the roles of nitrogen, potassium, phosphorous – that's a chemistry class. And we get into designing tools that can harvest sweet potatoes without damaging them and losing money – that's an engineering class. This way, young people who are interested in STEM can imagine themselves farming."

The school curriculum has reached about 2600 Trinidadian students under age 18. Alpha's new online video course, created in collaboration with the Thought for Food Foundation, "A Beginner's Mindset to Engaging Youth in Agriculture," will reach thousands more.

WhyFarm's university curriculum has been adopted by universities internationally, including by the Polytechnic College of Suriname. It also runs a university lecture series entitled "Grow After Graduation: Food and Agri

Series," and inspirational workshops on agribusiness in business schools. Participants have been inspired to enter farming and use innovative approaches like hydroponics. WhyFarm provides them with ongoing technical support and entrees to markets for their produce.

Other WhyFarm programs reach youth through non-school channels, like a youth theater program that teaches students about the global food crisis and the importance of local food production and native plants. Each year thousands of students in WhyFarm's "AgriKOOLture Kidz Klub" visit Alpha's farm, where they get practical how-to trainings and help with setting up their own school and community produce gardens.

Many WhyFarm participants go on to pursue farming as a career. Although it's difficult to attribute specific instances of this verifiably to WhyFarm, in the years since it was founded, Professor Ganpat has observed a 10% annual uptick in enrollment in the Food and Agriculture program at the University of the West Indies.

> *WhyFarm's catchphrase [is] "plant one tree and eat for free." One of its goals is to engage young people and sustain the agricultural sector through the continuity of generations of farmers who will institute sustainable agricultural practices. "WhyFarm is a catalyst for inspiration in the agricultural sector and encourages citizens to make changes to eat local and support local farmers," says Sennon.*

healthline

For those who decide to take up farming, WhyFarm conducts workshops in 10 countries for young professionals up to age 30 to sharpen their business skills and grow their operations. Alpha created the Agripreneur Mastermind Program (AMPITUP) where young agripreneurs are challenged to write a business plan to take their product or service to the next level, and hone their skills at innovating, fundraising, and financing it. Throughout the competition, participants are mentored and offered professional development resources.

AMPITUP winners receive cash prizes totaling $50,000 and their business plans are included in WhyFarm's Best Practices Road Map for Youth Engagement in Agriculture, posted online. For one winner who makes ice cream pops, AMPITUP helped her find suppliers like local coconut producers and wholesale printers for packaging. She won a grant from the US Embassy to further develop her product.

83% of participants reported growing their operations, thanks to AMPITUP, which helped them register their businesses, understand their export potential, and find more professional development, mentoring, and funding opportunities. The first AMPITUP pilot in 2019 was presented as a case study at four global conferences, and Alpha received support from the Inter-American Development Bank to scale the program across the Caribbean.

Alpha's WHYFARMers Collective, a growing network of young farmers who share ideas and resources and support each other's ventures, gives participants entrees to markets – for example, via a special supply relationship with Massy Stores, a leading supermarket chain, which carries WHYFARMers' produce.

Beyond WhyFarm, Alpha also collaborates with major partners, including consulting for FAO on how to stoke more youth interest and more innovation in Caribbean agriculture, and contracting with FAO to create a digital agriculture roadmap for Trinidadian farmers. Alpha builds hospital "medicinal food parks" in collaboration Trinidad and Tobago's Ministry of Health, and community gardens in collaboration with the United Nations Development Program (UNDP).

THE PERSON

Although Alpha grew up on a farm in Trinidad and Tobago, he didn't feel a personal connection with farming when he was young. "It just felt like chores," he said. "I was missing the connection to a great purpose. "Like many young people, for Alpha, working the land had become "a symbol of oppression, rather than freedom."

As a college student, Alpha stayed as far away from farming as he could, until, on a trip to Jamaica, he toured farms and factories, and saw how large-scale agricultural production could be managed as a business. This opened

PHOTO CREDIT: *Alpha Sennon – Because the future of food security depends on younger generations, WhyWeFarm has developed programs geared towards youth of all ages – from youth theater programs to university curriculum.*

his eyes to the innovative potential of agripreneurship as an exciting, purposeful, innovative career.

Alpha traveled more widely, witnessing sustainable farming techniques in India, and studying abroad in Thailand. As he visited more farms, Alpha began to envision implementing the practices he was learning about in his home country. He recognized enlisting young people was the key; they had to be exposed to agriculture before their negative attitude toward it hardened, and bring fresh eyes to the profession.

To that end, Alpha took leadership roles in college organizations such as the Executive Committee for Agriculture and the Agribusiness Society. As a Youth Representative for Agriculture, he noticed that older members of the Society were recycling failed approaches from the past and were resistant to new ideas proposed by younger members. Alpha decided the solution was to connect directly with youth and empower them to bring their innovations forward. That was the genesis of WhyFarm and Agriman.

Alpha's work has been recognized with many international awards including the Misk Global Challenge award, sponsored by the Bill and Melinda Gates Foundation. Alpha was named the 2021 national influencer by the prime minister of Trinidad and Tobago (the first time a farmer has received the accolade), one of 30 Under 30 Caribbean American Emerging Leaders and Changemakers, and one of 2016's Young Leaders of the Americas. Alpha is currently a Specialist Business Mentor for Agriculture with the Caribbean Centre of Excellence for Sustainable Livelihoods and serves on the Next Gen Council for the Thought for Food Global Foundation, where he is also an ambassador for the Caribbean.

Alpha Sennon created WhyFarm to address food insecurity in Trinidad and Tobago and promote sustainable agriculture among youth and children. WhyFarm aims to refocus the regional agricultural sector to prioritize youth engagement. The organization creates spaces for youth to be involved in agriculture-related decision-making, provides capacity building opportunities, and hosts programs to empower young agripreneurs.

CHERYL PERERA

Founder and President, OneChild

 www.onechild.ca

Cheryl is enabling young people, including survivors of sexual exploitation, to develop and deliver self-empowerment programs, policies, and educational curricula. By betting on young people to disrupt the sexual exploitation of children, Cheryl builds these children's resilience to protect their rights and inspires adults to follow their lead.

SCAN THE CODE TO READ AND SHARE THIS ARTICLE ONLINE

THE NEW IDEA

Cheryl Perera and her organization, OneChild, is educating and preparing the youth to lead a movement that disrupts child sex slavery and advocates institutional reform against human trafficking. Cheryl believes that because the sexual exploitation of children (SEC) represents one of the worst violations against the rights of the child, young people themselves are uniquely poised to take a stand on the front lines for their own rights. Cheryl enables the self-assertion of young people by providing a foundation of knowledge and tools for them to directly interrupt—through public education campaigns, targeted advocacy initiatives, and fundraising—the global sex trade's supply and demand.

As the world's first youth-led organization focused on ending the sexual exploitation of their fellow youth, OneChild shifts the narrative around child protection efforts by positioning young people at the forefront of advancing solutions. Instead of the standard "doom and gloom" approach that focuses on the vulnerability of children in these trafficking systems, Cheryl sees the problem as an opportunity to catalyze youth leadership; Cheryl helps young people see the world around them in a different way, one in which they have an important role in the fight against this sexual exploitation and have a seat at the decision-making table in transforming themselves and their world.

OneChild's approach is empowering a movement of children and youth to take action against child sex slavery through preventative education, survivor empowerment, and advocacy and mobilization for institutional reform and policy change. It begins with a peer-to-peer based education model that provides powerful preventive education. This education disrupts the sex trafficking pipeline by informing young people of the actual ways (including online) that traffickers lure children into sex slavery.

Through workshops, motivational talks, and social media outreach—all designed and delivered by young people—children learn how to protect themselves and their peers from sexual exploitation. At the same time, they learn the hard facts about the global child sex trade and the insidious ways in which the most vulnerable children become victims of human traffickers. This closes the knowledge gap and inspires students to take action. Motivated youth are engaged to receive changemaker training, where they obtain fact sheets and toolkits for both in-person and digital action campaigns to run at their schools or other events. These programs have had great success and have swept across high schools and elementary schools throughout Canada, especially in the largest province, Ontario, where the national rates of child trafficking are the highest in the country.

Cheryl undergirds her conversations with young people by drawing on the UN Convention on the Rights of the Child. In particular, she draws on Article 34, which claims that "all children are granted the rights to be protected from all forms of sexual exploitation," and Article 12, which states that children have "the right to give their opinion, and for adults to listen and take it seriously." By emphasizing to young people their rights to demand and take action, Cheryl enables them to see themselves as social and political actors with creativity, intelligence, and technical savvy who can help determine solutions, even in the face of closed doors and adults' resistance. Cheryl's aim is a world that regularly incorporates youth and children, including survivors, into mainstream discussions on the development of legislation, policies, and programs to fight, disrupt, and ultimately end child sex slavery. To accompany this shift in mindset, OneChild provides practical opportunities for young people to discover their power through education, advocacy, and survivor care and empowerment.

Informed of their rights and power to lead change, young people want to take action, and part of OneChild's work is to support them in leading public action campaigns (both in-person and digital) in their schools, communities, and nationally. One national campaign involved bringing OneChild's message to the travel and tourism sector of Canada. In Cheryl's conversations with law enforcement officials working on sex trafficking, she realized that a major part of the trafficking of children involved individuals (including Canadian citizens) travelling to foreign countries for the purposes of sexually abusing children. She also learned that some European airlines were showing videos to passengers alerting them to the problem and signs of child sex trafficking. Cheryl and her co-leaders decided to ask Canada's national airline, Air Canada, to join the fight. Cheryl lacked a budget and film equipment, but since she knew— from the awareness-raising she had done in schools—that she had strength in numbers, she circulated a petition calling on Air Canada to act and with young people at the center. The petition received thousands of signatures. So, Cheryl and her team went to Air Canada's corporate headquarters and convinced the company to take this youth-led action, making the company the first in Canada to address the issue of SEC in travel and tourism. Over 22 million people saw the videos that Cheryl and her "club of kids" made. But the impact didn't end there, as Air Canada went on to implement mandatory training for their flight attendants, joined with the Royal Canadian Mounted Police in flying trafficking survivors to their homes after rescue, and influenced other airlines (WestJet and Air Transat) to join the campaign. Air Canada then teamed with OneChild as a co-leader of the first-ever national campaign aimed at ending sex trafficking in the travel and tourism industry, a campaign that involved such partners as airports, travel agencies, tour operators, police, governments, consulates, and embassies. Young people both initiated and led all this work, including three major national trainings led specifically by trained children from OneChild.

Cheryl's unique approach to disrupting and ending child sex slavery centers around catalyzing a social movement in which young people take advantage of what Cheryl calls, "the most powerful time in their lives." Although she and OneChild are focused on eliminating the sexual exploitation of children, Cheryl encourages young people—in her workshops, trainings, and organizing—to follow their own passions and to address the social and environmental problems that matter most to them, whether that is LGBTQIA rights, climate change, world hunger, or women's rights. By modeling ways of getting informed and building leadership capacity, Cheryl and OneChild help youth understand that they don't have to wait to be powerful contributors to solving problems. Cheryl believes that young people have special powers to get the attention of adults, including perseverance and stubbornness: "If we speak up, people will listen."

Through a variety of global partnerships with groups working directly with survivors—like the Philippines' PREDA Foundation—Cheryl facilitates ways for young people to actively take part in supporting survivors' recovery and ultimately their empowerment. OneChild has raised hundreds of thousands of dollars which have supported the direct intervention in the lives of survivors and supported them in becoming leaders in the movement themselves.

To date, OneChild has impacted close to 100,000 lives in 11 countries. OneChild also offers a competitive opportunity for 10 young people each year to join their Youth Advisory Squad (YAS). These young people receive in-depth mentorship and coaching in public speaking, advocacy, and fundraising, as well as scholarship money. Through the YAS, OneChild constantly renews its youth leadership, reinvigorates its model, and creates a self-sustaining movement.

THE PROBLEM

The sexual exploitation of children includes the sale and sex trafficking of children, online child sexual exploitation, and the sexual exploitation of children in travel and tourism. Children in all countries are at risk of trafficking and forced prostitution, as well as online dangers such as grooming, sextortion, and proliferation of child sexual abuse videos and images, and these forms often overlap. While sexual abuse can happen to anyone, certain groups of children are more at risk. Statistics Canada (2016) has documented that First Nation, Inuit, and Métis women and girls, youth in foster care, runaway and homeless youth, persons with disabilities, children with mental illness, lonely individuals, refugees and migrants, and LGBTQIA persons are the most vulnerable.

While the scale of the problem is difficult to establish because of its clandestine nature and the fact that victims are often too frightened to report, a 2014 report from the Canadian Medical Association Journal showed that 10% of the population (corresponding to some 3.6 million Canadians) reported having experienced sexual abuse before they were 16 years old. 2018 law enforcement statistics indicate that most of the victims were women and girls (97%). They were trafficked predominantly for sexual exploitation purposes. Around half (45%) of these victims were between the ages of 18 and 24 and 28% were under the age of 18.

The sexual exploitation of children has lifelong and devastating effects. In Sri Lanka, where Cheryl first encountered the harsh realities of the sex trade firsthand, perpetrators were forcing the victims, with whom she spoke, to have sex up to 26 times a day. In the case of online sexual exploitation, a child can potentially become re-victimized millions of times—every time another person watches, sends, or receives an image or video. Children can experience trauma from both contact and non-contact sexual abuse, and these effects can become generational, if left untreated.

Long-term impacts on survivors include substance dependency and addiction; mental illness; prolonged feelings of guilt, shame, and anger; hypersexualization; unwanted pregnancy; sexually transmitted diseases; trauma bonds and Stockholm syndrome; self-esteem issues; fistulas and other health issues; and suicidal tendencies.

OneChild helps children and youth understand that there is no cookie-cutter definition or profile of a child sex perpetrator or a human trafficker—they could be any age, gender, ethnicity, or sexual orientation. The perpetrators might be pedophiles or perpetrators completely unknown to the victim, though most demand for SEC comes from individuals who children know and trust—these individuals identify and leverage their victims' vulnerabilities to create dependency.

At the same time, Statistics Canada (2018) has identified that four in five persons accused of human trafficking from 2009-2018 have been men. 35% of Canadian sex traffickers or pimps were between 18 and 24 years old and 31% were 25 to 34 years. Expanding access to the Internet, mobile technology, and cheap travel makes this crime easier to commit; it has never been easier for perpetrators to contact children, share images and videos of the abuse, hide the profits, and carry out these criminal acts anonymously. In Canada, Ontario is the province with the vast majority of cases. SEC occurs at schools, parties, coffee shops, and malls, and social media platforms have now become hunting grounds, where someone often plays the role of a "Romeo" pimp to lure victims. Juvenile recruiters often receive the job of bringing in more minors.

Historically, the world has largely tackled this problem through the prosecution of perpetrators and the protection of survivors. This response includes disrupting criminal networks, holding criminals accountable, and securing justice for survivors through amendments to the legal system. The protection of children who have become victims of SEC largely includes palliative services for survivors, which stops survivors from becoming future abusers as well. While these interventions are critical, the lack of robust, youth-centered prevention tactics weakens the fight against SEC.

Although there have been many isolated prevention efforts, such as government and citizen sector awareness campaigns, they have mostly failed to reach the people most impacted: Children and youth. When these prevention efforts do reach children, they are often based on a framework of "protection," which views children as helpless and needing supervision and assistance from adults. As long as society is organized this way, children only really have the option to "snitch" to the police or other adults about what they see amongst friends. These tactics fail to appreciate that young people themselves are the experts of their own experience and are in the most powerful position possible to protect themselves and their peers.

> *Through workshops and visits to Canadian and U.S. schools, Ms. Perera says that she and her team have helped to educate some 35,000 young people on issues around child sexual exploitation, a crime whose underground nature makes it difficult to assess.*
>
> THE WALL STREET JOURNAL

THE STRATEGY

During her three-and-a-half month trip to Sri Lanka, 17-year-old Cheryl was exposed to the hidden reality of the child sex exploitation industry. What further shocked her was the fact that citizens from her birth country, Canada, were tourists perpetrating the problem. Upon her return home to Toronto, Cheryl wanted to share with other children about what she had seen, heard, and experienced. She traveled from school to school, presenting to thousands of students and was met with motivated youth who were devastated to learn of the exploitation of their peers and wanted to be a part of the solution. Looking to engage these students, Cheryl reached out to established citizen sector organizations, explaining that she was a teenager with an army of teenagers eager to help. However, Cheryl's emails went largely unanswered. She grew frustrated with witnessing what felt like a waste of youth passion, intelligence, expertise, creativity, and talent on this critical issue.

In 2005, and at 19 years old, Cheryl, together with her family and friends, founded OneChild to empower a youth-led movement against SEC through education, advocacy, and empowerment. She incubated OneChild in her family home; her mother cooked for volunteers, and Cheryl and her mother worked multiple jobs to donate to their own citizen organization. OneChild's primary access point for youth was, and continues to be, through classroom-based workshops and motivational speeches at school assemblies. OneChild engages young people through child – and youth-friendly educational workshops, activist trainings, toolkits, action campaigns, and youth events and conferences. Through these forums, young people learn how to look out for each other and themselves and thus eliminate the supply of potential victims of the SEC.

OneChild covers themes such as recruitment tactics and vulnerable demographics, as well as root contributors to child exploitation, such as mental health, gender inequity, social constructs, and media representation. The presentations and workshops also include topics of well-being, healthy relationships, and finding self-worth, as well as toxic masculinity and the objectification of women. OneChild partners with ARISE Ministry, as well as the Ontario Provincial Police, to provide trauma counsellors at every session. By 2021, OneChild's prevention education had reached just over 36,000 youth in 230 schools. Cheryl designed these speeches and workshops to make it easy to get in front of young people, with the potential to have a long-lasting impact. Her 2021 survey data indicates that following OneChild's presentations, 89.9% of students claim that they now know how to spot a victim of SEC, 88.3% of students say that they now recognize the warning signs of SEC, and 55.8% of students feel prepared to take action against this issue.

While building broad awareness amongst youth through school outreach programs, OneChild nurtures their Youth Advisory Squad. This includes a group of extra passionate young people who demonstrate a need and/or desire to be an agent of change on the topic. These young people undergo activist training with OneChild and serve as speakers for the organization. They are equipped to close the knowledge gap with other stakeholders such as parents, teachers, social workers, corporations, and policymakers.

OneChild facilitates opportunities for young people to participate in policy dialogues to call for more effective child protection policies. Most recently, in 2021, Cheryl launched a campaign with Canadian known survivor, Tamia Nagy, to rally tween brands in a new pledge that committed them to not using sexualized images as part of their marketing strategies for young people.

Altogether, as of 2021, OneChild's work has impacted over 100,000 at-risk children, child survivors, parents, social workers, citizen sector workers, and law enforcement officials through prevention education, advocacy, and survivor empowerment. Notably, between 2005 and 2018, the volunteer labor of young people solely produced much of this impact. In 2018, OneChild hit a point of inflection when it successfully fundraised to start paying staff salaries and to bring on Cheryl fulltime.

> *Her career in child protection began at age 17, after playing the main role of the decoy in a STING operation with Sri Lankan authorities to apprehend a child sex perpetrator.*

Going forward, Cheryl aims to increase the guidance for and by children and youth against SEC and to continue to foster the conditions for child-adult partnerships with parents, educators, and other adult supporters. For example, OneChild builds relationships with different members of Parliament in Canada, creating space and support for OneChild's movement of young people to petition for meetings with MPs to share recommendations. The first agenda item is to garner support for mandatory trainings on recognizing and reporting child trafficking in Canada's hospitality sector—where much SEC takes place and therefore a key point of leverage. In 2021, Cheryl secured a partnership with the Peel Region of Greater Toronto to fight human trafficking. Peel Region has the highest rate of human trafficking in the GTA. OneChild's programming is now at the heart of the area.

As relationships build, OneChild and their Youth Squad plan to seek more values-aligned corporate and government sponsorships to scale their in-school program to other underserved parts of the province of Ontario (where 2/3 of all abuse cases in Canada exist), and other provinces in Canada. Cheryl and her organization are targeting the provincial Ministries of Education, Ministries of Children, Community and Social Services, and Anti-Trafficking Coordination Offices to demonstrate how OneChild's "Break the Chains" school programing and youth-led partnerships prevent child sex trafficking and advance provincial curriculum objectives. In 2021, OneChild joined forces with Ontario Physical Education Curriculum to co-apply for provincial funding to create 7th and 8th grade gym curriculum around SEC prevention. Internationally, OneChild plans to join ECPAT, a worldwide network of over 100 organizations working to end SEC, so that they can share knowledge and resources for prevention as well as build their growing movement of young people and adult allies. Together, these strategies are putting Cheryl on track to her end-goal: to build young people's capacity to protect themselves and their peers in the fight against SEC and to be advocates for the change they wish to see.

THE PERSON

In 2001, at age 16, Cheryl learned about the child sex trade while researching for a high school project. She recalls being filled with anger that people were exploiting children her age and younger in such a heinous way, and she resolved to stop it. Realizing that her native country, Sri Lanka, was considered a "pedophile's paradise"—with 40,000 sexually exploited children— she decided at 17 to organize a solo, three-and-a-half month, fact-finding mission to Sri Lanka. She wanted to consult child victims, social workers, NGO workers, law enforcement, and government officials to get an insider's look into the child sex trade.

When Cheryl arrived in Sri Lanka, she contacted and managed to partner with the National Child Protection Authority and convinced them to let her play the main role of the decoy—a sexually exploited teen in an undercover sting operation. The operation was successful and ended in the apprehension of a 40-year-old Canadian perpetrator and father of two. During her stay, Cheryl brought her experiences from meeting various stakeholders, as well as going undercover, to a meeting with the Advisor to the President of Sri Lanka on Social Infrastructure. At the conclusion of this meeting, the President offered Cheryl a place in the Presidential Secretariat to serve as the President of Sri Lanka's Nominee on Child Protection and asked her to assist them with building a children's parliament as well.

Through her discussions with the children, Cheryl learned about their suffering, as well as the change they wished to see. During that trip, Cheryl made a silent promise to every child she met that she would do everything in her power to fight for their rights. By going undercover, Cheryl understood—even for just a sliver of a moment—how it felt to have one's childhood commodified. These experiences motivated Cheryl to return to Canada to start her years-long journey of bootstrapping, while working at McDonalds, to launch OneChild from her parents' basement. Cheryl's commitment was solidified in her early years, when she partnered with the PREDA Foundation in the Philippines to construct a rehabilitation center for rescued girls and with Action Pour Les Enfants to build a prevention education and training center for law enforcement in Cambodia. Cheryl is committed to using OneChild as a means to empower young people to protect their rights.

IARINA TABAN

Director and Founder, Ajungem Mari (Growing Great)

 www.ajungemmari.ro

When communism ended in Romania, images of neglected children found in overcrowded orphanages shocked the world. In response, Iarina founded a national network that marshalled volunteers, helping professionals, and other resources to serve the long-term educational and developmenal needs of institutionalized children and youth. Her work not only changes their lives; it changes the care system and shifts intergenerational patterns of trauma, poverty, and institutionalization.

SCAN THE CODE TO READ AND SHARE THIS ARTICLE ONLINE

THE NEW IDEA

Iarina Taban engages and weaves together committed volunteers, care staff, educators, specialized helping professionals, and other resources into a dynamic, creative team of teams and a community of care serving the developmental needs of institutionalized young people. Her approach empowers participants to become changemakers in the lives of Romania's disadvantaged youth and its institutional care system. Together, they are not only transforming young people's lives, but also mindsets, institutional cultures, and the care system itself.

A legacy of the communist era, Romania has one of the largest institutional care systems in Central and Eastern Europe. Orphanages with outdated facilities and approaches still operate there.

Youth in state care often experience trauma, have low levels of educational attainment, and lack social integration outside the institution. Iarina recognized that as they aged out and left the institution, the cycle of poverty, trauma, and institutionalization would likely continue into the next generation – especially if they had children themseves – – unless they were shown a different path.

Iarina forged one. She co-founded Ajungem Mari or Growing Great, Romania's only national program dedicated to the broader educational and developmental needs of institutionalized and disadvantaged youth.

Existing care institutions in Romania serve young people's immediate needs like food and shelter, and provide a basic level of education. But Iarina's work recruits and

PHOTO CREDIT: *Iarina Taban – Iarina's Ajungem Mari connects community members to institutionalized young people to provide them with the necessary support, care, and education that they need.*

equips volunteer "life mentors" to serve their critical developmental needs, providing the key dimension missing from institutional care: emotional bonding with a trusted, caring adult who can be a consistent, long-term presence and a positive role model, and provide a bridge to an independent life beyond the institution.

Mentors undergo specialized training in how to build trust and lasting relationships with young people who have been through trauma and are connected to a network of psychologists, educators, and other professionals who lend their expertise and support. Mentors have creative license to implement their own ideas about how to customize their activities to meet mentees' needs, but they also have to work within the rules of state care institutions.

Volunteering is not common in Romania and where it occurs, it's typically short-term. But Iarina has managed to attract a growing number of citizens to volunteer for long stretches of time and commit to changing the lives of institutionalized children. Mentors volunteer for a minimum of eight to 12 months – enough time to establish a consistent presence in the life of a child and to form a secure attachment to a significant adult. But the bond typically lasts for years, until after they leave state care. This is transformative for young people, and for mentors as well.

Growing Great has engaged 8500 volunteers so far, with than half of life mentors still engaged with their mentees years later. Exposure to the close relationship between mentors and children also influences state care workers, sparking their interest in adopting a similar approach. Iarina works to foster that, offering state care workers training and support resources. She encourages them to reframe how they see their role, not as "prison guards" or low-level vocational trainers, but as as caring, mission-driven professionals providing emotional support for institutionalized youth.

THE PROBLEM

Over six million children live in institutions worldwide – the majority of them in low – and middle-income countries. Institutionalization profoundly affects childrens' physical and psychological development and is associated with long-term mental health problems. Care institution staff typically have little training, low pay, and high turnover. This hinders effective relationship building, and is often insufficient to provide a basic standard of care.

In Romania, the problem is especially pronounced. In the communist era, poor families were encouraged to leave their children in state care, especially children with disabilities. When the communist regime ended in 1989, over 100,000 children were in living in state institutions. More than 16,000 children in state care were dying each year from treatable diseases and other causes.

Since then, care facilities and conditions in Romania improved, and the number of children in state care has fallen. But institutionalization remains widespread and still negatively impacts young people's health and development.

Five thousand children and young people enter Romania's childcare system each year. In 2018, there were

PHOTO CREDIT: *Iarina Taban – Iarina's model has spread throughout the country. Over 8,500 volunteers have contributed more than 500,000 hours helping children in 220 state care facilities.*

about 60,000 children in the state foster care system, of whom 18,500 were in state-run institutions, many of them ending up there because of family poverty, abuse, or neglect. Inside the system, many suffer from abandonment trauma, experience new or restimulated trauma, and act it out, engaging in negative, risky behaviors and sometimes becoming abusive or violent themselves.

Understanding and effectively working with their needs requires specialized training that staff and educators at state care institutions rarely have. They are often stretched impossibly thin, with 30 or 40 children per orphanage, and 60-70 children per case manager. Institutional culture is not geared toward developmental needs, fostering meaningful emotional bonds, or delivering personalized care. In fact, working in these challenging environments and constantly exposed to children's trauma, care staff are at risk for experiencing trauma themselves.

Though much reduced since the fall of communism, corruption's lingering influence tends to make state care institutions untransparent and highly political. It's common practice for employees to write detailed reports that don't acknowledge problems, tell officials what they want to hear, and give the impression of perfect conditions in order to maintain the status quo and protect their funding.

Consequently institutionalized young people don't get the support they need to build life skills, pursue their education, make good decisions, and become functional, independent citizens. Two thirds of those who age out and leave state care lack any occupation, and only 15% continue their education in any form.

This leaves them disconnected from society and puts them at high risk for poverty, homelessness, and human trafficking. Girls in Romanian state care institutions are particularly targeted by sex traffickers. Trafficking is by nature global and reliable data is scarce, but Romania ranks among the top five EU countries for the number of registered trafficking victims, and ranks first for the number of reported persons arrested, cautioned, or suspected for trafficking.

Ajungem MARI, the only national program that supports the long-term education of institutionalized children and young people from disadvantaged backgrounds, has started a new volunteer recruitment campaign. Children and young people in the protection system in Romania need people to support them, understand them, and give them confidence.

When formerly institutionalized children in Romania have children of their own, they often abandon them, recapitulating a cycle that leads to institutionalization and subsequent negative outcomes.

Such problems aren't unique to Romania; they're global. According to UNICEF, lack of individualized care and the lack of healthy bond with an adult figure are key factors inhibiting essential psychosocial development of children in institutions worldwide, which in turn leads to negative outcomes in adult life.

Since they aren't getting what they need inside care institutions, it stands to reason community members outside these institutions could be a resource to help young people integrate into society successfully. But lingering influences of communism have also made this culturally difficult in Romania.

Communist officials required Romanians to "volunteer" for national celebrations and other activities mandated by the government. This fostered resentment rather than feelings of personal responsibility or desire to serve the community. As a result, volunteerism was widely considered a waste of time, and socially engaged individuals were dismissed as "village fools." This attitude persists today, especially among the generation that remembers life under the communist regime.

THE STRATEGY

Iarina built a diverse team of teams for the welfare of institutionalized children that brings together volunteer mentors, care staff, educators, and helping professionals.

She co-founded Growing Great in 2014 and started recruiting volunteers in the Bucharest area as "life mentors" for young people in the state childcare system. Today, 3000 prospective volunteers across Romania, ages 16 to 65, apply to be life mentors each year.

Connecting community members to institutionalized young people is shifting norms and nurturing a growing desire for community service and a volunteerism. At the same time, connecting care staff and educators to the network of volunteers and expert resources is shifting the care system toward meeting children's developmental needs.

Educators and care staff are connected to volunteer mentors in their area, invited to online support groups, given access to psychologists to advise them as needed, and offered certificates for completing trainings in subjects institutionalized youth need to learn about, such as online safety, civic education, financial literacy, sexual education, and more.

County-level mentoring communities self-organize into peer-to-peer learning networks with their own coordinators, debriefing and supporting each other on their work with children.

Life mentors commit to spend at least two hours a week with the children for a minimum of eight to 12 months. That may not seem like a long time, but given the relative lack of volunteerism in Romanian society, it's actually an ambitious place to start. And for most, it's just the beginning. The majority of Growing Great life mentors stay engaged with their mentees for three to five years, motivated by a genuine mutual bond, rather than the initial volunteer commitment.

Iarina Taban is the founder of the Ajungem MARI Educational Program for children from foster care centers and disadvantaged environments. Since 2014, her team has attracted thousands of volunteers to be with institutionalized children for the long term.

Republica

"Children in foster care need relationships with people who understand, listen and accept them as they are, people they can trust, says Iarina. "And trust can only be built over time, by keeping promises."

Life mentor applicants undergo a rigorous psychological clearance and orientation process, then an eight-hour training program on safe and effective ways of communicating with the children, handling tense situations such as fights, and developing educational activities. They are then tested to determine how they would react to various situations – i.e. encouragingly or judgmentally. Those who make it through the vetting process sign contracts, are partnered with another mentor, and they are assigned to children in the state care system.

PHOTO CREDIT: *Iarina Taban – Ajungem Mari provides young people with resources to help them transition out of state care and prepare them for the realities of adult life. They receive vocational counseling as well as professional training courses.*

Mentors work in pairs, supporting and keeping each other accountable. Starting by helping children with their homework, they build trust and learn more about their mentees' needs and desires, then create a personalized program around them. Helping professionals in Growing GREAT's network – educators, vocational trainers, psychologists, speech therapists, etc. – – are available for individual courses, one-on-one tutoring, and therapy sessions. Mentees are also offered internships and local extracurricular activities that help them explore a wide range of interests (circus school is one example) as well as trips, summer camps, and social activities that connect them to and prepare them for life outside the institution. During the pandemic, Growing GREAT tapped its networks to offer children a rich array of online courses in dance, theater, singing, and robotics, among other subjects.

Life mentors are free to innovate and create their own individualized programs for mentees, but they also must understand and operate within rules and protocols governing state care institutions. Mentors file paperwork on their interactions with children, which is compiled and tracked by Growing GREAT, helping build trust with care institutions. Proposed activities need sign-off from the institution's director or from county officials, and life mentors are encouraged to work closely with them, exchange ideas, and cultivate collegial, two-way relationships.

The experience of mentoring and the bonds life mentors form with mentees can be just as transformative for them as for the young people they serve. In fact, some mentors have adopted their mentees. Others changed their careers to become teachers, psychologists, therapists for disadvantaged children.

"For three years, on Mondays at 4pm, I would arrive at the care home, and they would be at the window, waiting for me," said one life mentor. "The children have grown up, but I feel that I have also grown up. I learned new things with them, I attended classes to keep up with them, and I had to read more myself so I could answer their questions. I met open-minded, young people who gave me confidence in myself. I saw that there is room for everyone, any helping hand is welcome, and any skill can find its usefulness."

The end of the mentor-mentee relationship is handled with care. Since life mentors work in pairs, if one of them must stop volunteering, the other can maintain their bond with the child. And whenever a mentoring relationship ends, the Growing GREAT community facilitates a comprehensive closure process where mentors let the child know what they love and appreciate about them. The process allows for healthy separation and prevents further trauma for the child.

Partnering with other civil society and public sector organizations, Iarina recently launched an independent living guide for young people, mentors, and teachers. It has practical information explaining young people's options and legal aspects as they age out of the care system, which they otherwise wouldn't know. For example, the guide points out they can stay in care centers until age 26 if they are studying or have a job.

> *The Ajungem MARI educational program...has brought a significant and visible change in the lives of thousands of children in the protection system. Volunteers prepare them for an independent life [by] doing homework, meditation, going on camping trips, and practicing kindness every day.*

But even as they prepare to leave the system, many have trouble making decisions and directing their lives. Iarina puts particular emphasis on providing resources to help them transition out of state care and establish themselves in the world, such as vocational counselling, professional training courses, site visits to explore different jobs, and help with getting driver's licenses. One measure of her success is that children who went through the Growing GREAT program have even gone on to become life mentors themselves.

Launched in Bucharest eight years ago, Iarina's model was designed for rapid uptake. In 2016, Romania's Ministry of Labor recommended the Growing GREAT be extended to as many vulnerable children as possible. Today, it has expanded throughout the country. Organizations in the Republic of Moldavia are also working to spread Iarina's approach. So far she has engaged over 8,500 volunteers contributing over 500,000 hours helping children in over 220 state care facilities.

With mentoring communities widely established, Iarina is focusing on her role as a field builder, including by deepening her relationships with and support for workers and educators in state care facilities. Their own trauma from working in these settings needs empathy and redress in its own right, so that they can be more fully present to children and become changemakers within the care system. Iarina uses online learning tools to engage state care employees, foster a closer relationship between them and life mentors, and create a better environment for institutionalized children.

THE PERSON

As the only child of well-educated parents, Iarina was instilled with a sense of the importance of education, and won national prizes for creative writing.

She started volunteering in high school and in her first year of university joined the Volunteer Brigade, where she coordinated volunteers at concerts and festivals. In a culture where volunteering had not been valued historically, the experience convinced her that a critical mass of volunteers could achieve meaningful change.

In her early 20s, Iarina worked as a communications staffer for an English language education company. She was given the opportunity to oversee a pilot project for which she recruited, trained and coordinated 27 volunteers to teach English using non-formal methods for disadvantaged children in Bucharest daycare centers. The volunteers were high school students. Working two hours a week with the same group of children, she came to realize that the relationships they formed with the children had other benefits besides improving their English. The children demonstrated higher self-esteem, more motivation to learn, and better developed social skills.

The next year many more volunteers signed up and the project was set to expand to three more counties. But the company didn't support the effort properly, so Iarina quit her job to start her own volunteer education project for disadvantaged children. She left with 150 euros in her bank account, a small group of close friends who offered to help, and zero restrictions on her creativity.

At age 25, she made her first visit to a state care institution. She was shocked by the continuous screaming of a three year-old boy who was abandoned at birth and then abandoned again by a foster parent. The suffering and loneliness of the children she encountered there, most of whom couldn't even express their feelings, was overwhelming. The experience crystalized Iarina's mission to revolutionize and humanize care for disadvantaged, traumatized children.

ARUNDHUTI GUPTA

Founder and CEO, Mentor Together

 www.mentortogether.org

Arundhuti Gupta enables disadvantaged young people to escape the "lottery of birth". Through systems, both in person and online, she can deliver anywhere that ensures successful mentoring for them as teens and as young adults.

SCAN THE CODE TO READ AND SHARE THIS ARTICLE ONLINE

THE NEW IDEA

What disadvantaged – – whether by caste, class, gender, geography, or other causes – – young people cannot get sufficiently at home or in rote, narrowly focused schools and colleges, they might access through a third dimension: Mentoring. That they do is Arundhuti's life goal.

But how can one provide reliable, successful mentoring to the hundreds of millions of young people who need it? That's Arundhuti's entrepreneurial challenge.

She is succeeding. More and more schools, colleges, state governments, and others are signing up. Ninety percent of her young teen mentees have a better relationship with their mothers, 80 percent with their fathers. Over half see their school grades go up.

Arundhuti is successful because she is building for systems change. She studies and evaluates and iteratively improves how her mentoring works and is delivered all the time.

Between 2009-2018, Arundhuti first focused on scaling an in-person mentoring program for high-school students. This started as an action-research project at Centre for Public Policy at the Indian Institute of Management, Bangalore. The program then scaled up to five cities – Bangalore, Mumbai, Pune, Delhi, & Chennai. By 2018, the program would annually accept about 500 new high school students facing conditions of high risk into a 3-year mentorship program until they graduated high-school. Despite the success of the program, Arundhuti realized that the in-person model significantly constrained the supply of available mentors as it was difficult to meet the needs of mentees due to work travel, difficulties committing to the program duration, and language barriers.

Around the same time in 2018, Arundhuti noticed an economic and socio-cultural shift in India: older students

***PHOTO CREDIT:** World Economic Forum – Arundhuti's Mentor Together has partnered with 89 colleges and universities and 26 corporates to champion the platform in their respective organizations and institutions.*

– prospective mentees for Mentor Together – in universities began to own and access mobile technologies. The falling costs of mobile data and smartphones meant that mobile phones became ubiquitous and essential to the student experience in universities. The entrepreneurial mind of Arundhuti saw this as a unique opportunity to increase the access of mentorship using technology.

In 2018, she developed and launched 'Mentor To Go', a mobile and web-based mentoring platform that offers career mentorship to help young people – – across the age groups of 18-22, a period where such mentorship can be career-defining – who are primarily from low-income families.

The platform, via its data driven algorithms, matches best-fit mentors and mentees in either 1:1 or group formats and presents structured mentorship tools for teaching and learning. Through an array of language choices and audio/video communication channels, the platform has made the mentoring program extremely accessible and scalable. Beyond platform development, Arundhuti is orchestrating a coalition of governments, individual educational institutions, non-profits, and corporates, across India to champion this mentoring model.

Over 35,000 mentors and mentees have signed up to the platform in the last 4 years, from a network of over 150 educational institutions and 40 corporate partners. 65% of the educational institutions are in Tier 2 and Tier 3 cities, and 35% in Tier 1 cities, across 10 states in India. Formal government partnerships in Karnataka, Maharashtra, and Telangana help drive the bulk of student participation in the program. Close to 5400 mentoring relationships have been facilitated by the platform.

Mentors and mentees work through a mentoring toolkit of activities that supplements formal education with an emphasis on enhancing the mentee's work readiness skills holistically. Through research-backed sessions, mentors help mentees understand themselves, build social and emotional skills, set a career vision, plan roadmaps towards those goals, and discover personal & professional values.

> *Arundhuti Gupta believes that education alone isn't enough to help young people in developing the skills and mindsets they need to fully overcome their conditions. "Providing them life skills that can broaden horizons, build identity and connect to opportunities, is also necessary," she says.*
>
> **The Indian EXPRESS**

Arundhuti is gathering important information and data to support her work on policy change to embed mentoring as a critical element for youth development. In addition to her own efforts to expand scalable mentoring, Arundhuti has also registered a new non-profit organization to make the Mentor To Go technology platform available for companies and citizen groups looking to

PHOTO CREDIT: *Mentor Together – Mentors undergo a comprehensive training period before establishing a relationship with their mentees. Mentors learn interpersonal skills like active listening and empathy.*

institute their own mentoring programs to meet the enormous demand for mentoring across the world.

Her mentors and mentees benefit from a rich mix of learning techniques ranging from games, softly Socratic problem solving, all delivered in empathetic, mutually respected ways. They also benefit from close, objective management monitoring and help. Her approach for young teens is in person; for young adults, online (but still very personal).

In other words, Arundhuti has developed a system that can cover millions, which can be taken up by others (which she encourages), and that promises that those millions of young people can have full futures. This is a big step for India's future and for justice.

THE PROBLEM

As of 2022, 38 million young people are in tertiary education in India, with the highest ever enrollment rate of 30 percent of the youth population in the tertiary age-group. Furthermore, national education policymakers seek to increase that number to 50 percent by 2030. To meet this national goal, services and sectors are getting on board to support the vision. However, in their quest for meaningful jobs and a better life, first-generation learners battle systemic inequalities that prevent them from achieving upward social mobility, something that is exacerbated by a lack of economically and socially successful role models within their social and geographical reach.

In addition, job markets are changing rapidly, while India's continued dependency on standardized, textbook-based learning denies young people access to 21st century skills that are critical to surviving and thriving in emerging and future markets. Ill-prepared youth, especially women, struggle to find connection and mentorship in their immediate environments and many end up taking unskilled and low-paying jobs as a result. Many become unemployed.

There is some access to informal mentoring programs, but these avenues focus on connecting youth with elders in the immediate community, so there is neither any formal training or support for the mentor or mentee nor access to a wide set of mentors who have experience outside of these communities. As a result, many of these relationships fizzle out and young people become disillusioned with the benefits of mentoring.

THE STRATEGY

Arundhuti's solution is to help young people break out of socio-economic silos to achieve their potential. By integrating cross-disciplinary research, expertise, evidence, design, technology, and curriculum, she addresses the massive gap between the demand and availability of trained mentors for India's youth as they navigate the school-to-work continuum. Furthermore, she is developing a mentoring solution that is backed by evidence, developing the capacity of the mentor to offer the highest quality support and forming a community of learners and practitioners who are championing this form of mentorship.

To enable children and young people ages 13-21 to access a varied network of mentors, Arundhuti and her team have instituted two programs.

> *I don't know if she's like a friend, a parent or a guide. I think she's more than God to me," says Nayana (name changed), 19, who feels she can't thank her mentor enough for giving her life a new direction. Just like her, a few other girls from Karnataka's rural areas have been helped by Mentor Together to guide them academically and emotionally –*
>
> **The Indian EXPRESS**

First, the city-based school mentoring program is designed for high-risk adolescents in grades 8, 9, and 10. Anchored by in-person mentoring (at home or school), mentors counsel their mentees through the development of critical life skills – including self-awareness, self-esteem, motivation and perseverance. A randomized control trial carried out in 2018 by the Centre of Budget and Policy Studies demonstrated a 90 percent likelihood of a mentee having a better relationship with their mother and 80 percent likelihood of a better relationship with their father when compared with students who did not participate in the mentorship program. Further, a mentee is 58 percent more likely to have better emotional, social and school well-being, and 55 percent more likely to have better grades in math, social sciences and sciences.

Second, the Mentor To Go work readiness mentoring program for underprivileged college and university students opens up opportunities for young people who are transitioning into the world of work to build skill sets and open new and important networks they will need to shape long-lasting careers. This is a virtual program through which mentors and mentees connect online.

Both programs are defined by strong evidence-based curriculums, mentoring that is facilitative and not prescriptive, allowing for an equal stake of mentor and mentee in the successful outcome of the mentoring process, robust processes, and partnerships that lay the ground for a vibrant mentoring ecosystem.

While the in-person school program has been dormant due to the pandemic since 2020, the Work Readiness mobile mentoring platform – Mentor to Go – has grown exponentially, as documented above. Arundhuti and her team have developed a research-backed curriculum benchmarked against global excellence standards. Working through the curriculum, young people set work readiness goals and access personalized coaching.

To be eligible for mentoring, both mentees and mentors must commit to a minimum six-month timeframe. Uploading their college ID and proof of income, mentees submit basic information – their current academic courses, subjects, work readiness, need areas, hobbies, preferences and available times for mentorship. Before they are matched, the students must complete a set of self-learning exercises, demonstrating their commitment to the process. The algorithm then offers the mentee a choice of mentors in sync with their preferences – only first names and profiles are shared. The selection of a final match is determined by the mentee.

PHOTO CREDIT: *Mentor Together – Access to formal mentoring helps young women obtain higher paying jobs and upwards social mobility.*

> *Altering the choices of India's disadvantaged youth also requires an expansion of their social networks. Their communities have few role models who can guide the next generation with professional advice. Mentorship has been a part of urban youth community programmes around the world for nearly a century but is a fairly new intervention with children and youth in India. When Arundhuti Gupta launched Mentor Together in 2009, there were only a couple similar programmes in the country.*

The Guardian

Mentors are also trained and prepared for the mentoring process through a series of modules that explain the process and support mentors' developing ability to listen, stay objective and empathize. This formal training provides an important and missing pillar in traditional mentoring initiatives across the country. The lack of such interpersonal skills among traditional mentors often leads to the breakdown of mentorship engagements because no amount of technical knowledge, resources, or network relationships can offset the need for soft skills that are needed to foster trust and connection. Arundhuti's robust training curriculum for mentors aims to fix this and take a more holistic – technical and interpersonal – approach to mentorship.

In virtual learning spaces – through scheduled or on-demand communication and powered by a range of exercises such as games, videos, toolkits, goal-focused activities and self-reflective discussions – the mentoring pair dive deep within and share reflections as they exchange thoughts and experiences. These conversations help mentees develop a sense of self as they identify core values and motivators. Gaining insights into the world of employment through the mentorship relationship, mentees are encouraged to express their career visions and pathways to actualize those visions. Once these are mapped out and identified, they take the first initial steps to becoming work ready – putting together their resumes, preparing for interviews, or applying for internships.

On the ground, the Mentor Together team ensures the effectiveness and success of the mentoring relationship before, during, and at the end of the mentoring journey. Mentees are asked to assess their motivation and commitment to the program before matching each pair. Then, a 'pair manager' tracks the mentoring relationship diligently and is alerted to issues about ease of navigation, safety, compatibility and comfort in the relationship. Responsible for catalyzing the relationship and championing mentors and mentees through regular check ins, the 'pair managers' are now able to expand their roles through the Mentor To Go platform. By professionalizing this process, a greater sense of trust and accountability is nurtured for all stakeholders.

Mentor Together staff adheres to global standards for effective mentoring with weekly team meetings to report on and analyze data on mentors, mentees, levels of satisfaction, and attrition. These data are measured against 5-6 indicators of outcomes with an emphasis on improving self-concept, career-focused self-efficacy, improving work readiness and career maturity. The metrics instill rigor in the process and help Arundhati to strengthen the system itself by continuously using the data to iterate the curriculums, trainings, and engagement practices. This data-informed process has been a key advocacy tool when convincing partners such as state education departments to adopt the model. Female mentees who comprise 61 percent of the total mentee pool are specifically tracked for increases in voice/expression, agency, understanding of gender socialization norms, and behaviors that apply to the workforce.

Mentor Together has signed MoUs with governments of three Indian states, and agreements with 89 colleges and universities located in Tier 2 and Tier 3 cities. 26 corporates with a huge workforce have signed up to champion the mentoring platform within their organizations. The partnership with Telangana's TASK (Telangana Academy for Skill and Knowledge) has enabled mentoring opportunities to reach over 6,000 students (including pilot programs with people from indigenous backgrounds) across the state since 2018. Through the partnership with Karnataka's Department of Technical Education, Arundhuti is reaching 14 government colleges in rural Karnataka, covering over 1,000 students since 2020. Lastly, with the more recent partnership with Maharashtra's Department of Higher Education, Konkan Region, Mentor To Go has already reached over 1,000 students since March 2022.

Furthermore, Arundhuti has reached new groups through employee engagement programs and existing mentors are serving as ambassadors. Responding to the demand from mentees, Mentor to Go is being made available in more Indian languages, ensuring that the model can reach the most disadvantaged youth across the country. Topic-based speed mentoring over shorter time periods will also be introduced, allowing mentees to dip into work related experience with mentors. Arundhuti also plans to track the mentee's successful transition into the workforce in the long-term alongside other impact indicators over a person's lifetime.

Moving forward, Arundhuti has set three clear goals for herself: 1) to reach a 100,000 young people with Mentor Togethers' services in the next five years 2) create a mentoring ecosystem by training citizen groups and organizations and making her technology open source, 3) influence policy to further embed mentoring as a critical element for youth development. Arundhuti is setting up the networks and infrastructure to achieve these goals. Having rigorously proven her solution through service delivery since 2009, Arundhuti is now looking to ramp up the ability for her model to be widely replicated and scaled across the country.

THE PERSON

Having personally experienced the positive power of mentoring and its influence on her life choices, Arundhuti started Mentor Together as a way to pay it forward.

Growing up in Bangalore, Arundhuti's early life was dedicated to academics. She was a very strong student and eventually joined one of Bangalore's premier colleges known for its emphasis on holistic personal development. There, Arundhuti discovered a world beyond academics as she participated in many activities and found great joy and a sense of purpose in volunteering.

At age of 20, encouraged by her professors, Arundhuti participated in a student leadership program held by the Goldman Sachs Global Leadership Institute in New York City – one of only two Indian students selected. Interacting with peers from 50 countries, she was both stunned and inspired by their life choices as well as their actions and ambitions for a more equitable world. For the first time, Arundhuti learned about different youth identities and power outside of academics. This was a turning point for her.

Energized and brimming with new ideas, she returned home to explore her own ability to make change happen. A meeting at a conference with Dr. Rajeev Gowda, then a Professor at the Indian Institute of Management – Bangalore, pivoted her into the world of youth development and youth empowerment. Expanding her leadership skills and own experiences in a mentoring relationship, she volunteered with Dr. Gowda, and supported his efforts to host career exploration events for young people. Through these experiences, she learned not only about young people's hopes and dreams, but also about their fears. These early insights helped draw the blueprint of Mentor Together.

After university, Arundhuti took a position with Goldman Sachs as an operations analyst at a bank. However, after a year, she felt reaffirmed that her life's purpose was working with young people, but her current job didn't offer a fulfilling path forward. She decided to return to school and pursue a Master's in Finance. While studying in Manchester, she shared with two close friends about her experience, her passion and her dream of accessible mentorship for India's disadvantaged youth. Together, with Arundhuti's leadership, the small group went on to establish her design for a standalone youth mentorship program for young people in India.

Impressed and inspired by her entrepreneurial zeal and determination, Dr. Gowda signed on as co-trustee and, in 2009, at the age of 23, Arundhuti launched Mentor Together with a mission to help underprivileged students gain access to formal mentorship opportunities.

ENVIRONMENT

JAGDEESH RAO
India

NANI MORÉ
Spain

CARLOS NOBRE
Brazil

DYLAN TERREL
Mexico

TASSO AZEVEDO
Brazil

JAGDEESH RAO PUPPALA

CEO, Foundation for Ecological Security (FES)

 www.fes.org.in

Jagdeesh Rao has championed a replicable framework that enables self-governing village communities to uplift themselves by effectively and sustainably utilizing the natural resources around them in a way that restores ecosystem productivity. His respectful, science-sharing approach shows how to end villages (and all of us) the 'tragedy of commons'.

SCAN THE CODE TO READ AND SHARE THIS ARTICLE ONLINE

THE NEW IDEA

Jagdeesh is working to end the spiraling modern tragedy of these villagers' forests and other commons and move instead to "the promise of the commons." His organization – The Foundation for Ecological Security (FES) – helps secure rights to the land and assists the local communities in strengthening and building local institutions, restoring degraded ecosystems, and cultivating local volunteers to take on the stewardship and preservation of the forest and water resources around them. These common property resources provide a single platform that anyone can leverage to address issues of social justice, ecological restoration, and poverty alleviation.

These activities also reduce hunger and poverty while reviving democratic functioning in the village. Jagdeesh ensures that the local communities that use "common" lands have the information needed to choose options and run ongoing decision-making wisely. That's the only way to get sustainable decision-making reliably that will ensure ongoing livelihoods and ecosystems.

By recognizing that the forests, water, and other natural resources are part of the village's ecological, social and economic landscape, conservation efforts are always informed by local needs and contexts. Instead of considering farming as crop production alone, FES works with communities, so they see the interconnections between the larger farming system and resources beyond the farm, such as forests, pastures, bodies of water, livestock, pollinators and pest predators more clearly. This kind of systems understanding is innate and latent within farming communities, so efforts to connect agriculture, livestock, pastures, and forests have resulted in vastly improved collective decision making on crop choices, the treatment of groundwater as a common property, and the nurturing of pollinator and pest predator habitats to improve crop productivity. Besides scaling

PHOTO CREDIT: *Foundation for Ecological Security (FES) – Jagdeesh's model brings together reliably scientific data and community cohesion and self-governance.*

up such measures, FES also plays an equally important role in motivating government and research institutions to integrate the commons into their systems thinking and to screen their sector-based programs for any unintended and undesirable consequences.

Rao has been working on the problem since 1984, when he first visited Hyderabad as an undergraduate studying agriculture sciences. Through FES, he has collaborated with more than 7,000 villages to bring 3.7 million acres of common land under local management.

THE PROBLEM

The Tragedy of the Commons refers to a situation in which individuals with access to a publicly held resource (known as a common) act in their own self-interest and, in doing so, ultimately deplete the resource. The Tragedy is often applied to discussions of environmental issues and is a model for a great variety of society's current resource-based problems, including over-irrigation, habitat destruction, overfishing, and traffic congestion. Around the world, and in India in particular, the degradation of Commons has been identified as a key contributor to poverty, conflict, corruption and limited economic growth.

The commons in India face widespread degradation, leading to falling crop yields, increased cost of cultivation, depleted water tables, shrinking forests, and the unregulated use of pastures. Everyone in India depends to some degree on the ecological functions of these commonly held lands, but the vast numbers of the most marginalized people in India depend entirely on commonly held community land for every aspect of their lives. While the majority of this common land in India is owned and managed by the government, the poor communities that live on these lands have long standing relationships and practices associated with their management and use of the lands, but ensuring the community works to conserve the land depends on whether their rights are protected. Without any formal tenure rights or legal claims to the land, the community has very little incentive to maintain the health of the ecosystem, despite its importance in

PHOTO CREDIT: *Foundation for Ecological Security (FES) – FES provides capacity building workshops and legal assistance to help community members claim their rights to use, manage, and protect the Commons.*

their lives. The issue of legal rights to the land become particularly acute when outside private interests or government forces exploit the land, and all of the hard work that a community has invested in the land provides them with no benefits. At the heart of the situation is the even more tragic fact that the government lacks belief in the community's ability to be effective custodians and stewards of the land, and chooses the short term economically viable option, such as giving the land to industries (e.g, mining and logging) to destroy the land and forests completely while ignoring the greatest protectors of the land, the people themselves.

Forests represent the second largest land use in India after agriculture, covering 23.57 percent of the overall landmass of India (378 million hectares). Local people depend on forests and other common lands for fuel wood, fodder, timber, forage, food, drinking water for animals and other household requirements. About 275 million of the country's rural poor in India depend on forests for at least part of their subsistence, with the collection and processing of Non-Timber Forest Produce (NTFP) alone estimated to be worth between USD 208 million to 645 million per year. Despite their criticality, forests across India are besieged – previously inaccessible areas are now open to exploitation, and subsistence hunting and gathering in forests has given way to large-scale extraction of forest resources to cater to industrial and distant market demands.

Forest destruction has also contributed to a serious and alarming rate of groundwater depletion in India, which has resulted in around 75 percent of India's dryland districts being declared "dark zones" meaning post monsoon water levels in the aquifers are inadequate to sustain farming practices until the next monsoon season. Practically speaking, forests and other Commons need to be maintained for the ecological functions they serve, the ecosystem services they provide, the biodiversity they contain, and the ways in which they reduce the harmful effects of greenhouse gasses, as well as to preserve local agricultural and water systems. Compounding the problem is the fact that conservation and developmental efforts of the government to improve land usage practices are often administered by different government branches and levels, and tend to be fragmented and piecemeal, and at times they even work at cross-purposes, giving rise to further negative consequences. What is required instead is an integrated methodological framework for conserving forests, grazing lands, and bodies of water that can span across habitats and administrative domains, and which are led by self-governing communities of women and men, who are sensitive to local needs and the long term health of the environment and the village.

Entrepreneur Jagdeesh Rao Puppula is definitely disrupting status quo. . .[His] foundation helps villagers improve the soil, water and other conditions in what had been regarded as wasteland. So they're able to grow more crops and bring in more revenue. Wildlife benefits, as well, from the changes.

THE STRATEGY

Recognising that the vast majority of common lands sit in unique geographical regions, with very specific cultural norms, Jagdeesh and the Foundation for Ecological Security (FES) have built an adaptable model which puts the onus of the future of the Commons in the hands of the community members, and brings together principles of self-governance, community cohesion and justice. At the heart of the model are three interconnected elements that vitally connect local communities to the Commons, and enable them to better understand and respect the inter-relationships of biodiversity and natural systems: First, is to help local communities retain their rights over the Commons; second is to move these communities towards sustainable land-use practices that aid conservation; and, third is to foster collective action that creates sustainable economic opportunities. By securing community land rights, establishing community based resource management and governance plans, and creating access to resources and finances, the Commons become the source of resilient livelihoods and improved ecological health.

To achieve and multiply impact on community-led governance of shared natural resources, FES works to enable system-level shifts by providing system-wide thought leadership and by embedding the Commons in debates on policies and programs. By advancing thinking around community property rights and groundwater management, they advance the dialogue of the Commons at local, regional, national and international levels, rooting the conversation in the larger goals of climate action and sustainable development while at the same time linking it to local thematic groups in neglected domains, like pastoralists and small livestock keepers. FES is also at the forefront of promoting informed action by improving access to knowledge, analytics and tools, for greater transparency, civic engagement and informed decision-making.

As Jagdeesh has observed, "if you put a map on the floor, people start talking and local people know everything about the land." So, in collaboration with organizations and initiatives across India, they aggregate and contextualize data, analytics, and tools to supplement the decision-making of rural communities. By providing better information to villages, including spatial and satellite imagery, locals can approach the management of the Commons with a birds-eye view that helps them account for the land's history, current usage, threats, and potential. At the community level, Jagdeesh begins his intervention by identifying natural resources which have been degraded over time, such as forests, grasslands, or bodies of water. FES then conducts extensive studies of the area and the surrounding communities around the degraded lands, and completes an analysis of the land's condition, history, and use. Once the studies are concluded, Jagdeesh brings together and engages local organizations who already have trust with the communities living near the natural resource. Depending on their level of awareness of the role that the common lands play in their lives and larger natural ecosystems, FES conducts capacity building workshops to help the community members better understand their importance in managing the Commons, even if they do not directly use them.

Jagdeesh then assists these united communities in using provisions of affirmative legislation such as the recently-enacted Forest Rights Act, to claim their rights to access, use, protect and manage commonly held forests and other natural resources. Because the degradation of Commons can be attributed to weak tenure rights, the erosion of local institutions, and the misplaced belief that local communities are ineffective managers of their shared natural resources, FES aids communities in securing tenure over their Commons. Where the Forest Rights Act applies, communities are supported to claim rights over Commons as community forests. Where there are wastelands, they help village communities acquire long-term leases, and claim for increases in pastures. They also enable local communities to map their common

PHOTO CREDIT: *Foundation for Ecological Security (FES) – FES has restored over 11.38 million acres of common lands benefitting over 22 million people.*

lands (wastelands and pastures) and to legally register them to limit their diversion to other uses.

In this work of advancing the communities' capacity for local self-governance in managing resources, Jagdeesh works to improve gender parity by promoting the participation of women and increasing their involvement in governance processes. By working with Panchayats (a common system of local self-government in rural villages throughout India) to develop Gram Panchayat Development Plans that place restrictions on groundwater mining, better sanitation, and protection of grazing land, they help restore the agency of rural communities while improving collective action, democratizing the functioning of local institutions, and devising institutional spaces that safeguard the interests of the poor. To further enhance local capacity for policy and program implementation, FES developed the Prakriti Karyashala (Rural Colleges), which are designed to serve as local centers for the exchange of ideas and experiences, and to provide large-scale, cost-effective and quality learning opportunities. The Karyashalas train rural communities, village institutions, Panchayats, as well as government and NGO officials, who can then provide training to stakeholders in other locations. To achieve the learning outcomes, the Karyashala employs experiential learning methods in the form of sequential training modules in combination with field-level applications. The modules include filing claims on community lands; effective planning, and implementation of natural resource management through the national rural employment government program; strengthening the capacities of Panchayats; and, accessing social security benefits. The overall focus is on enhancing local stewardship, improving rigor of action, and building the necessary leadership and collaboration skills to bridge local practice and program imperatives.

> *Jagdeesh emphasizes that with the development of the land comes the development of the people. 'A vital part of this is enhancing the capacity of local people, the power of collective action, and harnessing these high quality leaders who address these serious ecological, economic, and social deficiencies.*

Since its beginning, FES has worked with 36,407 villages across 10 ecological regions of India, restoring 11.38 million acres of common lands and impacting the lives of 22 million people. With an ambitious aim of restoring 30 million acres of common lands in the next five years (and with an overall potential of restoring 200 million acres), FES aims to scale their work to 100,000 villages through collaborations with various local NGOs, government partners, researchers, practitioners and changemakers. By creating a collective platform and exchange forums, FES is elevating the debate about the Commons and giving a voice to the issues of the degradation of common lands while also participating in the development of products to facilitate widespread change across many sectors and communities – like groundwater monitoring tools, a Geographic Information System enabled entitlement tracking system, an integrated forest management toolkit, a crop water budgeting tool, tools that identify and demarcate shared lands, create designs for soil and water conversation, and provide quick summaries of socioeconomic and environmental parameters of any chosen state, district or block, as well as documentaries, research studies, and reference manuals.

THE PERSON

Jagdeesh was born in Andhra Pradesh and in his years growing up he experienced harsh treatment due to the dark color of his skin. His own experience opened his eyes to the many other forms of division all around him – mistreatments related to race, sex, and social status – and with this awareness grew a fierce determintation to fight for the underdogs and to make room for the voices of the people who are not heard. He also grew up next to a river which brought him calmness and serenity; so, in choosing his professional life, he knew he would want to live close to water and to nature.

While finishing his schooling and undergraduate degree in Agricultural Sciences from Baroda, Gujarat, he encountered a local guru who showed practically the ways in which social and ecological systems are interconnected with the economic systems. He then went on to study Forestry for Rural Management in the Netherlands. In 1986, Jagdeesh was part of a pilot project on Tree Growers Cooperatives by the National Dairy Development Board. He was responsible for project design and conceptualization in the first year, which brought him face-to-face with the political and bureaucratic hurdles that face rural India.

While engaged in this work from 1986-1994, however, he began to see the pitfalls of the cooperative system model which defined a successful cooperative by the profits it generated from cutting and selling trees, and reduced the natural landscape to a commodity. It was during his work with TGCP that he began to understand the politics and power struggles associated with the Commons, and especially the dynamics of ownership. While with TGCP, the core of the work he was doing was arranging land from the government and passing it to the villages to help manage and protect them. While doing this, he realized that the villagers were strongly disproving the theory of tragedy of Commons when the land was brought under their management. He learned up close in the villages that "just because people are financially poor doesn't mean they are intellectually poor." In 2001, he moved away from the cooperatives project and founded Foundation for Ecological Security.

PHOTO CREDIT: *Foundation for Ecological Security (FES) – Women's active involvement and participation in the governance process improves gender parity in their communities.*

NANI MORÉ

Chef, Founder & Director, Menjadors Ecològics

 www.menjadorsecologics.cat/ca/coneix-nos/

Nani Moré has pioneered and grown a new ecosystem supplying sustainable, nutritious food at an affordable cost through collective kitchens in schools, hospitals, civic centers, and care homes across Spain, where food deficits are surprisingly widespread. By connecting kitchen chefs, staff, and municipal food procurement procedures with local organic food producers, she has turned Spain's collective kitchen system into a powerful strategy for fighting malnutrition, building spirit, and helping the environment.

SCAN THE CODE TO READ AND SHARE THIS ARTICLE ONLINE

THE NEW IDEA

Public kitchens in Spain were originally conceived as a way of feeding infants. Today Spain's nationwide system of collective catering kitchens in schools, hospitals, civic centers, and care homes serves 5 million meals each day. They are the chief resource for feeding vulnerable populations including children, the sick, and the elderly. But for cost reasons, they typically serve low-quality overprocessed, unhealthy, and unappetizing food.

Nani Moré's work is changing that. She understood that collective kitchens in Spain could be the key to a reimagined food system centered on quality, nutrition, and health. And she knew from experience that high food prices need not force kitchens to serve food of low quality. By linking the chefs and staff of collective kitchens with municipal procurement and local agriculture, she formed a new ecosystem that delivers healthy, nutritious food inexpensively.

Her approach integrates an otherwise siloed food system from end to end, connecting the local farmers growing the food, the municipal workers who procure it for collective kitchens, and the cooks who prepare it. She knew from experience that one determined chef could transform her own kitchen and reasoned that a network of determined chefs working together could transform the whole food system, so she built one.

She focuses on locally produced organic and seasonal foods, and how to get it into collective kitchens within their current budgets. Her method involves exposing lack of transparency and hidden costs in the current food procurement system, and replacing this with alternative planning, open bidding, and billing procedures. They facilitate three-way, collaborative relationships between farmers, municipalities and kitchens, instead of the usual top-down relationship where procurement decisions are based on cost, then imposed on kitchens.

> *Nani Moré [is a] founding partner of Menjadors Ecològics ("Ecological Eaters"), which brings together professionals from different fields (production, food, and education), to promote local organic production, and with it a healthy, educational, sustainable, and fair model [for combating hunger] in Spain, [where] 5 million people eat in schools, hospitals, and residences each day.*
>
> **Forbes**

This sets up a local virtual circle or closed loop which stimulates and sustains demand for local, organic produce, making it possible for local farmers to commit to producing more of it to meet demand and selling it at affordable prices, which in turn making it possible for procurers to order more of it and for public kitchens to serve more of it. In the long run this will also extend to local shops and markets, making healthy food available and affordable for the whole community.

Nani Moré calls these local loops "short supply circuits." She also calls her approach "climate cuisine," because it aligns local, sustainable, and organic farming, which shrinks agriculture's climate footprint, with high food quality and healthy diets.

One well= framed municipal purchase order can supply all collective kitchens in a municipality with fresh, local food, incentivizing more local food production and sourcing, guaranteeing a high volume of high-quality food, and enabling high standards to be met across the collective kitchen system. Taken together, the local and

PHOTO CREDIT: *Nani Moré Ramon – Nani is transforming the food system by using local, sustainable food and creative management.*

PHOTO CREDIT: *Nani Moré Ramon – Menjadors Ecològics connects lòcal food producers with collective kitchens to make healthy food available and affordable for the whole community.*

regional networks form a new ecosystem delivering local, organic, and seasonal food at scale. In this way, collective kitchens that adopt healthy, sustainable menus become drivers of positive change in the food system.

THE PROBLEM

Spain has the potential capacity to produce up to 80% of its food needs, yet it imports 60% of its food. Shipping food accounts for 25 – 30% of global greenhouse gas emissions, according to the Intergovernmental Panel on Climate Change (IPCC).

Local food has a much smaller environmental and climate footprint than imported food, and Spain has favorable conditions for producing it sustainably. But a history of low demand for local food lowers the supply and raises the price, so that it's considered a luxury item.

In addition, hidden costs and lack of transparency built into food procurement systems tend to put the cost of local food furthermore out of reach, further limiting demand for it. To invest in ramping up sustainable production, local farmers need to know there will be sufficient local demand and market access for their products. Since this is lacking, it keeps local food production well below its potential, making the overall food system less sustainable than it could be.

Limited local food production means vulnerable populations that can't afford luxury item prices and have limited access to quality food. They also lack education as to how food is connected to their health. It's estimated that more than 80% of Spain's adult population will be overweight by 2030, costing the healthcare system €3 billion a year. By 2050, half of Spain's total population, children included, are expected to be obese unless the trajectory changes.

Nani Moré's motto is that "there is a difference between filling belies and feeding people." She has created a healthy and sustainable culinary concept connected to local food producers.

EL PAIS

When making procurement decisions for collective kitchens, municipalities typically prioritize food cost over quality, and there has been little in the regulation of public food procurement to challenge this way of thinking. There are also procedural problems that make food costs opaque and make procurement decisions untransparent. For example, instead of itemizing food prices, decisions are based on a total price that includes transportation and kitchen services, so the price of the food itself is unclear.

Recent consolidation among food suppliers has made the sector less competitive and less accountable. Today 54% of municipal food is bought from just 10 companies. Growing privatization of public services has served to increase the dominance of these companies and made the problem worse.

As a result, municipalities tend to default to buying lower-quality, cheaper food from a handful of suppliers, so chefs and kitchens in the public system lack the ingredients to prepare healthy meals and have to make the best of the supplies they're given.

Most kitchen workers lack the training to use their ingredients optimally. Of the 200,000 collective kitchen workers in Spain, only about 10,000 have undergone specific training in operating catering kitchens. Most of the rest have only basic training in food preparation, so they mechanically prepare food as directed instead of using ingredients creatively or efficiently to increase nutrition and lower costs. Since these workers do little more than assemble meals, they are increasingly getting replaced by food companies that transport meals directly from industrial kitchens.

> *Despite their problems, Nani Moré's insight is that collective kitchens can become the lynchpin of a new system that delivers local, healthy, nutritious food to those who need it on a large scale. "The dining rooms are not the problem but the solution," she says. Nani Moré informs us that [hunger] is happening not only in Andalusia, but in most communities [in Spain]. Many educational centers have chosen to keep their dining rooms open throughout the day... "We can feed the population," Moré says. "Community kitchens are a precious resource that we cannot waste, especially in these hard times for our society."*

THE STRATEGY

Together with her organization Menjadors Ecològics ("Ecological Eaters"), Nani Moré has a multi-pronged approach to converting collective kitchens from part of the problem into a solution for making healthy food available at scale: conducting studies, working with food producers, providing training and support to kitchen staff, consulting with local governments, and doing public education.

Nani Moré and Menjadors Ecològics conduct feasibility studies to demonstrate how collective kitchens can adopt healthy and sustainable menus without charging more for meals. They also assess the potential benefits. For example, they recently launched a two-year study in collaboration with the National Pediatric Association to quantify the benefits of healthy foods in municipal nursery schools.

They work to connect local food producers with collective kitchens, creating reliable local demand and "short supply circuits." That enables local farmers to ramp up sustainable production and assure sufficient supply of healthy foods at an affordable price.

And they work with community kitchen staff, from the managers who place purchase orders and set the menus, to the kitchen workers who prepare the food, providing training and support to help them plan and execute healthy, sustainable menus without raising meal prices. For catering kitchens under public authority, Nani Moré and colleagues help design menus adapted to the production potential of local food, highlighting local products (crops, fruits, livestock, etc.) along with training and support for implementing them affordably.

Nani Moré's initiative to change Spain's food model by linking collective kitchens (e.g., small groups of people who pools resources together to cook for large groups, often in school, university, hospital, army, and group residences) to local organic food productions has been remarkable.

A key dimension of this work is consulting with government administrators on incorporating health and sustainability criteria into procurement procedures, analyzing the costs involved, and framing specifications for food ratios, itemized food prices, and kitchen equipment that support healthy and sustainable meals at an accessible price. Nani Moré and colleagues are currently working with 13 local governments and counting.

One tool she uses to accelerate uptake is a 2019 Spanish federal law which requires, among other things, that municipal food procurement decisions be based on a ratings system with 51 points for food quality and 49 points for food price. Her team, which includes a pro bono lawyer, monitors and reports on compliance. That nudges local governments to adjust their procurement practices. In cases of recurrent noncompliance, Nani Moré's group initiates legal action.

It also works to educate the wider public, for example through local health centers and local programs such as parenting classes, building awareness about the need for change in the food model, connecting consumers to local food production, and helping shift production-consumption dynamics toward health and sustainability.

To help scale her approach nationally, Nani Moré formed Chefs 2030, a collaborative network of collective kitchen chefs across Spain. They work to adopt healthy, sustainable menus in their kitchens and change local procurement procedures. Working together they created a free, downloadable, practical guide for kitchens called Menu

2030, which offers detailed examples and tools to help kitchen professionals everywhere make these changes. As Nani Moré says, it's a deliberate effort to "transform the menu in order to transform the food model."

To facilitate further scaling, Nani Moré is making her knowledge and experience accessible via a digital platform. It offers a searchable directory of local producers, videos demonstrating recipes for large groups, advice on measuring and managing supplies and cost control, and a planned feature that enables users to audit bidding parties for compliance with healthy and sustainable food requirements. With no additional training or staff time, any collective kitchen can use the platform to make impactful changes in their local food systems.

THE PERSON

The daughter of farmers, Nani Moré grew up in Spain's countryside, helping care for her family's orchards, helping her grandmother in the kitchen, and going to buy food at the local market. Nani Moré came to share her grandmother's passion for good food, which led her to study catering and hospitality in school.

On graduating, she worked in catering restaurants with various specialties, including a stint as a chef traveling with Cirque du Soleil, which introduced her to a variety of different local foods and producers. In 2006, the year she became a mother, she was head chef at a slow food restaurant where she worked long hours, including holidays. She resolved to find a way to balance work and family life.

She took a job at an eldercare facility, where she found herself cooking for 225 residents. She was shocked by the low quality of the ingredients she had to work with, and the menus which were not adapted to residents' dietary needs. She created new recipes with fresh, seasonal, and local food but was told that these meal plans were over budget and that she had to continue to cook with frozen and processed foodstuffs.

As she sought creative ways to improve the ingredients and the menus at the facility, she discovered the larger problem: the whole catering kitchen system was oriented toward cheap, low-quality food, and the model itself needed to change in order to improve the quality and nutrition of the meals.

That experience inspired her vision for collective kitchens in which chefs could work together to transform the food system by using local, sustainable food and creative management. She quit the eldercare facility for a job at a nursery school, which she convinced to let her implement her idea. There she honed her approach, for example learning how to make changes in procurement procedures to support local, healthy, sustainable food.

Her next step was to write and direct the well-known documentary "El Plato o la Vida" ("The Plate or Life") which exposed the problems with the current food system, and got schools interested in changing their approach. That interest in turn allowed her to create *Menjadors Ecològics*, Spain's first and still its only organization dedicated to building a healthy, sustainable food system through collective kitchens.

PHOTO CREDIT: *Nani Moré Ramon – Nani created a collaborative network of kitchen chefs across Spain to build public awareness about the need for change in the current food model.*

CARLOS NOBRE

Earth System Scientist, Nobel Peace Prize 2007

 www.theamazonwewant.org

As the needs of the Amazon and the world forest have evolved, Carlos Nobre has found systems solutions. Now he is helping the Amazon's residents develop attractive new livelihoods that depend on a healthy forest.

SCAN THE CODE TO READ AND SHARE THIS ARTICLE ONLINE

THE NEW IDEA

Before Carlos Nobre dedicated himself to changing mindsets on climate change, the global scientific community did not know that there was a tipping point – – a point of irrecoverability – – beyond which the Amazon would dry out. Since his discovery, Nobre's pioneering work has been fundamental to a better understanding of the relationships between deforestation, biodiversity, and climate change, and it and he have inspired collective, global action at the scientific, political, and civic levels ever since. He envisioned and has been central to building the climate science field and the fight to protect the Amazon Basin from crossing the tipping point.

Carlos' drive to produce data, influence national and international policies, and get science into the hands of policymakers, businesses, and citizens alike, has helped bring Brazil to a point where 90% of its citizens today consider climate change a "catastrophic risk." Carlos has also played a leading role in the climate science field globally, including as co-chair of the International Geosphere–Biosphere Programme and as a contributor to the Intergovernmental Panel on Climate Change (IPCC) assessment reports. In 2007, Carlos received the Nobel Prize.

> ***Carlos's leadership inspires action and encourages multilateralism, providing a framework to allow us to move towards a more sustainable and equitable future, together.***
>
> *– Emma Torres, UN Sustainable Development Solutions Network*

Carlos has now pivoted to a new and significantly different and very big challenge: inventing and entrepreneuring into being a series of new ways people in the Amazon can live good and improving lives that make them allies of the forest. The forest cannot vote. If the people living in the Amazon do not have a vital interest in protecting it, it will disappear. Carlos is using his understanding of all of science, along with technology, economics, community organizing, and broader organizing to invent a new human/forest economy that will be mutually beneficial.

> *We cannot take the rain forest's resilience for granted. We are on a path to destroying the Amazon. Turning it into a savanna would get us closer to an uninhabitable Earth. Instead, we can create a standing-forest, flowing-river bioeconomy that fuses scientific and traditional knowledge, preserving biodiversity and improving livelihoods for generations to come.*

– Carlos Nobre

The New York Times

Carlos is convinced that a sustainable pathway exists in the Amazon and that one need not choose between conservation and unsustainable exploitation of natural resources (which now notably includes many common forms of agriculture, energy, and mining). As a result, Carlos is now working to revolutionize the model for development in the Amazon by promoting the use of emerging technologies, such as artificial intelligence, robotics, blockchain, genomics, synthetic biology, DNA editing, nanotechnology, energy storage and quantum computing, as well as bio-mimicry – all managed by local populations to add value to natural assets found in the rainforest and thereby turn the region into a hub for sustainable innovation. Here's one example: The use of mobile genomics labs, with portable genome sequencers, can produce great value to science and medicine. Forest communities can learn to sequence the genome of plants, animals, and even microorganisms, based on their knowledge of species with particular properties, which they could then register through blockchain systems and monetize. A genetic library of microorganisms would also be key to tackling pathogens – coming from the Amazon or anywhere.

Elected as a Senior Fellow (a highly successful social entrepreneur who enriches the Ashoka network and its collaborative work), Carlos is not just working on a big project. Instead, he is building a whole new pattern of developing new sectors whose cumulative impact will be a new, synergistic human/forest economy and politics.

THE PROBLEM

The Amazon is one of Earth's most important ecosystems, housing nearly a third of the world's remaining rainforests acreage and between 10 and 15 percent of all the known wildlife species. Amazon biodiversity plays a critical role in supporting global ecosystem services, absorbing up to 120 billion tons of carbon and generating 15 percent of freshwater that flows into the oceans. Yet over the past 50 years, human activity has increasingly destabilized ecosystems in the Amazon region. Vast swaths of land have been cleared for cattle and commercial crops. Additionally, rising temperatures due to global warming have led to more frequent and severe droughts. The combination of deforestation, higher temperatures, and more extreme droughts has increased the forest's vulnerability to fire and has accelerated global climate change.

Before the 1980s, neither the government nor Brazilian society recognized the value of rainforests. Policy towards the Amazon was dominated by the belief that conservation was a barrier to economic progress, and there was little concern for the issue of climate change. There was virtually no climate research in Brazil and minimal involvement in international environmental policy.

Carlos's pioneering research demonstrated that failing to curb rainforest degradation could increase warming in the region by two to three degrees Celsius by 2050. The resulting disruption of the hydrological cycle could lead to a tipping point, converting large parts of the tropical forest into dry savannah and risking ecological collapse on a continental scale.

> *The "bioeconomy"... concept, is seen by researchers today as one of the main alternatives to bring wealth and development to the Amazon without the need for cutting down trees or polluting rivers.... Carlos Nobre, founder of Amazônia 4.0, highlighted that it is possible to further develop the region to bring wealth and development to those who live there.*

That process, known as savannization, would devastate biodiversity and threaten the livelihoods of more than 30 million people who inhabit the Amazon, notably including especially vulnerable indigenous communities. But the effects of savannization would reach much further than the basin, irreversibly affecting ecosystem services that are essential to human life globally. Savannization of large portions of the Amazon would result in emissions of more than 200 billion tons of carbon, overtaking the amount it now absorbs, thus reducing the forest's crucial role as a carbon sink and protector against climate change. Finally, given that deforestation can cause the displacement of disease-carrying animals from their natural habitats in search of food, there is now growing concern that severe ecological degradation might be a strong driver of infectious disease transmission, as well.

THE STRATEGY

Carlos has worked at strategic national and international levels to increase understanding of the relationship between the Amazon and climate change, providing guidelines on how to build the technical and institutional infrastructure needed to take action. His groundbreaking research has provided critical evidence that the Amazon is worth vastly more if it is substantially preserved than if destructive extraction continues.

PRIOR WORK

In 1995, Carlos led the establishment of the Brazilian Center for Weather Forecasting and Climate Studies, which became the most advanced center for monitoring climate changes in Latin America and for the coordination of international projects related to climate and Amazonia. Then, in 1998, Carlos launched the Large-Scale Biosphere-Atmosphere Experiment in Amazonia (LBA), the world's largest international environmental science program. Specifically, he united an interdisciplinary network of 280 global institutions, including NASA and the European Union, to better understand global environmental change and the role of the Amazon. This widely heralded study—which continues to date and has engaged over 1,000 researchers—contributed to building the collaborative research infrastructure that was critical to developing effective policies and galvanizing the public and the media towards action.

Recognizing the need for translating scientific knowledge into practical solutions, Carlos then harnessed the media, public events, and high-level international fora to communicate the science of climate change in a language that a wider audience could easily understand. Carlos raised public awareness about the effects of deforestation on climate change and, conversely, how climate change may affect the Amazon and its inhabitants. By making the numbers relevant to people's daily lives and showing them that there was a way out, Carlos helped trigger a paradigm shift in public opinion that galvanized grassroots campaigning and organization to push for policy change in Brazil. At a global level, Carlos leveraged foreign media to bring attention to the universal significance of the Amazon, which fueled international concern and put the spotlight on Brazil. The political and economic costs of external pressure, combined with growing demands from Brazilian civil groups, were decisive in inducing the government step up and try to curb deforestation.

Further, in 2008, Carlos launched the Center for Earth System Science in Brazil, institutionalizing the field of earth system sciences. The Center expanded the local scientific community's vision beyond climate to encompass multiple, interlinked dynamics affecting global change. The Center's integrated systems model now forms part of the IPCC's global climate assessment process. In Brazil, this model became the standard for calculating the costs and

PHOTO CREDIT: *Leticia Valverdes/Silverback – Carlos is revolutionizing the model for development in the Amazon through pioneer research and community organizing. He is creating a new economy that will benefit humans and the environment alike.*

benefits of any proposed project's impact on the national agenda for sustainable development.

In early 2011, massive landslides and floods caused by record-breaking rains claimed more than 900 lives in the hills of Rio de Janeiro state. That devastation provided the sense of urgency Carlos needed to successfully push for the creation of the National Center for Monitoring and Alerts of Natural Disasters. Early warnings of the risks of natural hazards issued by this Center are in great part responsible for an 80 percent reduction in deaths caused by natural disasters since then.

NEW SOCIAL ENTREPRENEURSHIP

In his latest initiative, Amazonia 4.0, Carlos seeks to promote social justice and wellbeing for Amazonian populations by building local capacity and employing new physical, digital, and biological technologies to increase the value of renewable resources and create new industries. Once again, Carlos is applying his masterful organizing skills to orchestrate a large number of players, including several universities—such as the University of São Paulo— citizen sector organizations, grassroots organizations, and funders to design a new model of inclusive bioeconomy in the Amazon. The collaborative is setting up mobile Creative Labs (LCA) and a Rainforest Business School to create long-lasting capacity in the Amazon. The LCAs, which operate like mini factories, leverage technological advances and local knowledge to innovate new products.

The first LCA to be implemented in order to add value to forestry products is modernizing production and the uses of cocoa and cupuacu. By utilizing small computers with special software and sensors that are connected to each of the machines used in chocolate production, they are able to achieve fine control of the process. The LCA platform allows users to bring their own characteristics to the process by adding other biodiversity ingredients to the recipe, choosing the fermentation and roasting point, and even printing molds with their own design. (A concrete example of how revolutionary the concept is for the process lies in defining the roasting point of the seeds, which is crucial for the final taste of the chocolate. Today, the control is done in manual ovens. Inside the LCA, the oven is equipped with temperature sensors and a computer, with a program that controls the electrical resistors, allowing a roasting curve to be drawn where the temperature varies over time. The entire process is tracked end-to-end, and the data is stored in a database using blockchain technology that could become publicly accessible via a barcode. – a factor that will be important for the viability of these products in the international market, which is becoming increasingly demanding in terms of product provenance and supply chains.) The Amazonia 4.0 team expects the average value of a kilogram of cacao from the forest to go from R$15 for the raw product to R$300 for the processed fine chocolate it will now produce. (USD3 to USD56).

Another Creative Lab (LCA) under Amazonia 4.0 aims to engage local communities in genome sequencing myriad forest species. The initiative has the potential to protect public health by identifying new biomedical benefits that can come from species growing or living in the forest and enabling disease surveillance that can be monetized. The focus of this initiative is to empower local populations with the necessary technical, business, and legal skills needed to make decisions about how to do the work, share the resulting data and ensure the fair compensation of indigenous communities for their intellectual property. The project is also designed so that the locals running the business will have strong incentives to protect the forest source of its samples. In doing so, Amazonia 4.0 also seeks out how to harvest these benefits in ways that are synergistic with forest health overall.

> *We stand exactly in a moment of destiny: The tipping point is here," Brazilian climatologist Carlos Nobre wrote ... "It is now.*
>
> The Washington Post

THE PERSON

Carlos grew up on the outskirts of São Paulo. He became interested in environmental issues as a teenager, yet the conventions of the time narrowed his career options. Always up for a challenge, he selected the most difficult course: electrical engineering. As a student in the 1970s, he had the chance to visit the Amazon at a time when deforestation was rare. The undisturbed rainforest captivated Carlos and inspired him to transition his studies to climate science and to earn a PhD in Meteorology at the Massachusetts Institute of Technology (MIT) in 1983.

After completing his PhD, Carlos joined the National Institute for Space Research in Brazil, where he began collaborating on research in the Amazon that would become a turning point in his career: a British-Brazilian pioneering experiment on forest-atmosphere interactions. Two years later, Carlos was participating on major scientific projects in the Amazon with the U.S. National Aeronautics and Space Administration. Carlos then returned to the United States, where, during postdoctoral studies at the University of Maryland, he conducted and published the groundbreaking "point of no return" research on the impact of the Amazon's deforestation on global climate.

> *Dr. Nobre has contributed to the scientific understanding of the Amazon rainforest as a globally important ecosystem and as part of the irreplaceable ecological and cultural heritage for all of humanity.*

UN Sustainable Development Solutions Network

The scientific breakthroughs Carlos advanced helped deepen the understanding of the role of the Amazon and its deforestation in the global environment. These experiences cemented Carlos' position as a leading figure in the field and as one of the most important scientists in the world. Such recognition opened the doors to leadership positions at some of the most important scientific institutions, both within and outside Brazil, giving Carlos a platform to push the national and global agenda on advancing the research and protection of the environment.

He worked to communicate the complex science of climate change to a broader audience, using his storytelling ability and influencing skills to inform public debate and mobilize different sectors.

Carlos is one of those extraordinarily, rare scientists who causes galvanizing systems changes—who unites different players for the common good. He bridges his passion for rigorous science and research with his entrepreneurial vision and unstoppable persistence.

Carlos has now launched nothing less than creating a new economy for the Amazon. This entails creating one new economic sector after another. Each enriches its human participants in ways that protect the forest and that make its people its champions.

DYLAN TERREL

Founder and Executive Director, Caminos De Aqua

 www.caminosdeagua.org

By weaving together highly economic water collection and filtration innovations, community leadership, bringing in the data and making it accessible to all, and by connecting the fractured actors, Dylan is making safe water available to all. A huge change

SCAN THE CODE TO READ AND SHARE THIS ARTICLE ONLINE

THE NEW IDEA

Dylan uses simple pioneering technologies that deliver affordable, adaptable, and durable solutions to communities suffering from water scarcity in Mexico. These simple and low-cost technologies are implemented through a model in which leadership is held by local communities. Through his organization, Caminos de Agua, Dylan provides both immediate solutions for water-stressed regions, and long term strategies to address the root causes of water shortages and contamination.

Existent solutions to provide clean water for the challenges facing rural communities in arid regions were both out of reach financially and technically unfit. Big agriculture exporting its products to North America and Europe is responsible for most of the water usage, which means that communities are literally exporting their very precious water resources. To address what has emerged as one of the most urgent environmental and public health issues facing Mexico and other areas with inadequate water supplies, Caminos de Agua develops and delivers low-cost technologies that enable entire communities facing water scarcity to collect and purify water.

Half the Mexican population doesn't have reliable access to safe water, a giant threat to them and their communities – and to health. Bottled water is too expensive, and many conventional responses don't work. Dylan has researched and prototyped both technical solutions and successful ways of organizing through local communities. This does work.

Through his wide network of grassroots partners, Dylan trains and involves community members in designing solutions that meet local needs, and which he monitors and evaluates to track progress and improve over the long term. These solutions are then made publicly available – meaning anyone in the world suffering from similar water challenges can use their designs and data to develop their own solutions.

PHOTO CREDIT: *Caminos de Agua – Caminos de Agua also advances community health and wellbeing by removing one of the biggest barriers to promoting sustainable management of water resources: the lack of information and transparency regarding water systems and usage.*

To date, Dylan and his team have developed two main technologies: Aguadapt (a ceramic water filter), and a Groundwater Treatment System (known by its acronym, GTS). Both technologies have received national and international awards, as well as academic recognition. Through their installation in households Caminos de Agua is creating estimated savings of $220,000 USD per family over the 30-year guaranteed life of the systems.

Caminos de Agua also advances community health and wellbeing by removing one of the biggest barriers to promoting sustainable management of water resources: the lack of information and transparency regarding water systems and usage. They do this by developing a comprehensive education program for communities, schools, citizen groups, and governments that raises everyone's understanding of local and global water problems and possibilities. Additionally, they have created low-cost methods to produce more accurate, detailed, and updated data on water issues at community and national levels, and they offer this data openly to ensure informed decision-making by stakeholders across sectors and regions.

Dylan leverages his experience in low-income rural and peri-urban areas that face extreme water stress to influence public policy at the local and national levels, through a variety of strong networks and the vision to create collaborative, systemic solutions. He also works with local and federal level policy makers to improve water management and climate change resiliency, and to educate other organizations in the field on how to effectively monitor water quality and replicate their systems that work.

PHOTO CREDIT: *Caminos de Agua – Once invited to a community, Caminos de Agua implements a participatory process that enables communities to take the lead in designing, building, and maintaining smart water collection. Caminos de Agua has eliminated arsenic and fluoride-contaminated water consumption in impacted communities and increased overall water access by 26%, with all families reporting sufficient water for drinking and cooking.*

Caminos de Agua is creating estimated savings of $220,000 USD per family over the 30-year guaranteed life of the systems.

In other words, Dylan has now reached the moment when he is beginning to tip the whole system. He's having this impact because he has the leverage of – uniquely – having brought together his singular combination of state-of-the-art technology, community-led approaches, and collaboration with a multiplicity of partners in a notoriously fragmented sector.

THE PROBLEM

In Mexico, 52 percent of the population (67 million people) live with some form of water scarcity. More than 47 million do not have daily or continuous water access, and an estimated 9-11 million have no water service at all.

At the same time, agriculture accounts for over three-fourths of total groundwater usage in Mexico, the second-highest level among OECD countries, with usage continuously increasing. In the state of Guanajuato, for example, over-exploitation by industrial agriculture reduces groundwater levels by two to three meters per year—which is 30 times greater than the eight-centimeter loss per year that qualifies as "extreme water stress".

The decrease in groundwater levels forces wells ever deeper into the geological substrates, which results in the emergence of dangerous naturally-occurring chemicals in local groundwater supplies, resulting in a serious public health crisis. In Guanajuato, arsenic levels are 22 times higher than World Health Organization recommendations, and fluoride levels are more than 12 times higher. Arsenic and fluoride are closely linked to dental fluorosis, crippling skeletal fluorosis, chronic kidney disease, skin disease, and various cancers. Chemical pollution of the water poses the greatest risk to children, as their growing bodies absorb these minerals at much higher rates, and exposure to high fluoride in utero has severe impacts on children's cognitive development and learning ability later in life. Globally, 300 million people suffer from excessive levels of arsenic and fluoride in the water supply, with up to 21 millions of them living in Mexico. However, due to the lack of adequate water monitoring, the problem is largely unknown and therefore hugely underestimated – – and all too commonly untreated.

Beyond polluting groundwater, over-exploitation causes even the deeper wells to eventually dry up, leaving entire communities without access to water. This forces residents to find water at alternative sources that are often unreliable, expensive, or unsafe, which puts their physical and economic wellbeing at great risk—especially for women, who are usually responsible for fetching water. This kind of water stress sows the seeds of social conflict. It has contributed to forced displacement within Mexico and around the world. Other ways of getting water often don't work. Bottled water is too expensive, in water harvesting, is often insufficient, especially in dry. Dylan believes that this crisis must be faced with both innovative, low-cost short-term solutions that address the current needs of marginalized communities and long-term systemic strategies to tackle increasingly complex water challenges.

THE STRATEGY

Dylan combats water scarcity and contamination in marginalized communities through two parallel strategies: (1) Developing community leadership and low-cost technologies that together provide safe water; and (2) assembling multi-stakeholder collaborations to drive long-term policies and solutions while raising awareness at all levels about local and global water challenges. He supports both strategies with robust monitoring and evaluation systems, which prove the effectiveness of the model in the long term and provide open data to inform systemic solutions.

Dylan's design and testing work starts with monitoring and mapping water quality and scarcity challenges at the community level. Caminos de Agua partners with grassroots and community organizations that already have a deep understanding of local challenges and can facilitate the work through existing relationships of trust with locals. This broad network allows a birds-eye, yet detailed view of the water situation in communities across Mexico, which enables the networks members to identify and direct the right resources towards those most at risk. Once invited to a community, Caminos de Agua implements a participatory process which enables communities to take the lead in designing, building, and maintaining smart water collection and filtering systems. Caminos de Agua then share their findings on local water quality and explain the available options. If the community decides to take action, they provide technical training, a seven-module educational program and support to community members in designing and leading projects.

Caminos de Agua uses an unusually collaborative approach in addressing this complex problem: in addition to local communities and grassroots organizations, they have partnered with leading international universities and with Engineers Without Borders to develop appropriate solutions. Through its Technical Fellows program, Caminos de Agua has created pioneering technologies such as Aguadapt (a certified ceramic water filter, used for treating rainwater), and the Groundwater Treatment System. Both are simple and low-cost, utilizing universally available, inexpensive materials so they can be easily replicated in different contexts.

There are times we go one to two weeks without water. I can go down to the river with my daughters when it has water, but when it doesn't have water, we are all struggling. We are always without water.

Local resident, Juana Reyes Bocanegra, in journal of Values-Based Leadership, 2020.

PHOTO CREDIT: *Caminos de Agua – 92% of households that have partnered with Caminos de Agua have lowered their annual spending on potable water from 22% of their income on average to less than 2%, creating estimated savings of USD 220,000 per family over the 30-year guaranteed life of the systems.*

Local resident, Juana Reyes Bocanegra, in journal of Values-Based Leadership, 2020.

Existing low-cost water filters are limited in scope and unable to adjust to the unique water problems and context of each community. Aguadapt is an award-winning, low-cost ceramic water filter that removes 99.9% of all biological contaminants in under five minutes, attaches to universal plumbing, and is easily installed in all common containers, making it ideal for disaster relief. Each filter is about the size of a liter of bottled water but can produce upwards of 30,000 liters of safe drinking water over its four-year life, at a price accessible for a family living on less than $2 USD per day. Most importantly, Aguadapt can be adapted to treat regionally specific organic chemical contaminants that disproportionately affect low-income communities around the world. This adaptability lowers costs by avoiding overengineering to remove contaminants that do not exist locally. As chemicals are poised to become the world's most serious water contamination challenge, Aguadapt is the first low-cost technology designed to be flexible enough to tackle the problem in any context. To date, more than 7,000 Aguadapts have been distributed through citizen sector partners across Mexico, impacting more than 11,600 people. These filters are also used in Caminos de Agua's rainwater harvesting systems, which have created more than 3.2 million liters of rainwater storage capacity and 125 million liters of filtering capacity in 68 communities and 30 schools throughout Mexico.

Dylan has also developed the Groundwater Treatment System (from now on, GTS) together with Technical Fellows from leading universities, to remove arsenic and fluoride from contaminated community water supplies at a very low cost—the first such tool in the world. For roughly the same initial cost of one rainwater harvesting system that would only serve one to two families, and 100 times cheaper than buying water, a GTS can be installed to provide clean safe drinking water for up to 15 families in a community. After directing contaminated water to an elevated storage tank, the contaminated water passes through a series of filters to remove sediment, arsenic, designed and adapted to address a given population's needs, size, and levels of arsenic and fluoride.

After a successful year-long trial, Caminos de Agua is in the midst of the first full-scale pilot system trial in a rural community that faces water deprivation and excessive levels of arsenic and fluoride contamination. In this community, the GTS is already providing 300 liters of drinking water per day to ten households. Dylan and his team are currently in talks with the State Health Secretary of Guanajuato to roll the system out statewide once the pilot is concluded.

By empowering communities and local partners to co-lead solutions from day one, Caminos de Agua has achieved exceptional levels of sustainability. Involving communities at each step—rather than installing pre-made, top-down solutions—fosters ownership and builds local capacity to maintain the systems. For example, follow-up research on rainwater harvesting systems installed in 2018 showed that 100 percent of households were using the systems and around 90 percent were correctly maintaining them. This participatory approach promotes sustainable behaviors as community members become more aware of the quality of the water they drink.

Long-term monitoring and evaluation has shown concrete results around Mexico. In community after community children born after the installation of rainwater harvesting and filtering systems no longer suffer from the severe stomach pain and dental fluorosis that were prevalent before. Caminos de Agua has eliminated arsenic and fluoride contaminated water consumption in impacted communities and increased overall water access by 26%, with all families reporting sufficient water for drinking and cooking. As a result, 92%of households have lowered their annual spending on potable water from 22% of their income on average to less than 2%, creating estimated savings of $220,000 USD per family over the 30-year guaranteed life of the systems. This interventions also encourage social cohesion as a result both of the collaborative approach and by reducing conflict due to water scarcity. Community members report closer relationships with their neighbors, which has led to other community-based projects.

As well as developing and implementing technical solutions for the short and medium term, Dylan is tackling the systemic causes of water issues by promoting education, building networks, and improving access to data to influence policies and strategies at the national level. To raise awareness about modern water quality challenges, Caminos de Agua provides its educational program and materials to communities, citizen groups, schools, and government agencies. All of the materials created by the organization are available to the public through its website. They have also developed international university-accredited courses, and function as a "field school" that prepares young aspiring engineers to be socially responsible professionals. So far, 29 "Technical Fellows" from Mexico and eight other countries have spent six months to a year gaining the hands-on technical, social, and political experience necessary to lead systemic solutions to water-related problems.

Prosperous Mexican Farmers Suck Up Water, Leaving Villages High and Dry. "As far back as the 1980s, even before NAFTA, the government imposed a ban on most new wells in Guanajuato. But water extraction increased exponentially. What allowed that to happen is "a pretty well-known system of bribes and corruption," Mr. Terrell said."

The New York Times

Dylan has improved the general understanding of water issues by providing rich, open-source data that the government can use to make policy decisions and that citizens can use to hold authorities and industries accountable. By leveraging their network of grassroots partners, they continuously monitor water quality, scarcity, access, cost, and conflicts on the ground at over 600 sites. In one municipality of Guanajuato, a study of all the local wells ultimately pushed the administration to build 100 large-scale rainwater harvesting systems and treatment plants in the most impacted communities. At the state level, they work with the Department of Environment and Sustainability to provide an extensive monitoring and evaluation program of the state's own rainwater harvesting projects. Caminos de Agua then aggregates their own data with that from other organizations, institutions, and the government and makes it available in

their own data with that from other organizations, institutions, and the government and makes it available in a free interactive map that can be easily accessed and understood by the general public.

Convinced that increasing citizens' understanding of water issues is essential to drive bottom-up solutions, Dylan engages strategic partners to develop mechanisms for communities to produce their own, contextually relevant data independently and make it easily available to all.

To scale his impact, Dylan is focusing on engaging and mobilizing multi sector partnerships from the local to international levels to co-create systemic solutions. He has joined the National Inventory on Water Quality Network where he works with academic institutions and civil society organizations to extend his map of water quality issues (especially arsenic and fluoride pollution) to other regions of the country. Further, Caminos de Agua has become one of the few CSO members with voting power on the National Consultative Council for Water, where they influence federal policies. In Guanajuato, Dylan spearheaded a new coalition of 14 local CSOs, the Agua Vida Network, to promote a coordinated and unified voice in the battle for healthy potable water in the region. Together, they successfully influenced the government of San Miguel de Allende to turn it into the first city in all of Mexico to require the installation of rainwater harvesting systems in all future housing and commercial developments.

Now, Dylan is focused on building high impact collaborative networks and influencing policies to raise awareness and address the systemic issues at the root of the problem, especially restoring watersheds, increasing groundwater infiltration, limiting consumption by water abusers, promoting reforestation, and pushing citizens and industry alike to invest in water conservation and capture for the good of all.

Moving forward, Dylan seeks to bring Caminos de Agua's approach and technologies to more communities in Mexico and beyond. He is considering forming a subsidiary (fully owned by the nonprofit) to manufacture and market their solutions, particularly to other CSOs as well as to governments, which would enable them both to scale and to generate an income stream to reinvest in the organization. He also plans on partnering with municipal and state governments to provide the Groundwater Treatment Systems as an ongoing service business. While in previous years his organization has grown slowly due to the intensive research and prototype development work, they now have the infrastructure and concrete solutions to rapidly increase their impact exponentially.

THE PERSON

Dylan grew up in the United States in a family that greatly emphasized working to create a better world for everyone. He volunteered with his grandparents' community organization from a young age, where he was exposed to diverse social problems ranging from immigration to housing. He is constantly inspired by his grandfather's words: "If you're not finding a way to help improve the lives of real people, every day, then you're missing the point." This ethos has helped him to take risks and make difficult choices to continue serving others, even when it meant going against the tide.

At 17 years old, Dylan took an unusual path before starting college: he traveled to Guatemala to volunteer and learn about the country. He became enamored with Latin America but was struck by the rampant inequality throughout the region. This stop became the first of several Latin American countries where he would later live and work in. While working in an orphanage in Peru, he became passionate about promoting sustainable development and decided to pursue a master's in Global Sustainability and Rural Development. During his master's program in Colorado, his work with a grassroots nonprofit took him to Chiapas to work with indigenous communities on social development projects. However, in splitting time between Mexico and the U.S., he grew frustrated by the lack of effective and deep impact over his short visits.

That is why, after meeting like-minded people in Guanajuato, he decided to build up a new project to develop solutions based on real community needs. From day one, he fully committed to the work by moving permanently to live in Mexico. Initially, the aim of his organization was to respond to local issues with sustainable technologies, training, and support. But it was through partnering with—and listening to the needs of—local communities and grassroots organizations that he understood water scarcity and contamination as the most urgent problems in the region and decided to launch Caminos de Agua.

TASSO AZEVEDO

Forester and Sustainability Activist

 www.tassoazevedo.blogspot.com

A chief architect of innovative environmental protection systems in Brazil, Tasso has repeatedly created original, strategic, far-reaching solutions that align sustainable livelihoods with protecting forests and the climate. He also built and manages collaborative technology platforms that accurately measure greenhouse gas (GHG) emissions and map land use, land degradation, land cover, and forest loss across Brazil. They make high-quality, real-time images and data available for free to anyone who wants to use them, enabling targeted, evidence-based, effective interventions to protect the climate, forests, soil, water, and biodiversity.

SCAN THE CODE TO READ AND SHARE THIS ARTICLE ONLINE

THE NEW IDEA

Ashoka Senior Fellow Tasso Azevedo has repeatedly blazed new pathways and forged strategic alliances connecting sustainable livelihoods with conservation, so that instead of fighting powerful economic disincentives, people are powerfully motivated to protect and sustain the ecosystem that sustains them. Tasso has been a chief architect of a new management system for Brazil's land sector. His innovations shaped environmental policy, connected conservation and sustainable livelihoods, balanced stakeholder interests, and empowered actors across society. In a subsequent phase of his work, he has focused on supplying a broad range of actors with monitoring data they need to identify environmental losses rapidly and precisely, so they can take action to stop them. By opening up the flow of information and resources, he has forged productive relationships among civil society, government, and the private sector, aligning and empowering them to take collaborative, effective action to protect the environment. That approach has become influential globally.

Tasso's career revolutionized Brazil's approach to environmental protection, applying insights which have become influential globally: Defending the environment is ultimately in everyone's interests, and requires alignment of the needs of people (who vote and ultimately decide society's course regarding the environment) with the needs of the environment. Interventions require the support of diverse stakeholders and the work of a broad range of actors to succeed. They also require accurate, current information about where and when losses are occurring so defenders can act quickly and effectively.

Just out of college, in 1995 Tasso co-founded the CSO Imaflora, the leading sustainability certification organization in Brazil, where he pioneered the basic systems and mechanisms for certification of sustainably produced forest and agricultural products in Brazil. His work brought together different stakeholders from farmers and foresters to indigenous communities and CSOs to forge an agreement on protecting sustainable livelihoods while conserving forests. At a time of great distrust between business and civil society in Brazil, this shifted mindsets from focusing on division toward acting on shared interests.

Tasso Azevedo founded MapBiomas in 2015... The network publishes annual monitoring data on land use and land cover, as well as alerts on deforestation, degradation, and regeneration. In August, 2021, it launched the MapBiomas fire, water and mining platforms. [MapBiomas data shows that] mining on indigenous lands increased by 495% in the last 10 years; 20% of Brazil's territory has burned at least once since 1985; agriculture has advanced 81 million hectares in the last 36 years.

In early the 2000s, Tasso joined Brazil's Ministry of Environment, where he was a highly effective intrapreneur creating systemic change from within. For example, he wrote and passed landmark bills for forest preservation, balanced with permits for extracting resources sustainably. He spearheaded the National Plan to Combat Deforestation in the Amazon which helped reduce deforestation in Brazil 75% between 2004 and 2014 – representing the most significant decline in deforestation and CO2 emissions globally. One critical aspect of the Plan was partnering with Brazil's space research institute to use technology to monitor deforestation in real time, which proved to be one of the keys to stopping it.

On leaving government, Tasso expanded monitoring by founding two open-source, multi-actor technology platforms that closely track greenhouse gas (GHG) emissions and land use changes on a national scale: the Brazilian Annual Land Use and Land Cover Mapping Project, better known as MapBiomas, and the Greenhouse Gas Emission and Removal Estimating System (SEEG).

SEEG continuously monitors all types of GHG emissions across all sectors in Brazil, and publishes annual assessments of them. MapBiomas is a collaborative network which includes CSOs, universities, Google, and tech startups. It uses remote sensors and satellites and digital mapping technology to reveal land use changes and deforestation across Brazil in real time. It makes high-quality imagery and data freely available to scientists, governments, indigenous communities, civil society, the private sector, and anyone else who wants to use it.

THE PROBLEM

The land sector (agriculture, forestry and other land use) accounts for 23% of greenhouse gas emissions globally, and it accounts for half of Brazil's emissions. Tropical forests are an especially powerful factor that need careful management.

Brazil is the second most forested country in the world, with more than half a billion hectares of forest. In addition to its crucial value as a carbon sink and a biodiversity hotspot, Brazil's forests are essential to the country's economy, livelihoods, and food security. The Amazon alone releases 20 billion tons of water into the atmosphere each day. That accounts for 75 percent of Brazil's rainfall, on which its agriculture and energy sectors depend (its main source of electricity is hydroelectric power). Yet Brazil today has by far the highest rate of deforestation globally, driven by the production of commodities such as timber, soy, beef, and palm oil.

In the early 2000s, Brazil faced historically high levels of deforestation. Weak governance coupled with corruption hindered sustainable management of public lands, which comprise 75 percent of the Brazilian Amazon. This led to a spike in illegal logging and land grabs encroaching on the rainforest.

You can't manage what you can't measure or even see. Tracking greenhouse gas emissions and sources nationally is challenging, and monitoring deforestation and other changes across vast landscapes in real time can be like finding a needle in a haystack. Gathering accurate data on emissions and changes in land use and forests has been a perennial problem. In the early 2000s monitoring mechanisms were limited and data was lacking, resulting in limited, ineffective policies and enforcement. Conservation efforts also failed to reconcile the imperative to protect Brazil's forests with their economic value and communities' need for livelihoods.

Tasso changed this equation. Recognizing that any hope of protecting the Amazon requires that people living there be able to make a decent, environmentally sound living, he worked to realign conservation and economic interests as the key to avoiding deforestation. His monitoring platforms generating accurate monitoring data on environmental losses to make them transparent, and guide interventions to stop it. Thanks in large part to his work, around 2010, deforestation in Brazil plunged to historically low levels. But today, as a result of subsequent policy changes, new economic pressures, and a kind of feedback loop driving more forest loss as the planet warms, deforestation levels are back up again.

Rising temperatures have led to more frequent and severe droughts and fires in the Amazon, accelerating deforestation. Climate change is also causing more intense flooding, faster spread of invasive species, and biodiversity loss, further destabilizing Brazil's forest ecosystems.

Tasso points out that these changes are directly or indirectly caused by humans. "In general, when you take the big transformations that happen, for example, in the loss of forest, conversion to agricultural use, in the urbanization that advances in rural areas – they are all transformations guided by human action," he says. "And even those transformations that are not direct, such as the reduction in the volume of water, are indirectly impacted by human action."

The net effect has been a return to historically high rates of deforestation. MapBiomas reports that in 2021, Brazil's deforestation rate increased by 20%, more than twice the rate of increase compared countries with the next worst deforestation problems (DR Congo and Indonesia). But, says Tasso, human decisions and collaborative actions can drive it down again.

[Azevedo's] work in preventing deforestation continues to produce dramatic results in South America, and his eagerness to involve all parties in preservation efforts is an example for all who strive to protect our environment.

Stanford | News

"We know how to reduce deforestation, but we need to make the decision to do so," he says. "If there is one thing that is different at this moment, it is an important behavior of a significant part of the business and economic sector.... There is the Climate, Forest and Agriculture Coalition and other initiatives that aim to bring together those who were agents of destruction, and engage them to be agents of [protection], an example of those who do it right."

THE STRATEGY

Tasso has been instrumental in developing and refining the field of environmental and climate monitoring, generating data that diverse actors – – government agencies, banks, local forest communities – – are using to make bold environmental commitments, and that civil society organizations use as an evidence basis to support their advocacy.

He founded and leads two multi-actor "platforms of platforms" which track and share data on greenhouse gas emissions, land use changes and land cover, with the long-term goal of building a global comparative database with granular, up-to-date information on each country's emissions status and trends, and the most efficient ways of driving them down.

SEEG, launched in 2013, is the world's largest digital platform for monitoring emissions across a national economy. It produces annual assessments of Brazil's emissions at the state and national levels, across all emitter sectors: agriculture, energy, waste management, land

PHOTO CREDIT: *Rainforest Alliance*

use change, industrial processes, and consumer product use. It considers all GHGs in the national inventory, including carbon dioxide, methane, nitrogen oxide, and hydrofluorocarbons, and reveals emissions trends over time. One of its datasets became an influential standard adopted by the Intergovernmental Panel on Climate Change AR5 report to convert other GHGs into carbon dioxide equivalents.

Using a methodology Tasso designed, SEEG generates detailed monitoring data on 600 emissions sources at the state and national levels. Whereas previous monitoring regimes produced reports only every five years, SEEG reports annually. Its data demonstrated the need for updating emissions targets and making them more ambitious, and became a key tool for measuring compliance and progress against the National Policy on Climate Change, and for spotting emissions trends or deviations that argued for correcting or adjusting policies.

SEEG recently launched a new system that allows Brazil's municipal governments (there are over 5,500 of them) to review local emissions data from 2010 to the present free of charge, enabling them to focus their resources on cutting emissions. To help with this, SEEG's annual reports include a progress and gap analysis, and make policy proposals for new emissions targets and strategies to meet them. The reports and their recommendations have become influential and encouraged local authorities to set more ambitious goals.

SEEG's data and reports are posted transparently and accessibly. Anyone can search the database, and pinpoint how specific emissions sources are tied to specific economic activities. SEEG is currently working to upload concrete proposals for mitigating each emissions source which will also be easily navigable and searchable. The proposals will include an action plan, case studies, and potential funding sources. SEEG's methodology is open-source and offered to collaborators and adopters via a web portal.

Tasso founded MapBiomas in 1985. Since then, it has produced thousands of reports each week, including mapping land use changes, deforestation, regeneration of vegetation each year, and monitoring surface water and fire scars each month. Since 2019, it has verified and reported on every single deforestation event detected in Brazil.

Today, the field of environmental monitoring Tasso helped develop has grown, and there are a dozen alert systems from various providers that monitor illegal deforestation from various providers that can trigger legal action against deforesters remotely, without on-site inspections, greatly extending enforcement of forest protection. The MapBiomas Alert system validates and refines these alert systems, enhancing their medium-resolution imagery to high-resolution, supplementing them as needed with field checks, so they function as ready-to-use documentation to guide government enforcement actions, similar to the way a license plate photo documents a traffic violation. So far MapBiomas validated platforms have prompted over 8,100 actions to protect forests in Brazil.

MapBiomas also furnishes businesses with the metrics they need to make ambitious commitments to reduce their impacts. For example, Brazilian banks consult with MapBiomas on how to conduct due diligence to make sure their investments don't fund companies involved in deforestation.

Both models are intensely collaborative and transparent, and they share their methodologies on accessible digital platforms so that more collaborators can use them. So far the SEEG system has been implemented in India and Peru. The MapBiomas system has been adopted across the Pan-Amazon and Gran Chaco regions, as well as by Uruguay and Indonesia. To scale up faster, Tasso is building and training coalitions of grassroots organizations to use available technologies to produce their own local data independently.

THE PERSON

Tasso traces his love of forests to a road trip to he took in the late 1980s to Brazil's Paraná state with his father, an electrical engineer, to visit a pulp plant he was helping build amid the forest. This was the time when the burning Amazon and the assassination of Ashoka Fellow Chico Mendes were making headlines. For Tasso, the idea that forests could be simultaneously protected and productive, so that they could support both biodiversity and livelihoods, was a revelation. It inspired him to study forest engineering at the University of São Paulo.

As a university student, he had his first encounter with the Amazon when he went with a friend to visit her family's property in the state of Montelus. He was shocked to see loggers clear cutting part of the property. "I was experiencing a mix of conflicting feelings," he said. "There was this wonder at the exuberance of the forest, full of life and megabiodiversity. And at the same time, there was despair hearing the sound of the chainsaw and the cracks of the trees falling down, followed by a sort of deafening silence."

On the drive back to camp, Tasso heard the farm administrator explaining that clearing the forest was necessary to expand the cattle raising since the old pasture was getting degraded and dry. When Tasso asked if this was legal, he was told, "No, nobody sees or cares about it and that's the way we develop land here." Nearly 30 years later, Tasso says, "those sounds and words still echo in my head every time I put my feet on a forest."

> *Mapping project MapBiomas is working with state governments, prosecutors and even state-controlled Banco do Brasil to flag illegal land clearances and bring the culprits to account with consequences including fines, lawsuits and loan refusals.... While best known in Brazil, MapBiomas is running similar projects in almost all South American countries and in Indonesia, working in partnership with local scientists.*

While at university, Tasso displayed his talent for convening people around a shared endeavor that would define his career. He went abroad to attend a symposium of the International Forestry Students' Association, and finding it personally transformative, he was determined to share it with others. Most students he knew lacked the funds to travel, so he mobilized them to host the next IFSA symposium in Brazil. He built teams to plan, coordinate, and fundraise, pulling off a event that brought together 140 students from 90 countries. Tasso also holds the record of the highest number of internships (20+) that a student has ever taken at the university, reflecting his polymath bent and his penchant for making cross-disciplinary connections.

In 1993, Tasso teamed up with his professor Virgílio Viana to help establish the Brazil chapter of the newly created Forest Stewardship Council (FSC), a sustainability certification regime that set global standards for forest management encompassing social, environmental, and economic criteria. Tasso realized that the forestry professionals doing the certification tended to be Americans and Europeans travelling to the tropics. He and Virgilio believed that certification had to be truly global and incorporate local knowledge and expertise. Two days after his graduation, Tasso and Virgilio launched Imaflora to build that vision. It's now the leading certification organization in Brazil, certifying more than 3 million hectares of forest, and influential globally. The regime works by bringing diverse stakeholders together and balancing their interests, facilitating dialog and aligning goals. That became a core theme of Tasso's career.

In the 2000s, Tasso joined Brazil's Ministry of Environment, where his game-changing intiatives included:

- Writing and helping pass a landmark bill creating and regulating government forest preserves to prevent illegal logging, instituting a concessionary system that ties permits for extracting forest resources to compliance with socio-environmental standards.
- Launching a major initiative to stop the illegal trade in mahogany, auctioning off seized wood to raise money for community projects in the Amazon.
- Designing and creating the the Brazilian Forest Service, which brought diverse stakeholders together to facilitate enforcement and strengthen tracking mechanisms.
- Conceiving and leading the development of the Amazon Fund, currently the world's largest forest protection fund.
- Spearheading development of the National Plan to Combat Deforestation in the Amazon. The Plan helped reduce deforestation by 75% between 2004 and 2014. It included a partnership with Brazil's space research institute to track deforestation in real time, enabling government, CSOs, and businesses to quickly identify and respond to illegal logging. Tasso later built on that experience to create SEEG and MapBiomas.

Tasso's belief that everyone is accountable for social and environmental change is reflected in his strategy of engaging and equipping people from all sectors and walks of life to take action. Tasso has established multiple systems which empower others to lead positive change, and which will endure and flourish without him – the mark of highly effective social entrepreneurs.

HUMAN RIGHTS

ANNA-LENA VON HODENBER
Germany

MARIANA RUENES
Mexico

PETRA MASOPUST – SACHOVA
Czech Republic

LIZZIE KIAMA
Kenya

ANNA-LENA VON HODENBERG

Founder, HateAid

 www.hateaid.org/spenden/

Recognizing that a growing pattern of hate-filled online attacks on those who speak out makes them withdraw and weakens democracy and civility, Anna-Lena's HateAid brings both perpetrators and digital platforms to account.

SCAN THE CODE TO READ AND SHARE THIS ARTICLE ONLINE

THE NEW IDEA

Anna-Lena von Hodenberg developed the first national-scale infrastructure to support and empower people to stand up to online attacks, seek redress, and hold perpetrators accountable. A former broadcast journalist, she co-founded and leads HateAid, based in Berlin, to support victims of digital violence and empower them to reclaim their rights and the digital space.

"For me, digital violence is the greatest threat to our democracy," Anna-Lena says. Her answer to it goes far beyond the standard procedures of blocking unwanted contacts and reporting attacks to tech companies, which hasn't prevented digital violence from exploding. She founded HateAid, which empowers users to stand up against digital violence, and is changing laws, law enforcement and jurisprudence, shifting norms toward holding perpetrators and tech companies accountable.

> *Today, HateAid supports around 200 people per month. It is important to [von Hodenberg] to emphasize that hatred does not only affect individuals. "It always has a dimension that endangers democracy (English translation)*
>
> **FrankfurterRundschau**

HateAid responds to attacks by providing victims counselling to process their trauma and technical support to protect them and their data. And it works proactively to stop attacks, holding perpetrators accountable through law enforcement, providing clients with free legal representation and helping them press their cases. So far HateAid has helped 2200 victims, including hundreds who took legal action against their attackers.

It also raises public awareness to build a positive online culture of solidarity and civil courage where users actively

PHOTO CREDIT: *Anna-Lena von Hodenberg – Anna-Lena's organization HateAid is the first support service for victims of digital violence in Germany. It helps them and others to recover their agency. It encourages them to report online crimes and take legal action.*

support each other instead of passively tolerating or ignoring digital violence against others.

Anna-Lena and HateAid have been highly effective in changing laws, regulations, and tech company practices. Her work was instrumental in reforming German laws so that perpetrators of digital violence could be identified and prosecuted, and in framing the European Union's new Digital Services Act, which holds online platforms to a new level of accountability for illegal content.

THE PROBLEM

The term "digital violence" was coined by Anna-Lena and the HateAid team to distinguish it from "hate speech." Like other forms of hate speech, digital violence includes racism, sexism, ableism, insults, defamation, and threats. But it also extends to anonymous perpetrators installing spyware on phones, weaponizing pornography to intimidate and encourage attacks, "doxing" or publishing a target's private information and home address, and "brigading" or flooding victims with so much abusive and illegal content that it's impossible to push back.

Such attacks are increasingly widespread and disrupt and traumatize many individuals. But they also disrupt society and democracy. They deter civic engagement and punish public servants, journalists, activists, and others for speaking out. They pressure them to self-censor, target them for non-virtual attack, and seek to drive them from the digital space altogether. This turns what should be the key locus of civic engagement into a lawless, unsafe, untrustworthy place ruled by bad actors.

Increasingly, digital violence isn't exceptional; it's endemic, part of an emerging, toxic norm. Some groups are more targeted than others. 80% of online hate messages are directed at women. Anti-Semitic, anti-Muslim, and anti-LGBTQI online content is rampant and growing. But it's not only certain groups which are victimized. All segments of society are affected.

A 2019 Eurobarometer survey found 80% percent of all those who follow or participate in online debates have witnessed or experienced abuse, threats, or hate speech. Over half said that this discouraged them from engaging in online discussions in the future.

HateAid surveyed a cohort of 2000 citizens of three EU countries and found that two thirds had witnessed hate and incitement on the internet, including over 90% of young adults 18 to 35. Across all age groups, 30% of men and 27.5% of women reported they were personally affected by online hate. Half of young adults reported this. Over 80% of respondents said Facebook, Twitter, and other social media platforms don't do enough to protect users from digital violence.

This has serious consequences online, including loss of freedom and self-censorship. Many are deterred from saying what they think or taking stands. 52% of women and 43% men of said they express their opinion less because of online hate. 43% of women and 35% of men said

PHOTO CREDIT: *Anna-Lena von Hodenberg – To date, HateAid has helped 2200 victims, including several hundred that took legal action against their attackers. Last year alone, it served 969 clients, funded 16 civil suits, and supported the filing of 255 criminal charges. These cases change and free the overall digital universe's culture.*

they are generally more cautious and anonymous on social media for fear of attacks.

Digital violence planned and carried out by extremist groups has destabilizing real-world effects. In Germany attacks against local and national politicians, journalists, and women are on the rise. Germany had long been one of the safest places for journalists according to Reporters Without Borders, but its ranking slipped recently because online and offline hate.

"Online attackers target pillars of society like politicians and journalists deliberately," says Anna-Lena, a former broadcast journalist herself. "There's a certain framing that goes with this: fake news, you can't trust the media, elite politicians lie to you. When they are attacked, key voices, even journalists and politicians, withdraw from digital spaces. Then who contradicts the false news and smear campaigns?"

HateAid works with elected officials across the country and has found that 90% of mayors in Germany have thought of leaving their jobs because of online and offline violence.

Because he defended Angela Merkel's pro-refugee stance, Walter Lübcke, a regional politician in Germany's conservative party, had been the target of virulent online attacks since 2015, including numerous death threats. His name appeared on a neo-Nazi hit list. His private address was published on a far-right blog. In June 2019, he was shot and killed in front of his home by an attacker with a violent neo-Nazi past. It was the first far-right political assassination since the Nazi era, and a shocking demonstration of how extremist digital violence translates into real-world violence. Prosecutors in the case found a causal relationship between the murder and incitement to violence on right-wing online forums.

> *With limited resources, authorities only prosecute a fraction of posts considered illegal speech, often because the person behind it cannot be quickly identified.... "People withdraw from debate more and more and don't dare to express their political opinion," said Josephine Ballon, legal director at HateAid, a nonprofit in Berlin that provides legal aid for victims of online abuse. "Too many cases are abandoned."*
>
> The New York Times

Despite the salience and urgency of the issue, most online hate crimes in the European Union go unreported and unprosecuted. Reporting them to the platform might get a post removed or occasionally an account suspended, but it doesn't stop the deluge of attacks and illegal content.

Due to free speech concerns, laws, regulations, and enforcement restraining digital violence have long been weak and inadequate, though in Germany this is starting to change. But since victims are usually unaware of their legal rights, intimidated, and/or overwhelmed by the number of attacks, only a small fraction of them gets reported to police, even in Germany. In the rare cases where victims want to press charges, legal costs are often prohibitive.

It's a cascading, systemic failure. But Anna-Lena and her team are turning it around.

THE STRATEGY

Anna-Lena's organization HateAid is the first support service for victims of digital violence in Germany. It helps them recover their agency, empowering them to report online crimes and take legal action.

The service is totally free and completely digital, offering online consultations three days a week aided by social workers and psychologists specialized in counseling people traumatized by digital violence. It also offers online digital security experts who provide technical support, conduct privacy checks, and work out a comprehensive strategy with clients to unwind the lingering impacts of online attacks. It includes advising on whether and how to respond, managing passwords and social media profiles, and conducting deep Google searches to find and remove posts that are fake, illegal, abusive, or invasive of privacy.

Often the only way to document digital violence is by taking a screen shot of the offending post before it's taken down. But with practices such as brigading designed to overwhelm targets with the sheer quantity of attacks (one HateAid client received 4000 abusive messages in 14 days), this can be a full-time job beyond most people's capability, so Anna-Lena's team does it as a service to clients.

Armed with documentation, HateAid clients are connected to legal representation and encouraged to press charges in criminal or civil court. The organization works with prosecutors to file charges and draws on a network of specialized lawyers who advise clients and represent them in court. Clients are not charged for these services, removing the cost barrier that would otherwise prevent victims from seeking legal redress. Instead, HateAid finances the legal fees partly with the damages awarded to clients who prevail in civil suits. To date, HateAid has helped 2200 victims, including several hundred that took legal action against their attackers. Last year alone, it served 969 clients, funded 16 civil suits, and supported the filing of 255 criminal charges.

HateAid works with lawyers who take civil legal action against those who post hate comments. The initiative...is financed in the long term by the damage claims that have been won, as well as by donations.

DER SPIEGEL

"With every victim, the goal is to give them their agency back and keep them online, to have them not withdraw from digital space," says Anna-Lena. "We can't lose them! We give them the support they need to feel they can go back in, even if they withdraw temporarily. We make them feel safe and more in control of their digital environment, and we enable them to go against perpetrators in court and get justice. The combination works very well to keep people online. Although most know they will likely be attacked again, they are better prepared. And they know it's possible to get justice. So, they stay online and start claiming their rights." She estimates about 80% of HateAid clients don't stop engaging the digital space, with another 10% leaving for a few months before coming back. In fact, many HateAid clients do more than just stay in the digital space; they become digital change agents by staying visible online and telling their stories. Politicians, journalists, and prominent activists are often targeted because of their visibility and influence, but the fact they have online followings cuts two ways. It also positions them to push back powerfully against digital violence and inspire others to do the same.

One well-known example is Renate Künast, a former national minister and one of Germany's leading politicians. She was targeted on Facebook (now known as Meta) with an image-text post containing an offensive fake quote that became a widespread meme, accompanied by a flood of virulent personal insults and misogynist content. Künast tried in vain for many years to get Facebook to delete the posts, but the company didn't intervene. Künast sought HateAid's help, and together they took Facebook to court, and after setbacks in the lower courts, pursued appeals all the way to the highest court in Germany. It required Facebook to find and delete the posts, and to hire a sufficient content moderation team to do it, without relying on automated upload filters. The court also awarded Künast damages for personal suffering.

The ruling established a new precedent that all politicians have personality rights, so courts must review their cases accordingly.

"You cannot believe how big a relief this was and how big a response we had," Anna-Lena said. "The court said there is a limit to what kind of criticism politicians must endure. That's important because if they must put up with digital hate as part of the job, people won't do this job. But now other politicians know that they can seek justice."

Another example of a prominent HateAid client whose case inspired others is Luisa Neubauer, a German climate activist who is one of the main organizers of Fridays-ForFuture. FFF is a powerful, youth-led and – organized movement of high school and university students demanding climate action.

Neubauer was targeted by right-wing extremists and flooded with sexist and misogynist content. Attackers tried to hijack her social media accounts to send fake messages, dox her, and publish her home address. She sought HateAid's help, and together they sued an attacker, winning a $6,307 USD judgment. When he refused to pay, his account was frozen, and the money was taken from him. A smart, outspoken young woman with a large online following, Neubauer celebrated her victory on social media, setting a powerful example for others.

"Her case was widely publicized via traditional as well as social media," said Anna-Lena. "It's important to have people like Luisa at the forefront of being outspoken about digital violence. That way, you reach so many more people." One ramification of these court victories has been national policy reform. Germany's Network Enforcement Act previously allowed platform owners to withhold the identities of the authors of offending posts, even if a court ruled the posts were illegal, making prosecution impossible. Anna-Lena and her team kept arguing against this in court, in legislative hearings, and numerous meetings with policy makers, until the law was changed.

> "
>
> ***The case of Künast is not an isolated one, stresses HateAid managing director Anna-Lena von Hodenberg. Local politicians, journalists and activists are particularly affected by defamation campaigns, hate speech and violence on the Internet – the majority of them women. They are people who are committed to democratic values, the rule of law, climate protection, equality or ending racism.***

DER TAGESSPIEGEL

"Before, digital rape threats were not illegal in Germany; now they are," she said. "Social media companies are now required to reveal the identity of users posting content that is ruled illegal." Companies are also required to report such cases to the Federal Criminal Police Office. Identifying and reporting them clears the way to prosecuting them.

Building on its success in Germany, HateAid established a policy and advocacy branch in Brussels which participated in negotiating the EU Digital Services Act, agreed in April 2022. The DSA holds online platforms across the European Union to a new level of accountability for illegal or harmful content.

Beyond accountability for perpetrating or enabling digital violence, Anna-Lena is working to build a positive, proactive culture of solidarity among online bystanders who witness it. "We have statistics showing many people witness digital violence against others, but how many report it, call the police, or try to help the victim?" Anna-Lena asks. "When people know they can literally call the police, things change. You can now send law enforcement a link with something that looks illegal. You can press charges anonymously. You can also send victims supportive messages. We call this digital civil courage."

It's a mindset shift and a new norm Anna-Lena is working to establish. She is expanding options for bystanders to stand up against digital violence, including through HateAid's online reporting platform. She is also working with law enforcement to establish their own platforms.

As a result of HateAid's work with them, public prosecutors' offices in Berlin, Hamburg, and Saxony now have their own online reporting platforms. The Hessian Ministry of Justice established a specialized public prosecutor unit on digital violence and a new department in the Central Office for Combating Internet and Computer Crime (ZIT). Four other German states are following suit. Many hundreds of prosecutions have resulted.

HateAid convenes digital violence fora with policy makers, civil society organizations, and tech companies. Anna-Lena is working to strengthen collaboration with social media platforms in particular as key partners in changing digital culture, ending digital violence and strengthening civil courage.

Anna-Lena believes achieving these goals are pivotal for the future of democracy. "The digital civic space counts as much – and maybe with covid even more – than the analog civic space," she said. "This hasn't fully sunk into society – – yet. But we are working on it."

THE PERSON

Anna-Lena grew up in a politically active German family during the 1980s. Her mother and father were part of "generation '68," in which students questioned their parents' generation's role in Nazism. "My mother and father became politicized during that time," she said. "That was extremely important in my family. We were taught not to look away and to do everything possible to ensure that nothing like Nazism ever happens again in society." As a child she was inspired by peace movements and took part in demonstrations.

She also grew up with an awareness of gender inequality. Her mother came from an old aristocratic family from Lower Saxony. Because she passed the family name of von Hodenberg to her husband and children, the rest of the von Hodenbergs excluded and ostracized them. "But by passing her name to us, my mother only did what men do routinely," Anna-Lena said. "It was part of '68 spirit and standing up for democratic rights. I saw her as brave."

As a student Anna-Lena lived in South Africa and Argentina, where she witnessed the consequences of oppression, discrimination, and injustice on a daily basis. At university, she founded and led the press office during a major student strike protesting the advent of general tuition fees in Germany. It became clear to her that protest alone is unlikely to lead to social change.

On graduating, she became a television journalist, working with major networks. But in 2015, when the Syrian refugee influx triggered the rise of xenophobic attitudes across Germany, she left journalism to become a political campaigner for one of Germany's leading anti-racism organizations. It found and leveraged opportunities to influence legislation to help counter rising right-wing extremism.

Ashoka social entrepreneur Anna-Lena von Hodenberg — founder of HateAid — had a precedent-setting win of her own: a German court ruled that Facebook (now known as Meta) is accountable for removing "identical and core similar" illegal hate speech from their platform once detected.

Forbes

That work showed Anna-Lena the dimensions of the extremist threat, but it also made her realize the limitations of the legislative approach. "A legislative strategy to achieve less bad laws wasn't enough," Anna-Lena said. "The new threat of organized hate came from social media, so we needed a holistic approach to understand and propose solutions – not only legislative change, but changes in how social media platforms were regulated. The whole field was blank then, the mechanism of online hate wasn't even fully understood. That's why we founded HateAid."

Today Anna-Lena is a recognized pioneer and expert in the field of countering digital violence. Policymakers seek her advice, and she was appointed to an expert commission on police misconduct.

MARIANA RUENES

President, Sintrata

 www.sintrata.org/en/

Mariana Ruenes exposes, confronts, and disrupts the human trafficking pipeline that exists alongside everyday people doing everyday things. She does this by engaging leading industries used by traffickers (e.g., transport, hospitality) and community members broadly in disrupting the traffickers' systems and relationships.

SCAN THE CODE TO READ AND SHARE THIS ARTICLE ONLINE

THE NEW IDEA

Mariana makes visible what we do not see as we walk through our daily lives – an invisible infrastructure of human trafficking hiding "in plain sight." In her grassroots work supporting human trafficking victims and survivors since 2011, Mariana came to realize that 99 percent of trafficking victims go undetected, even though they could easily be identified, since traffickers use common tourism, transportation, and technology services. Based on this insight, Mariana shifted her strategy towards breaking the "production chain" of human slavery at multiple levels. In partnership with targeted industry leading organizations, she has created new roles for thousands of front-line workers and enabled them to report trafficking activity without fear and to contribute real-time data to a shared trafficking database. By complicating the logistics of a crime that uses the infrastructure of cities to operate, Mariana and her organization SINTRATA have made human trafficking riskier, more difficult and less profitable.

As Mariana came to realize that businesses have a unique potential and responsibility to disrupt human trafficking, she began to form partnerships with key players in strategically identified industries that make it more difficult for traffickers to operate. Mariana focused on engaging industry leading companies such as Marriott International and Uber that have the power to influence their entire sector. When she partners with these companies, she conducts a diagnostic evaluation of their activity which uncovers the ways in which their services are vulnerable to exploitation by human traffickers. She then develops a customized plan for engaging their employees as workers and citizens who can improve the communities in which they live. By working with companies to develop and implement the conditions and tools needed for frontline workers to respond effectively and

PHOTO CREDIT: *Mariana Ruenes – By expanding the understanding of how, when, and where traffickers operate, Mariana has uncovered and mapped what previously was a largely undocumented, largely invisible phenomenon.*

safely, Mariana and her organization, SINTRATA, have increased workers' willingness to spot and report victims and perpetrators of human trafficking. The result? Victims are identified and provided justice while trafficking is disrupted, slowed, and prevented.

Studying patterns in the reported data led Mariana to see that the best people to report and intervene in real-time were those likely to come into contact with victims and traffickers. For example, based on patterns she identified where victims were being moved between cities within a trafficking network through ride-sharing services, Mariana partnered with Uber. Studying their business models and operations helped her put together customized approaches that use technology and tailored communications that would resonate with the needs and concerns of Uber drivers. By putting these pieces in place, SINTRATA was able to provide training and updates to over 300,000 employees, which enabled Uber drivers to report and gather real-time data from the local communities for SINTRATA. The increased reporting rates and more systematically collected data from the Uber drivers translated into increased responses from law enforcement. Disrupting the trafficking networks also means less dependence on the justice system to process and respond effectively to crimes of human trafficking.

Mariana's database on trafficking operations also enables more precise interventions. By expanding the understanding of how, when, and where traffickers operate, Mariana has uncovered and mapped what previously was a largely undocumented, largely invisible phenomenon. Her system for data gathering illuminates the activities of networks that strive to operate in the darkness, and this information is now being used to generate best practices, inform decision-making, guide technology supports, and foster large-scale and local coordinated action. Mariana's approach is also leading to the reallocation of society's resources towards the most effective, long-lasting solutions while providing an evidence base to influence policy and address long term structural problems across sectors.

THE PROBLEM

According to the Global Slavery Index, on any one day, human trafficking affects more than 40 million people worldwide. In Mariana's country of Mexico alone, there are believed to be more than 340,000 victims of modern slavery. However, the true magnitude of trafficking is unknown, for statistics like these only show identified cases, and this lack of data and information is one of the key reasons why human trafficking seems so intractable. It is estimated that less than 0.1 percent of victims – both in Mexico and globally – are reported; further, according to the International Organization for Migration, 80 percent of trafficking victims who have crossed borders have gone unnoticed at official checkpoints.

PHOTO CREDIT: *Mariana Ruenes*

Identifying victims gets further complicated by the coercive nature of the crime of trafficking. Traffickers take advantage of human vulnerability, poverty, and despair and use physical threats and violence to force people into collusion or silence. In Mexico, they typically prey on girls from the countryside who live in poverty, have little education, and have repeatedly been abused at home. A psychological tactic traffickers use involves threatening their victims' families with kidnapping or death. These and other factors make human trafficking fast growing and highly lucrative.

Traffickers rely on cities' infrastructure, services, and common goods, including buses, planes, taxis, hotels, and the Internet; yet businesses in these key industries are not actively involved in resolving this issue despite their central involvement and potential leverage. Through her research, Mariana found that front-line operators, such as drivers and hotel clerks, lack the knowledge and tools to safely identify, report, and respond to cases, thus allowing traffickers to continue moving people and money unnoticed. The U.S. Department of State attributes this to the fact that there is not a standardized protocol for these workers to report human trafficking; furthermore, workers lack training in looking for signs of trafficking like poor hygiene, malnourishment, physical abuse, or submissive behavior among suspected victims.

> ***"Good traffickers will not get caught."***
>
> *Mariana Ruenes, interview*

Insufficient data and a lack of coordinated action within and across countries has allowed traffickers to operate invisibly, as outsiders' limited understanding of the scope and mechanics of the problem has led to a limited capacity to identify and protect victims or to think through policy. Governments around the world report inaccurate and false numbers – an issue that has been highlighted by the U.S. Government Accountability Office which has criticized the inaccuracy of trafficking data, including its own, due to "methodological shortfalls." One of the weaknesses in current estimates is that terms such as 'trafficking victims,' are not defined or used consistently. Plus, data regarding the number of people being trafficked gets conflated with other data of exploited people, such as migrants being smuggled into the country or sex workers. These barriers to accurate information on trafficking operations inhibit the work of governments and civil society anti-trafficking practitioners around the world. In Mexico, the National Human Rights Commission conducted a study in 2020 which stated that the nation needs (1) to improve research and data collection on human trafficking patterns, traffickers and victims, and (2) to increase its allocation of resources for citizen organizations working in this area to achieve greater impact.

Strategies to fight trafficking also lack systematic impact measurements that would enable evidence-based decision making. As a result, interventions tend to be too broad, such as national media campaigns, and/or they keep repeating mistakes.

THE STRATEGY

Mariana's approach starts with developing a fuller understanding of the patterns of modern slavery. To do this, SINTRATA collaborates with data scientists, teams of multidisciplinary experts, and target populations to investigate how trafficking networks operate within different sectors and contexts. Using these insights, the organization develops best practices, policies, and digital tools to support key actors in the private and public sectors in taking evidence-based action against human trafficking.

Mariana also partners with businesses in key industries to reach citizens who can help reveal the hidden numbers of trafficking cases, and then uses this data to provide actionable insights for improving response and prevention. SINTRATA develops tools for documenting cases that can be used easily and safely by frontline responders – people who are most likely to come across potential victims at strategic touchpoints, such as airports, hotels, consulates, etc. For example, they developed a digital questionnaire called SINTRATA Survey Solutions to immediately log details of identified victims: Who they are, where they were found, and how they got there. Engaging citizens and employees as frontline responders allows Mariana and her team to have "eyes everywhere" and generates a continuous stream of information about how trafficking is functioning and moving in real-time on the ground. Meanwhile, citizens in these key sectors are invited to see their role and impact in society in a new light and are motivated to become part of the solution for the safety and welfare of their local communities.

Mariana complements and cross-checks this crowdsourced data by fostering intelligence sharing with national and international citizen groups, companies, and governments. As data and patterns emerge, they are added to a regional database to make the methods and true scope of the industry more visible. For example, Mariana's analysis of recent data found that over 10 percent of recently reported cases of trafficking involved victims who had previously been reported as missing children.

This more cross-connecting, accurate, detailed, and timely information can then be leveraged to move policymakers and the private sector.

Critically, trafficking survivors are involved at each step of Mariana's process as consultants who validate materials, provide feedback, and help map the realities of trafficking. Their collaboration helps SINTRATA learn where to search for victims and how to approach them most effectively to offer help without putting them at greater risk. Mariana hopes this focus on evidence will promote a culture of impact measurement and innovation in the field.

> *Sexual exploitation is identified as one of the main focuses of this crime [human trafficking], however, there are other forms of exploitation, such as labor, forced begging or the removal of organs.*
>
> **EL UNIVERSAL**

On-the-ground impact Mariana uses communication and partnerships to approach and help companies align. They in turn are key to Mariana scaling and disseminating. Armed with examples of success, she makes the case to potential partners for getting involved: Conducting a diagnostic of current or potential risk, considering all actors and potential impacts, developing a plan of implementation, and collecting data to refine the process over time. Throughout, SINTRATA aligns its work with the incentives of corporate social responsibility, risk management, and competitiveness. In only three years, she has secured partnerships with several multinationals

PHOTO CREDIT: *Mariana Ruenes*

including Marriott, Telefónica Movistar, Facebook, and Uber. These partnerships allow SINTRATA to feed data back to frontline responders at scale as recommendations and tools to improve their ability to identify and report cases. is clear in Mariana's partnership with Uber Mexico through which SINTRATA used available communication channels to teach 300,000 drivers and couriers in priority areas across Mexico what human trafficking is and how to identify and report victims. Uber's digital infrastructure made it possible to conduct a Randomized Controlled Trial that showed which messages, timings, and formats were most effective for digital campaigns. The result was a tailored call to action that led 90 percent of participants to agree that (a) they have an important role to play and (b) they have the knowledge to be a part of the solution. To translate awareness into action, Mariana's team also created a mechanism that facilitates reporting – a dedicated button in the Help section within the Uber app that eases safe, anonymous access to the National Hotline Against Human Trafficking – and helps coordinate the activities of federal and local law enforcement. By the end of the pilot, there was a 50 percent increase in willingness to report suspected cases. This success led Uber to integrate the program into its global security initiative. To date, the campaign has reached around 1 million people across Mexico, Guatemala, Panama, Costa Rica, and Canada.

Further, in 2021, SINTRATA launched a highly segmented online campaign for prevention education, and in partnership with Telefónica Movistar, they developed strategies to build capacity in the Cybercrime Prevention Police of the Public Security Ministry.

> ***Partnering with Sintrata has been essential in generating trust and showing that we are a company that cares. With Sintrata's guidance, we have been able to educate drivers and couriers about what human trafficking is, how to spot it, and the actions they can take if they suspect someone is being trafficked.***

Matt Olsen, Chief Trust & Security Officer

Uber

Building upon these successes, Mariana is currently focusing on enhancing and replicating successful strategies with new partners in other countries. She wants to establish working groups that bring together businesses, organizations, and institutions in key sectors to continuously share learnings and best practices. For instance, she recently partnered with OYO Rooms and IDB Invest to develop a study on human trafficking and exploitation in Latin America's hotel industry. Findings will be used to co-create prevention guidelines that can be implemented by any hotel, starting with pilots in Mexico and Brazil. In the next 5 years, she hopes to position human trafficking as a pressing issue in the private sector's agenda. Mariana aims for trafficking prevention to become a competitive standard, so she no longer needs to seek out partners individually and make a value proposition each time. There are already signs of this potential: the success with Marriot and Uber led OYO Rooms, Didi, and Mexico's Ministries of Transport and Tourism to approach SINTRATA. She eventually seeks to influence policies in the private and public sectors across Latin America that significantly reduce human trafficking by making it so unprofitable and risky that it becomes rare.

PHOTO CREDIT: *Mariana Ruenes – Trafficking survivors are involved at each step of Mariana's process as consultants who validate materials, provide feedback, and help map the realities of trafficking.*

> *Sintrata promotes access to justice for victims in Mexico and Latin America. Its purpose is to publicize the prevention tools that exist through technology to avoid the crime of trafficking in persons and guide actions of public and private actors that can prevent this problem.*

EL HERALDO

THE PERSON

Mariana spent much of her childhood on a remote beach in Jalisco, Mexico where her father opened a hotel. The beach significantly changed because of the presence of her and her family. Mariana returned nine years later to visit the beach after her father's hotel had been destroyed by a hurricane, and she felt a strange relief. The thought that a single action – her family moving to the beach or the hurricane destroying the hotel – can change an entire ecosystem has stayed with Mariana and spurred her ever since.

At 17, Mariana met a woman who had been a victim of human trafficking for sexual exploitation. Her story opened Mariana's eyes to this invisible problem and inspired her to volunteer at shelters for girl survivors, where she hosted events and fundraising efforts. She also started giving talks at her university to raise awareness, going door to door to persuade professors to donate class time for her presentation. What started as a short intervention in the classroom soon turned into university-wide conferences and eventually into 12 lectures per semester, packed auditoriums, and a student movement that grew to other top universities. A year later, in 2012, this movement evolved into SINTRATA, an award-winning organization with over 500 volunteers.

However, Mariana was unsure of how to measure her impact and grew increasingly frustrated that she was not making a dent in the system. She concluded that she needed to find a more strategic approach and decided to pursue a master's degree. An experience as an intern in rural Maharashtra, India clarified for her that she wanted to put solutions in the hands of those most affected. Back in Mexico, Mariana planned to train hotel employees to identify cases of human trafficking in order to finance a new community-based project. A conversation with Ashoka Fellow Alejandro Maza helped her realize the power of that idea. To learn more about the use and impact of all forms of human trafficking on other economic sectors, she dove into forgotten police records, identifying patterns in survivors' testimonies that revealed how traffickers' operations intersected with key industries. This insight led Mariana to completely overhaul SINTRATA's strategy and has since grown her impact internationally.

PETRA MASOPUST-ŠACHOVÁ

www.restorativni-justice.cz/en/

Lawyer, Researcher, Academic, and Chairperson, The Institute Of Restorative Justice

Working in the Czech Republic and beyond, Petra is championing a shift in the criminal justice paradigm towards restorative justice, which centers on healing and empathy, taps agency, enables restitution, and brings deeper resolution for victims, offenders, and society than punishment alone. Her approach engages judges, prosecutors and other professionals connected to the criminal justice system to experience restorative justice firsthand and commit to implementing it in their practice. She is building a broad ecosystem capable of shifting mindsets towards a restorative approach and getting traction on a policy level nationally and internationally.

SCAN THE CODE TO READ AND SHARE THIS ARTICLE ONLINE

THE NEW IDEA

At a time when the Czech Republic has the sixth highest incarceration rate in Europe as well as a sharply rising recidivism rate, attorney, legal scholar, and advocate Petra Masopust-Šachová is championing an alternative, empathetic paradigm of "restorative justice" as a path to deeper resolution for victims and offenders alike.

Criminal justice in the country is primarily concerned with how the law has been broken, and with finding and punishing the offender. Yet it can result in a double victimization, where victims' trauma from the crime gets compounded by the complexity and coldness of the justice system. It also prioritizes harsh sentences for offenders that rarely consider their circumstances and have little impact on reducing crime.

Petra and the Restorative Justice Institute—which she chairs—work to build a new culture of justice, moving away from authoritative, top-down decision-making to a more participatory and empathetic approach.

Restorative justice shifts the focus from punishment to healing. This approach allows victims, their families, and

PHOTO CREDIT: Petra Masopust Šachová

offenders to engage with the legal process in a more empowering way. Restorative programs create a safe space for them to meet, where victims can voice their experience and how they feel the damage should be repaired while receiving support to heal from trauma.

> *Restorative justice focuses on compensating for the damage caused by a crime, accepting responsibility on the part of the offender and redressing interpersonal relationships.*

"One of the main impulses for the development of restorative justice is the effort to help victims of crimes to repair the harm caused, to ensure their rights and needs, and to create a space to talk about how they feel and what they experience," Petra says.

These spaces not only offer victims a chance to have a say in deciding how the case is resolved, but they also restore offenders' agency. Instead of relegating them to passive recipients of sentencing they are given an opportunity to understand the pain they caused, to take responsibility, and to plan how they will make amends and set a pathway for recovery. In this way, restorative justice enables closure for victims and offenders in ways that punishment does not, and is more likely to prevent recidivism.

Petra does not promote a specific process. Rather, she creates consensus for restorative justice by changing the role of judges, attorneys, and other professionals in the justice system from gatekeepers or remote authority figures to accessible, engaged partners working with victims and offenders through open dialogue.

To achieve this, she involves them in experiential training where they use restorative techniques to identify shortcomings in the current system and what actions they can take from their position. Professionals can therefore immediately implement this approach in the cases they handle instead of waiting for legislative fiats, or relegating restorative justice to the fringes of the system.

Petra champions the application of restorative justice across the board – – for serious crimes as well as less serious ones. She empowers victims, offenders, and professionals to embrace their power as changemakers, transforming the criminal justice system from within, one case at a time, which in turn is creating impetus for change at the national policy level.

PHOTO CREDIT: *Petra Masopust Šachová*

THE PROBLEM

The incarceration rate in the Czech Republic is 200 per 100,000 inhabitants – – twice as many as is common in the European Union. Recidivism is also high: more than 60% of prisoners were already in prison at least once for other crimes.

Past attempts to reform the Czech justice system focused primarily on increasing the speed and efficiency of case resolution, but that is not necessarily a reliable metric of justice for victims and offenders. Instead, a tendency towards harsher sentencing has significantly increased the prison population, adding stress to an already burdened system and increasing costs to the public.

Restorative justice was introduced in the Czech Republic two decades ago through special programs in the Czech Probation and Mediation Services, a unit within the Ministry of Justice created in 2001. However, the reach of those programs was limited. They were applied only marginally, for less serious crimes, so they had no impact on the bulk of criminal cases or on the system as a whole. Current efforts are mostly fragmented projects led by non-profits that have little influence either. Also, restorative justice processes are often perceived as lengthy and slow, which makes legal professionals think twice before using them.

For Petra, the current system is a reflection of Czechia's totalitarian past. "There is a strong pattern of obedience to authority, not only in the criminal justice system, but also in education, healthcare, and other institutions," she says. "That's a relic of the old regime, where people weren't treated as active participants. They were expected to listen to those in power who decided for them."

Today Czech democracy is well established and advancing. But to build a truly democratic society, citizens need the power and tools to participate in decision-making and help steer how key institutions develop, including the criminal justice system. Recent surveys suggest that there is fertile ground for this change in mindset: even those who support a harsher, top-down approach to criminal justice were shown to be more open to participatory, "benevolent" alternatives when they are well explained.

THE STRATEGY

Petra has advocated and implemented restorative justice techniques throughout her 15-year career working in the citizen sector, practicing as a trial lawyer, and teaching in law schools. In 2018, she founded the Restorative Justice Institute (RJI) to consolidate the work and provide support for other organizations to adopt restorative programs.

Her strategy for accelerating uptake is four-pronged: working with criminal justice and related professionals, creating practical tools for applying restorative principles to criminal proceedings, supporting other organizations to develop their own restorative programs, and public education to shift attitudes towards a less punitive, more participatory idea of justice.

Petra engages law students and legal scholars, including by establishing restorative justice as a course of study in the Czech Republic's two top law schools. Her book, Restorative Approaches to Resolve Crime, was published in 2019. RJI creates public-facing content explaining restorative justice such as videos, interviews, conferences, and even a picture book for children.

But the core of Petra's strategy is activating professionals in the legal system- – judges, lawyers, law professors, legislators, police and parole officers, correctional officers and social workers – – to adopt a new mindset that advances restorative justice.

Petra and RJI design and deliver "restorative circle" training workshops for these professionals, where they experience the restorative approach firsthand rather than reading or hearing lectures about it. Petra is highly intentional about mapping the key stakeholders and inviting participants who have far-reaching influence, so they are in a position to spread what they learned widely and benefit thousands of people. Petra has engaged over 200 participants so far, nearly a third being high ranking leaders and officials.

The workshops are intended to model what it feels like to go through the restorative justice process itself. Participants are engaged on an emotional level, creating a setting where they can examine and express their own motivations and feelings, where all voices are heard with empathy, and where they can engage in purposeful dialogue. Together, they identify shortcomings in the system, brainstorm how restorative practices might help, and identify concrete actions they can commit to apply in their own work. These conversations reinforce practitioners' sense of agency and purpose by making them recognize that even small changes in their practice can help improve the system. Some judges have committed to speak differently to victims and families in the courtroom: intentionally asking them about their experience, what they felt or what they would consider helpful for the offender to do in order to repair the damage done.

After getting a taste of what restorative justice looks and feels like in practice, circle participants are inspired to actively promote it. Many go on to host restorative circles at their workplaces and design their own programs. And as participants adopt restorative techniques, they often create templates for others to follow. For example, one judge found creative ways to schedule restorative sessions with victims and offenders so as not to slow his overall case resolution rate. His experience was written up as a case study and shared with other restorative circles. In another case, a high-ranking Prison Services official carried out a national survey of Czechia's prisons,

PHOTO CREDIT: *Petra Masopust Šachová – Petra and RJI design "restorative circle" training workshops intended to model what it feels like to go through the restorative justice process. Afterwards, circle participants are inspired to host their own restorative circles.*

PHOTO CREDIT: *Petra Masopust Šachová*

which Petra helped design, in order to raise awareness of and gauge openness to restorative techniques. Of the counselors, guards, and others who work with inmates surveyed, a majority said they would welcome integrating restorative programs into their work.

What emerges from the circle discussions guides other parts of the strategy. For example, circle participants said they felt the need for practical ideas and examples of how restorative justice techniques might apply to their own work, so Petra and her team made it a priority to supply them. They created materials with case studies and practical advice for legal professionals, assembled into the forthcoming Restorative Justice Handbook.

Circle participants also flagged that the standard performance metrics for lawyers and judges, which are how many cases they can resolve and the speed with which they are decided, create a disincentive to spend time on restorative justice techniques. So Petra and her team worked with them to create new performance metrics that are more conducive to restorative approaches, which will be included in proposals for national reforms. These take into account how victims of crime feel during and after the judicial process and how offenders are involved in creating a plan for redemption.

Petra emphasizes that advancing restorative justice is not about establishing more alternative programs; it's about fundamentally shifting the justice system itself. "Restorative justice is not only about programs, but about the procedure of all law enforcement agencies," she says. "It's about what you're going to ask at the hearing, whether you're going to allow the matter to be dealt with as part of a diversion and whether you're going to support mediation."

Learnings from restorative circles involving high-ranking judges, prosecutors, police officials, and the Czech Bar Association have been incorporated into a "restorative platform," a national strategy for shifting the justice system and criminal proceedings in the direction of restorative justice. The platform has been submitted to the Ministry of Justice, and Petra and her team are working with the Ministry, Members of Parliament, and academics to incorporate key features of it into the Czech Republic's forthcoming Code of Criminal Procedure (the existing Code dates from 1961, created under Soviet rule, and its revision is long overdue).

> ***Petra Masopust Šachová is the founder and president of the Institute for Restorative Justice. Her strategy of restorative justice for Czechia was reflected in the program statement of the new government. She considers the strategy a success, and says over time people will be able to imagine something concrete behind the concept of restorative justice. "It's moving forward," she said. "I've managed to establish a dialogue."***

INFO.CZ

Beyond the circles, RJI works to foster a wider ecosystem of organizations that can institutionalize and spread restorative justice themselves. For example, it helps entities including Probation and Mediation Services, the Police Academy, the Justice Academy, the Society for Criminology, and other civil society organizations, find funding and other resources for promoting restorative practices.

"Past restorative justice efforts have been disconnected from the core of the justice system and have had limited impact," Petra said. "Probation and Mediation Services have had restorative justice programs for 20 years. But we are now offering more than just programs; we're offering a broader approach that changes mindsets. We are shifting professional thinking in the criminal justice field about which procedural steps to apply, how to work with victims and offenders, accountability, sanctioning, what to do besides to sending people to prison or community service. It's a systemic shift that is questioning and changing the stated goals of the criminal just system."

Demand for RJI's help is growing, including from Slovakia and other neighboring countries, and Petra is working to accelerate uptake of restorative justice approaches internationally. She serves on the board of the European Forum for Restorative Justice, coordinating its working group on Gender-Based Violence and Restorative Justice, and she is the national coordinator of Restorative Justice: Strategies for Change, which works with 10 core countries to promote restorative approaches in Europe's criminal justice systems.

The presidency of the European Union rotates, and currently Czech Prime Minister Petr Fiala is at the helm. In the latter part of 2022, the EU is revising its Victims' Directive, establishing standards for the rights, protection, and support of victims of crime. In collaboration with another Ashoka Fellow, Dagmar Doubravová, Petra has advocated prioritizing restorative justice in this process, which the Czech government has pledged to do.
"We are bringing to Europe Czech knowledge about how to implement restorative justice here, which is kind of unique," says Petra. "We are meeting with the Ministry of Justice on how the Czech EU presidency can support the revision of the Vicitims' Directive to include restorative justice. This could potentially affect all of Europe."

THE PERSON

The law runs in Petra's family – her mother and grandmother were lawyers. She grew up around sophisticated discussions about justice and the causes of criminal behavior. Her uncle, Pavel Štern, together with Andrea Matoušková, founded Probation and Mediation Services in the 1990s, which introduced restorative justice programs into the Czech Republic. He described it as "a world without lawyers," where communities came together to support victims and restore the social fabric that crime tears.

> *When Petra was not even 20, someone put pills into her drink in a bar and raped her in her sleep. Today, she is one of the promoters in the Czech Republic of "restorative justice" which focuses more on the restoration of relationships than on punishing the guilty, for example by meeting the victims of crimes with their perpetrators.*
>
> **Pražská DRBNA**

Inspired by this upbringing, Petra explored restorative principles early in her journey. Her passion was truly ignited after studying with American criminologist Howard Zehr, known as the "grandfather of restorative justice." She participated in a restorative circle with other law students that enabled her to develop deep relationships and to connect with her purpose to change the criminal justice system. This experience showed her the power of "learning by doing" to galvanize support for implementing a restorative approach.

Later, Petra launched several initiatives to test restorative practices in her work as a professor, an attorney with civil society organizations, and then as a trial lawyer. Despite their meaningful impact, she became frustrated by the lack of influence on the wider system. Restorative justice, she felt, needed to be more than a collection of isolated, localized efforts; it needed to be understood and promoted as a fundamental, new paradigm for criminal justice.

Petra launched the Restorative Justice Institute to focus on building towards this large-scale transformation. Her cross-sector background and experience in facilitating multi-stakeholder dialogue has allowed her to mobilize a diverse spectrum of actors to advance her cause.

LIZZIE KIAMA

Founder, This Ability

 www.this-ability.org

Through targeted communications, advocacy and county-by-county recruitment of physically "this abled" women and girls across Kenya, Lizzie is constructing a new public narrative about their full potential, rooted in control over their own sexual and reproductive health, workforce access, and independence in choosing how and with whom they choose to live.

SCAN THE CODE TO READ AND SHARE THIS ARTICLE ONLINE

THE NEW IDEA

Lizzie understands the creative, problem-solving, innovative spirit commonly found in those who are differently-abled. When the world is designed for those that are able-bodied, those with disabilities are forced to create new ways, find alternative possibilities, and demand access to opportunities. These are strengths that add value and perspective to any organization or business. Lizzie's women-led organization, This-Ability, pursues a bold strategy to transform the public's perception of what it looks like for Kenyan women and girls with physical differences to live their lives to the fullest while contributing their strengths to the communities around them. The strategy includes a podcast series, PAZA! Conversations, which seeks to document and create visibility for the experiences of women and girls with disabilities. This-Ability also has a YouTube Program called 'Let's Talk' to encourage young women with disabilities to share their experiences accessing quality sexual and reproductive health care as well as family planning services.

Beginning in seven counties in the Mombasa-Nairobi corridor, the organization hosts advocacy forums featuring, so far, the challenges facing 400 "This-Abled" women. The forums include meetings with local advocacy and human rights partners (national and community-based organizations). These forums have provided the first opportunity in Kenya for press conferences to be held where physically challenged women share their sexual reproductive health issues.

This-Ability has used these forums to help build the first national Unstructured Supplementary Service Data (USSD) platform on women and young girls with physical challenges. The database contains more than 19,800 "This Abled" profiles and this aggregated information is

Photo Credit This Ability – Lizzie empowers women with disabilities by building their digital and leadership skills through local and virtual training.

provided to potential employers, to product and service providers, as well as to international, national and local organizations focused on providing programmatic as well as solidarity and networking opportunities for people with disabilities. Once new members register, This Ability provides access and information while gathering their data to help inform policy interventions with, for example, the Ministry of Health.

Often, Lizzie sees how people overlook disability, which is why her mission is to advance the rights and inclusion of women with disabilities and to make them visible.

The fact of the USSD platform coming to fruition has triggered an interest from other Kenya-based NGOs in contributing to, or replicating, this approach. And the fact of these ongoing conversations has drawn the interest of other organizations, international as well as Africa-based, in the usefulness of this information in serving the needs of "This-Abled" African women and girls.

THE PROBLEM

Kenyan society maintains an outdated set of attitudes in its health care system related to the false assumption of someone with a physical disability as somehow "ill" and, as such, needing to stay home until they are "cured," which effectively means never. This biased mischaracterization is paired with a "common charity" social approach that views such people as helpless and unable or unwilling to represent themselves.

For example, in 2017, the Kenyan Government created a report on women and girls which did not include any information about women and girls with physical disabilities. This prompted Lizzie to create a shadow report which was submitted to the United Nations Convention on the Elimination of Discrimination Against Women (CEDAW). As a result, Kenya is now measured by UN agencies for their ability to provide inclusion for women and girls with disabilities.

At the policy level, a weak law enforcement system limits opportunities to improve the conditions for women and girls with disabilities. For example, the 2003 "Persons

PHOTO CREDIT: *This Ability – This Ability equips healthcare providers across the country to bestow appropriate treatment to women and girls with disabilities.*

with Disabilities Act" sets forth a comprehensive law to cover rights, rehabilitation, and equal opportunities for persons with disabilities and requires both private and public sector employers to reserve 5 percent of all jobs for disabled persons. In practice, the government does not regularly collect such information from private employers, and when it sometimes does for public employers it does not make this information readily available. Enforcement actions taken against public and private employers pursuant to this law are rare.

THE STRATEGY

Lizzie is training women with disabilities county by county on storytelling and data collection techniques. This will contribute to an upcoming report, "National Agenda Anti-Corruption on Women and Girls with Disabilities," to coincide with the 2022 national elections. Lizzie is using the creation of these local stories by local women to organize and build the confidence of county-level teams of women to step forward and become leaders in their communities.

Lizzie organized the pre-ICPD25 (25th International Conference for Population and Development) meeting with the United Nations that brought together women with disabilities to discuss issues relevant to sexual and reproductive health. The conference, hosted in Kenya in 2019, brought together more than 8,000 delegates representing governments and advocates, health organizations, women, and youth activists from 170 countries.

Subsequently the United Nations Population Fund (UNFPA) appointed This-Ability as the implementing partner for disability programs in Kenya. In addition, Lizzie has co-authored opinion editorials with UNFPA Head of Office on issues related to disabilities before and during COVID-19 as well as being featured in reports and social media posts on several UN Agency channels.

In 2019 This-Ability launched 'Introduction to Digital Literacy,' a face-to-face course aimed at building digital skills among young women with disabilities focusing on their interactions with the internet and social media. Given covid-19 limitations, in 2020 Lizzie and team created an e-Learning platform and launched a program to equip more women with various disabilities on digital marketing skills. The success of the e-learning platform motivated the team to explore more opportunities. For this reason, they launched the first online program in Kenya to equip 64 healthcare providers with the necessary knowledge, both anthropological and medical, on healthcare needs for women and girls with disabilities in partnership with the UNFPA. The goal is to create a blueprint amongst healthcare providers all across the country for treating women and girls with disabilities.

To date, This Ability's collective efforts have led to tangible changes for people with disabilities with special focus on girls' and women's reproductive rights and healthcare. For example, organized forums and distributed updates now include new information on technology and market development tools as well as social media how-tos that support women's leadership efforts to hold policymakers and organizations accountable while making injustices visible.

> *"Even in modernized areas of Kenya, buildings lack crucial accessibility features, like elevators and ramps. These physical barriers are compounded by less tangible obstacles, like illiteracy. In the absence of public education, Kenyan schools are exclusive, costly, and primarily located in wealthier, urban areas. Moreover, students with disabilities (when they can afford schooling) are designated to specialized schools, many of which are crowded and insufficiently funded."*

GLOBAL SPORTS MENTORING PROGRAM

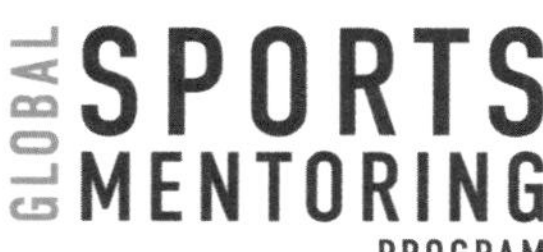

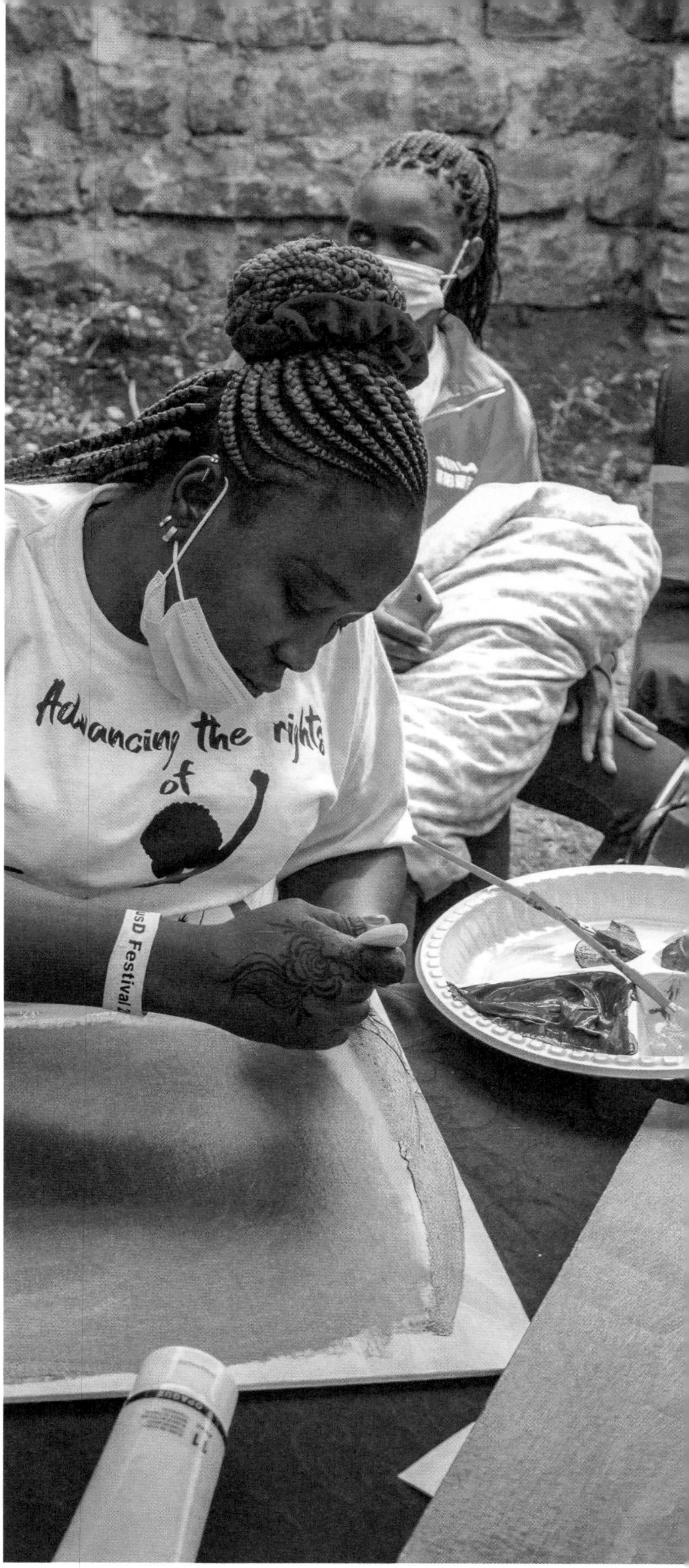

PHOTO CREDIT: *This Ability – This Ability equips healthcare providers across the country to bestow appropriate treatment to women and girls with disabilities.*

PHOTO CREDIT: *This Ability – Lizzie is training women with disabilities county by county on storytelling and data collection techniques.*

THE PERSON

Lizzie is the first born of a middle-class family from the coastal city of Mombasa, Kenya. In her teenage years, she excelled in arts, drama, poetry, acting and other creative activities. Lizzie was also very passionate about sports and participated in table tennis, distance running, and basketball.

When Lizzie was 18 she was in a car accident. When she regained consciousness her legs had been amputated. During her ensuing convalescence her mother played a critical role in helping Lizzie to resume her social life, including dating, and not view her difference in a way that would prevent her from ever finding love and family.

The delivery of her first child led Lizzie to more deeply confront the reality that she could not walk without the support of prosthetics. This was when Lizzie decided to fully embrace her identity as a woman with a physical disability. An internship at a government agency, the National Council for Persons with Disabilities, led to her being a Job Placement Assistant helping people with disabilities find employment. While she acquired insights into the challenges facing disabled people, Lizzie became frustrated by the "bureaucracy" that prevented her desire to innovate around obstacles. "Bringing new ideas was always met with hesitation," she explained. Due to this and her desire to learn more, Lizzie left her job and started This Ability.

COLLABORATIVE ENTREPRENEURSHIP

ASHOKA'S YOUNG CHANGEMAKERS & ITS "JUJITSU PARTNERS": THE FORCE TO RECKON WITH

How formidable changemakers across generations are joining forces to tip society

Ashoka Young Changemakers are highly empathetic, powerful teens who have had a dream, built a team, and changed their world. They are the best changemakers of their generation, and they are the "gold standard" examples of what now constitutes success in growing up. They also want to be and were carefully selected to be co-leaders in the "*everyone* a changemaker" movement.

At the same time, Ashoka is developing 80 to 100 "jujitsu partners" across the world. Quality, ethical, mega organizations, they are critical to the world's grasping and acting quickly and wisely to adopt the "*everyone* a changemaker" (EACH) reality. Ashoka helps them recognize that their members/customers/constituents all need now to understand that an everything-changing and – connected world requires them to perform differently in every dimension of life – – and that the jujitsu partner's helping those it serves through this life-changing transition is the most valuable thing it can do for them. Which means that doing so is their best core strategy (not just a project). Their core commitment gives Ashoka and the EACH movement the power to quickly change how society understand the new everything-changing reality and how to respond. These giant organizations also directly and indirectly impact the lives of hundreds of millions of young people in their countries and around the world.

Critical leadership inside these jujitsu partners comes from a team of their Next Generation Leaders, entrepreneurial individuals who are savvy and command respect within their organization and in the broader field they operate in. They have already led system changing initiatives and see themselves as serious changemakers for the good.

When we bring these two key constituents together, they multiply each other and dramatically, accelerate the changemaker movement.

No species would exist if the adults did not spend much of their life energy bringing up the young. That's why we are so moved when we experience a young person exercising his/her changemaking power for the good. Some people tear up. That's a power no adult has. Moreover, the AYCers see things and can lead in areas where a mega organizational leader can't. The mega leader also, of course, has special powers.

Both the young changemakers and the mega organization's next-generation leaders gain enormous power – – and satisfaction – – when Ashoka brings them together as co-leaders in the EACH movement. The impact of leaders of some of society's biggest organizations not usually seen together (e.g., a union and a publisher, and a city) doing interviews together, especially when joined by a super-powerful teen AYCer, all arguing that society must rise to the EACH challenge, is hard to overstate. And that's but one example.

AYCers are key to helping jujitsu partners' next-generation leaders move their colleagues, e.g., by helping them learn how to parent changemakers (which, it turns out, is the most effective way of turning the parents into changemakers). General publishers and AYCers need one another for many reasons, and this need is even more urgent for education publishers. A metro area working to become a region of the future needs them all working together. How can a school learn how to teach educators how to turn schools into "*everyone* a changemaker" cultures where changemaking is the norm, not a very tough slog only a few can overcome? AYCers know how because (1) they've done it, and (2) they typically have spread it. Since top entrepreneurs of both generations enjoy (they do!) entrepreneuring together, they keep finding more and more collaboration multipliers. In the process, of course, they are changing society so importantly for the good, which makes them love this new tie all the more.

Here are three examples of AYCers and Jujitsu Partner Next Gen Leaders co-leading the movement – – from Indonesia, Nigeria, and Brazil. Each sketch tells how the AYCer got their changemaking superpower and how they are now working with the right next generation leaders from Jujitsu organisations in their respective countries to tip society toward an *everyone* a changemaker culture. Each story illustrates how pivotal it is to bring these two seemingly disparate forces together.

AZZAM

Tuntungan & Ini Baru Keluarga – Indonesia

Growing up in the countryside of North Sumatra in Indonesia, Azzam spent most of his leisure time playing board games or participating in community services. He treasures the fact that these activities give him the space to interact and converse with his friends while learning new skills, especially problem solving and teamwork.

Sadly, as technology advanced, many of his friends turned to online gaming and rarely played together outside as they used to. Realizing this, Azzam felt challenged to create a fun board game for his peers that encourages empathy and constructive interaction. With a focus on process rather than outcome, the game is designed for small groups of 4-8 people to learn about and discuss the issues facing their communities.

The objective is to solve a problem, so the game begins with a social or environmental issue introduced by the "monster", and it is the heroes' responsibility to provide a solution using their respective abilities. Each of the heroes in this game represents a character in Indonesian folklore. So, while the objective is to teach young people about problem solving, they are simultaneously learning about Indonesia's literary traditions.

As of February 2021, when he was elected an Ashoka Young Changemaker, Azzam and his team had introduced Tuntungan Ground Board Game in six schools in four provinces, engaging 200 students aged 14-18. Although the COVID-19 pandemic has limited the growth of their in-person play activities, Azzam continues to promote empathy and the changemaker mindset through journalism and online discussions. This powered his co-leadership of the Spotify Podcast "Ini Baru Keluarga" (This is Family), co-produced by KBR Radio, a vast media network of over 600 affiliated local stations – – which was founded by Ashoka Fellow Tosca Santoso and is an Ashoka Jujitsu Partner

Through the KBR Radio partnership, Azzam leverages his expertise in journalism and gamification to influence the mindset of parents and to activate families all across Indonesia into a support system that helps young people grow up as changemakers. Azzam credits and takes inspiration from his parents for the sense of agency they gave him by introducing him to social issues in his early days and encouraging him to exercise his agency in addressing them.

Together with 13 other early adopters (from Ashoka Fellows, other Ashoka Young Changemakers, and the Jujitsu partners, Assam produces this podcast. It discusses relevant social issues and highlights the power of young people in the family context. The podcast series will soon be implemented in over 40 cities by organizing discussions at the grassroot level.

Ranging from a 16-year-old young changemaker to a 65-year-old social entrepreneur, everyone practices collaborative leadership that allows them to have an equal

footing and shared resources in a fluid open team of teams in achieving the central goals of the movement. Solidarity across generations is key for the *everyone* a Changemaker movement – – with emphasis on 'every-one' in the most inclusive sense.

AYOMIDE

Pink Diva Organisation – Nigeria

Ayomide is a 13-year-old changemaker from Lagos who started Pink Diva Talks, an initiative where young girls come together to discuss and raise awareness around menstrual hygiene. She saw young girls around her suffer from lack of access to right knowledge about periods and also the affordability issue. With the support of her parents as allies, she began to recruit young girls for her team and built an organisation that addressed period poverty in Nigeria.

They also teach young girls to collect and trade in bottles and plastics, enabling them to generate money with which to buy sanitary products for themselves. The Team now is also training girls in underserved communities to make reusable pads using sustainable materials, thereby reducing plastic waste and providing an affordable and safe alternative for girls from economically distressed families.

At her selection panel to become an AYCer, Ayomide met Bjorn Olatunde Lawal-Solarin (aka Tunde), the CEO of Lantern Books, West Africa's largest educational publishers and an Ashoka Jujitsu Partner. Deeply impressed with each others' dedication to changemaking for the good of all, the duo are now working to introduce concepts of menstrual hygiene education and girls exercising their agency in Lanterns' product offerings for primary and middle school students across Anglophone West Africa.

Ayomide alongside the inaugural cohort of Ashoka Young Changemakers from Nigeria

> ***Starting to take action made me feel powerful, confident and brave – it made me grow***
>
> *Ayomide*

Given Ayomide's age, such a partnership of equals needs a special set of parameters to be safe and effective. Firstly, their common understanding and commitment to the '*everyone* a Changemaker' movement enables them to explore this creative, collaborative and mutually beneficial opportunity. Secondly, all parties take care to

ensure Ayomide's success while protecting her privacy and image. Moreover, with Tunde as an adult ally Ayomide has been able to expand her superpower and show young girls the promise of Pink Diva – when you get started with your changemaking journey, the opportunities are limitless!

Another major contribution to the movement emerging from the cross-pollination of AYCers and our Jujitsu partners is the video series released by Trace TV – an African television media giant with presence in over 60 countries and another Ahsoka jujitsu partner. These videos present the journey of Ayomide and other AYCers through the stages of their idea, their team, and their changed world. By telling her story through the campaign, Ayomide has opened doors for millions of girls to see themselves as changemakers and learn the how-tos of practicing their agency for their menstrual health initially, and in then in many ways that serve the good of all.

SCAN THE CODE
TO WATCH AND SHARE AYOMIDE VIDEO STORY ONLINE

VINNICIUS

Cordel & InovaGRE | Brazil

Alongside a group of school mates, Ashoka Young Changemaker Vinnicius Rodrigo identified games and digital technologies as key opportunities both to develop better learning methodologies and to develop all students' changemaking skills. During high school, they created Cordel, a social startup that is already generating positive impacts in the Metropolitan Region of Recife, capital of Pernambuco state in the North-East of Brazil.

One of their products is InovaGRE, a program they designed in partnership with the Regional Management of Metropolitan Education South (GRE Metro Sul), which covers six municipalities and 95 schools. It seeks to boost teaching-learning strategies and better engage students.

The program offers trainings to educators, introducing them to concepts and tools to make the classroom a more changemaking environment. This includes project learning and improved digital culture, including the use of gamification. These resources are now available in the 95 schools of the six municipalities run by GRE Metro Sul. As next steps, the program plans to expand InovaGRE beyond the metro area of Recife, establishing new collaborations with the Pernambuco Department of Education.

"The feedback has been very positive, because many of these teachers aren't very connected to social networks and the latest technologies, so it's been a new experience," Vinnicius says. During the early stages, the team conducted a survey with the educators, and found that most of them did not consider themselves changemakers and did not feel prepared to use tech teaching tools. With the implementation of the program, Vinnicius says that he has seen real advances, "teachers have come to recognize that they have this power and these skills to promote their students' changemaking."

In addition, during the pandemic, Cordel developed EducaZAP, a tool that provides materials and exercises complementary to the content presented in class through a WhatsApp chatbot. When the student sends a message, the chatbot responds with the corresponding video lessons, PDF notes with explanatory content and exercises to be solved in the classroom.

Since internet access is limited and WhatsApp is the most widely used application, the team zeroed in on offering learning pathways through a simple chatbot rather than having multiple WhatsApp groups that teachers and students would find confusing and hard to navigate. The objective is to decentralize this communication and relieve the burden on educators, in addition to providing additional material to students in a direct and simplified way, appropriate to the lived reality of the young people who have limited access to the Internet and computers.

The pilot project was first implemented in two state schools in partnership with GRE Metro Sul: "GRE was very open to innovative projects. When they invited us, we encountered several challenges, such as the difficulty of student engagement and the uncertainties surrounding face-to-face teaching. Based on that, we started thinking together," Vinnicius says.

Marcos Moraes, GRE's manager and a key next generation leader in the Recife Metro area, says that he had been following the evolution of Cordel and its projects since their team started up. "With InovaGRE, we have worked together throughout the process, from the design of the project and its applications to the monitoring of all phases," he explains. "The idea is to bring an innovative program to schools, in which we use technological teaching tools that already exist, but which are not yet in the teachers' day, bringing an innovation that reflects the learning process of our students."

SCAN THE CODE
TO WATCH AND SHARE
VINNICIUS VIDEO STORY
ONLINE

ORGANIZING THE MOVEMENT

CONTENTS

ASHOKA LEADERS

World Council

Marjorie C. Benton

Marjorie, very much a fellow spirit, has founded and co-founded many socially important organizations including: the Chicago Foundation for Women; the Women's Issues Network; and The Peace Museum. She has been board chair of Save the Children, and she served as a delegate to the United Nations special sessions on disarmament in the 1970s, and then as U.S. Ambassador to UNICEF.

Vera Cordeiro

One of the early Brazilian Ashoka Fellows, Vera Cordeiro founded Associação Saúde Criança which addresses the root causes that prevent poor families from providing adequate care to their children when discharged from hospital.

Marian Wright Edelman

Marian Wright Edelman is a lifelong advocate for disadvantaged Americans and is the President of the Children's Defense Fund. Under her leadership, CDF has become the nation's strongest voice for children and families.

Anupam Puri

Anupam ("Tino") Puri founded and managed McKinsey's practice in India. In 1996, he was elected a managing director, and from 1998 onwards, he oversaw all of McKinsey's Asian and Latin American practices. Tino was a founder board member of Ashoka.

Sir Shridath Ramphal

Sir Shridath Ramphal is Co-Chair of the Commission on Global Governance and President of the World Conservation Union. He is Former Secretary General of the British Commonwealth, Chancellor of the University of West Indies and former Foreign Minister and Attorney General in Guyana.

Muhammad Yunus

Nobel Prize recipient, Muhammad Yunus, provided the global leadership that made micro-credit a universally accepted development tool. He went on to create a series of social businesses, including the largest telephone service in the region and now champions new forms of social-serving organization globally.

ASHOKA BOARD

Richard Cavanaugh (On Leave)
The Kennedy School of Government
Harvard University
Former President and CEO, The Conference Board
United States

Bill Drayton
Chair and CEO, Ashoka: *Everyone* a Changemaker
Chair, Get America Working!
Former Assistant Administrator, U.S. E.P.A.
United States

Sushmita Ghosh
Leadership Team Emerita
Former Ashoka President
India

Mary Gordon
Ashoka Fellow
Founder & CEO, Roots of Empathy
Canada

Roger Harrison
Newspaper Executive and Chair, Leading Charities
Chair, Royal Dance Academy
Former Chair, Asylum Aid
Former Chair, Toynbee Hall
United Kingdom

Fred Hehuwat
Founder, Green Indonesia Foundation
Former Director, National Institute of Geology an
Mining of the Indonesian Academy of Sciences
Indonesia

Sara Horowitz
Ashoka Member
Founder of the Freelancers Union
United States

Felipe Vergara
Co-Founder and CEO, Lumni
Peru

Kyle Zimmer
Founder and President, First Book
United States

NORTH AMERICAN COUNCIL

Marjorie C. Benton
Trustee, President's Commission on White House Fellowships
Former Chair, Save the Children
Former United States Representative to UNICEF

Richard Danzig
Former Secretary of the Navy

Peter Kellner
Founder and Managing Partner, Richmond Global
Co-Founder, Endeavor
Founder, Environmental Management and Law Association (Hungary)
Founder, Ural Petroleum Corporation

Eugene Ludwig
Former U.S. Comptroller of the Currency
Founder, The Promontory Financial Group

Alice Tepper Marlin
Founder & President, Social Accountability International
Founder, Council on Economic Priorities

Theodore R. Marmor
Professor of Public Policy and Management and Professor of Political Science, Yale School of Management

OFFICES WORLDWIDE

Ashoka Global and North America

2200 Wilson Blvd., Suite 102, Unit #313
Arlington, VA 22201
UNITED STATES
T: 1 703 527 8300
F: 1 703 527 8383

Ashoka East Africa

Nexus Co-Working
Ground Floor, Riara Corporate Suites
Riara Road, Nairobi
KENYA
T: 245 0 202 628 738

Ashoka Argentina

Teodoro García 2964
C1426DND CABA
ARGENTINA
T: 54 11 4393 8646
E: infoargentina@ashoka.org

Ashoka Anglophone West Africa

3rd Floor, Katia Towers
Plot 1676 Oladele Olasore Street
Off Sanusi Fafunwa
Victoria Island, Lagos
NIGERIA
T: 23 412 950 872
E: jnzerem@ashoka.org

Ashoka Austria and Central Eastern Europe

c/o Haus der Philanthropie,
Schottenring 16/3.OG
Vienna A-1010
AUSTRIA
T: 43 1 3840100
E: austria@ashoka.org

Ashoka Belgium

20 Rue Joseph II,
1000 Brussels
BELGIUM
T: 32 2 675 2219
E: ashokabelgium@ashoka.org

Ashoka Brazil

R. Araújo, 124 – República,
São Paulo–SP, CEP 01220-020
BRAZIL
T: 55 11 3085-9190
E: brasil@ashoka.org

Ashoka Canada

336 Adelaide Street West, Suite 606
Toronto, Ontario M5V 1R9
CANADA
T: 1 416 646 2333
F: 1 416 646 1875
E: canadainfo@ashoka.org

Ashoka Chile

Américo Vespucio Sur 952
office 1401B,
Las Condes region Metropolitana,
CHILE
T: 56 2 220 00232
E: bdominguez@ashoka.org

Ashoka France

Bayard Groupe
18 rue Barbes
92120 Montrouge
FRANCE
T: 33 1 40 26 30 83
E: france@ashoka.org

Ashoka Germany

Prinzregentenplatz 10
Munich 81675
GERMANY
T: 49 89 2175 49 754
E: ashokagermany@ashoka.org

Ashoka India, Bangladesh, and Sri Lanka

54, 1st Cross, Domlur Layout
Bangalore 560071
INDIA
T: 91 80 4274 5777
E: india@ashoka.org

Ashoka Indonesia

Jalan Pangkalan Jati 5 No. 3, RT 011 RW 05, Keluaahan Cipinang Melayu, Kecamatan Makasar,
Jakarta Timur 13620
INDONESIA
T: 62 81 1222 7201
E: indonesia@ashoka.org

Ashoka Israel

98 Ussishkin Street,
Tel Aviv 62031
ISRAEL
T: 972 52 6967722
E: israel@ashoka.org

Ashoka Italy

Mento Via Conte Verde
68 00185 Roma,
ITALY
T: 003 934 788 35904
E: italy@ashoka.org

Ashoka Japan

4-23-4 Denenchofu,
Ohta-Ku, Tokto 145-0071
Tokyo, 150-0012
JAPAN
T: 81 3 6459 3144
E: japan@ashoka.org

Ashoka Korea

HeyGround 3F
5 Ttukseom-ro 1na-gil Seongdong-gu
Seoul 04779
SOUTH KOREA
T: 82 2737 6977
E: korea@ashoka.org

Ashoka Mexico and Central America
Tuxpan 57
Colonia Roma Sure
Mexico, DF 06760
MEXICO
T: 52 55 5256 2820
E: ashokamexico@ashoka.org

Ashoka Middle East and North Africa
93 Abd El-aziz Alsaud Street
7th Floor, El-Manial
11451 Cairo
EGYPT
T: 2 02 253 285 86
F: 2 02 236 544 04
E: venture-assist@ashoka-arab.org

Ashoka Netherlands
De Ruijterkade 128
Spring House
1011 AC Amsterdam
NETHERLANDS
T: 221 33 825 43 43
E: info@ashoka.nl

Ashoka Nordic
c/o Norrsken House fack46, Birger Jarlsgatan 57c,
Stockholm 11457
SWEDEN
T: 0046 72 579 7376
E: scandinavia@ashoka.org

Ashoka Philippines
c/o co.lab
Unit 301, 3rd Floor, #3 Brixton Street,
Brgy. Kapitolyo, Pasig City,
PHILIPPINES 1603
T: 632 899 4587
E: philippines@ashoka.org

Ashoka Poland
Ul. Michała Paca 40
04-386 Warszawa
POLAND
T: 43 1 38 40 100
E: info _ pl@ashoka.org

Ashoka Romania
Strada Gina Patrichi 6
Bucureşti 010449, România
Găzduiţi de RAF
ROMANIA
T: +40 799 827 088
E: romania@ashoka.org

Ashoka Sahel
Cité Sipress II villa 176,
BP 15090 Dakar Fann
SENEGAL
T: 221 33 827 37 19
E: ctoure@ashoka.org

Ashoka Singapore/ Malaysia
141 Middle Road
GSM Building #5-05
Singapore 188976
SINGAPORE
T: 65 9154 890
E: singapore@ashoka.org

Ashoka Southern Africa
Office 4—b2 House
8, Tyrwhitt Avenue, Rosebank
2196 Johannesburg
SOUTH AFRICA
T: 27 011 447 1758
E: southernafricainfo@ashoka.org

Ashoka Spain/Portugal
Calle Alameda, 22
28014, Madrid
SPAIN
T: 34 91 448 9962
E: coordinador@ashoka.org

Ashoka Switzerland
c/o Quadia
Rue du Conseil Général 20
1205 Geneva
SWITZERLAND
T: 41 078 685 45 60
E: switzerland@ashoka.org

Ashoka Thailand
101/8 Phahonyothin 32 Road
Senanikom, Chatuchak
Bangkok 10900

THAILAND
T: 66 29 41 9294
E: thailand@ashoka.org

Ashoka Turkey
Asmali Mescit Mah. Mesrutiyet Cad.
Gen. Yazgan Sk. No:14
Beyoglu—Istanbul
TURKEY
T: 90 538 437 9498
E: turkiye@ashoka.org

Ashoka United Kingdom
First Floor, 65 Gresham Street,
London EC2V 7NQ
UNITED KINGDOM
T: 44 20 8980 9416
E: infouk@ashoka.org

Ashoka Venezuela/Andean Region
Av Francisco de Miranda
Mene Grande Bldg, 5th Floor
Office 5-4 URb Los Palos Grandes
Caracas
VENEZUELA
T: 58 212 421 9005
E: venezuela@ashoka.org

ENSURING THE FUTURE: THE ENDOWMENTS

Ashoka's endowments provide an enduring base of support for innovation across the globe. Their growth also helps ensure Ashoka's long-term ability to serve a field that will be critically needed as long as society must adapt and change. Ashoka's endowments have had positive investment results annually for all but two of the last thirty years. Managed with a five-year perspective by three endowment trustees, the trustees invest with a long-term perspective and are committed to maintaining the real value of the funds before agreeing to disbursements. Given by both institutions and individuals, Ashoka endowments often create a permanent statement about or memorial to someone the donor especially loves or respects.

The Amaterasu Endowment

For the support of women Fellows working outside the Americas in the areas of women's reproductive rights, women's empowerment, or sustainable community. Endowed by Katherine Victoria Randolph. Established in December 1999.

The Henry Beal Endowment

In memory of Henry Beal, a founding friend of Ashoka and, before his death, one of its Endowment Trustees. He was one of America's most inspired and effective environmental managers and leaders. The endowment is focused on environment issues and HIV/AIDS. Established in 1992.

The E. Noel Bergere Endowment

In memory of Noel Bergere who, though crippled by polio at three years old, became Master of the High Court. He was also a leader of the disabled and a patron of education in Australia. Focused on supporting a Fellow who is handicapped and/or whose work relates either to education or the law. Established in 1984.

The Joan Bergere Endowment

Joan Bergere came to America as a young musician and later helped other young musicians get their first career opening at major New York City public concerts. She was a loving parent and a citizen of the world with broad interests. Established in 1982.

The Benjamin and Anne Bloom Endowment

Ben Bloom was a successful lawyer and businessman who, as the son of immigrant parents, believed strongly in creating opportunities for others to succeed as he had succeeded. This endowment has been established to honor his desire to provide opportunities for those who are willing to work hard but need a chance in life. Anne, his lifelong partner, passed away in 2019, and thoroughly agreed with him about providing opportunities for others. Established in 1996. Unrestricted.

The Columbia Ashoka Fellowships I and II

The Columbia Foundation created two endowments to enable Ashoka to elect more women as Fellows. Established in 1986.

The C.M. Cresta Fund

Established in 1986. Unrestricted.

The Padma Rag Datta Endowment

Dr. Padma Rag Datta dedicated his life's work to using science to improve human welfare and preserve the environment. His father, Parasuram Datta, founded a wildlife sanctuary in Assam and was a strong believer in social justice. The family wishes that their legacy be continued through this endowment so that Ashoka Fellows may find their own path to the simple and profound acts that make a difference. Established in 1996.

The Sarah Dunbar Endowment

Sarah Dunbar had an enduring concern for downtrodden people whose environment had been destroyed or reduced by modern times, especially by war and industry. Contributing to maintaining a people-friendly environment was another of her passions. Established in 2000.

Endowment Fund B

Established in 1999. Unrestricted.

The Michael Fein Honorary Endowment

This endowment is in memory of Michael Fein and his tremendous ability to touch so many lives. He was very passionate about the social enterprises that Ashoka fulfilled. Established in 2001.

The Maurice Fitzgerald Ashoka Fellowship

Maurice Fitzgerald taught in the Philippines after the Spanish American War. He loved teaching and the people of the Philippines. Created for a teaching and education fellowship. Established in 1986.

The John and Eleanor Forrest Ashoka Fellowship

Established in 1986. Unrestricted.

The Fort Hill Endowment Fund

Established in 1993. Unrestricted.

The Fox Peace Endowment

The Fox Peace Endowment is inspired by the Peace Testimony articulated by George Fox in 1651 and by the commitment of Tom Fox, who was killed in Iraq in 2006, while serving as a witness for peace. Its purpose is to identify and launch social entrepreneurs and their projects dedicated to the development of structure, conditions, and communities that nurture peace.

The Buckminster Fuller Ashoka Fellowship

For Fellows working to alleviate hunger in South Asia. Established in 1983.

The General Endowment Fund for Ashoka

The General Endowment for Ashoka was established in 1998 from numerous individual contributions earmarked for endowment purposes. Unrestricted.

The Sanjoy Ghose Endowment

This endowment is a tribute to the work and sacrifice that Ashoka Fellow Sanjoy Ghose made in building a culture of volunteerism and a sense of citizen responsibility among the youth in India's northeastern state of Assam. It is a legacy of the work he began to reorient the area's youth away from violence and anarchy towards constructive and active social involvement in the face of ethnic strife, insurgent movements, and state repression. Sanjoy was abducted on July 4, 1997. The United Liberation Front of Assam (ULFA) claimed responsibility for this event. Unrestricted. Established in 1998.

William T. Golden Ashoka Endowment

Bill Golden helped launch Ashoka in 1980. Bill Golden held lifelong enthusiasm for science and the arts. He studied business and used his skills to accomplish useful work in diverse fields. He was a wide-ranging creator, himself an artist, repeatedly forging ingenious and effective ways to promote education, research, and understanding. If asked about his purpose, Bill would answer, with a twinkle in his eye, "to do interesting things." In common with Ashoka, Bill Golden brought opportunity to people with ideas for highly constructive ends. For over three decades, Bill was a close partner and advisor and also endowment trustee for Ashoka.

The James P. Grant Ashoka Endowment

Named for the late Executive Director of the United Nations Children's Fund (UNICEF) and created by his friends, colleagues, and family to "continue his life's work and world vision." The endowment's purposes include supporting innovative leadership that contributes to social development among children and the disadvantaged, developing new methods and low-cost technologies to further social development, and encouraging dialogue leading to policies that improve the lives of children and all humankind. Established in 1998.

The Jeroen Hehuwat Endowment

In memory of Jeroen Hehuwat, an easy-going young man, with many interests and many good friends. His greatest passion was the natural world and he loved hiking, climbing, and whitewater rafting. In April 2015, he was on a hiking and climbing expedition to Yala Peak in Nepal when an earthquake struck, causing a landslide in the Langtang Valley where Jeroen and his team lost their lives. The endowment will support Ashoka Fellows and Youth Venturers in Indonesia. Established in 2015.

The Albert O. Hirschman Fellowship

Given to honor Professor Hirschman's long leadership in the field of practical, grassroots development. Established in 1986. Unrestricted.

The Jimmy Hopkins Fellowship

Jimmy Hopkins was a Judge in the New York State Supreme Court, Appellate Division. He was known as a very kind man who was a master of the law. Many of his decisions and interpretations are the basis for important legal precedent. Created for a Fellow in the legal or judicial arena. Established in 1997.

The Harris and Eliza Kempner Fund Ashoka Fellowship

For support of Fellows working in Mexico. Established in 1989.

The Abdul Waheed Khan Memorial Endowment

Abdul Waheed Khan, who was elected an Ashoka Fellow in Pakistan in 2003, was assassinated in 2013, following death threats for his work. This Endowment celebrates his life and work. Abdul is remembered by his colleagues for his gentle, empathetic, persistent and values-driven approach to finding peaceful solutions to problems. He wanted all children to learn and be prepared to succeed in the modern world.

Because of his country's inadequate investment in education, poor communities often create their own schools, typically madrassas. Responding to what parents and local communities wanted, Abdul brought new approaches to and modern subjects to learning, including mathematics, science, computers and English. Abdul leaves a legacy of great courage and determination; a spirit that was committed to change in spite of risk; and work that will have a lasting impact through the many thousands of children who will be able to live far richer, more open lives because of Abdul. Established in 2013.

The Martin Klitzner Endowment

Marty Klitzner was an anomaly. He spent his life in the financial industry, most of it as president of Sunrise Capital Partners, a successful hedge fund. Yet he and his family lived comfortably, not opulently. The family's extra money was for others—in the local community and worldwide. Marty was one of the most loved and respected men in the American financial community. He was known for his integrity, ready smile and good humor.

In the mid-nineties when Marty learned about Ashoka. He said, "This is my kind of an organization." Until his death in 2012, he was a fervent fan and contributor. He was delighted to have dinner with Bill Drayton and discuss their shared ideal of helping others in the most effective way.

The greed and excesses of the financial industry are a shame on it and our society. Hopefully, the Ashoka Fellows supported in Marty's name will help start the reversal of this culture. Established in 2012.

Svayam Krishi Endowment

"The soul of India lives in its villages."
-Mahatma Gandhi

India has 640,000 villages, which saw three revolutions since the 1970s: rice and wheat, milk and poultry. As a result, India is number one in milk production and among the top five in poultry. Smart village revolution can be next in providing holistic and integrated development.

Svayam Krishi Endowment was created to support social entrepreneurs and changemakers to build models for sustainable villages and self-reliance among villagers and to spread the models across villages in India. Sustainability means that villagers are able to meet their human potential and flourish within the village on a long-term basis rather than needing to migrate to cities for sustenance. Self-reliance means that families and individuals within the village are able to meet their needs without external assistance. The Endowment meets these objectives: (1) through the election and support of Ashoka Fellows whose work strongly supports these objectives and who will bring significant pattern change across India, and/or (2) through enabling young people in the villages to play important roles contributing to these same objectives, first (a) by helping them to dream their dream, build their team, and change their world for the better, and second (b) by enabling them to be role models and to provide active and broad-impact self-reliance leadership.

Dr. Ratnam Chitturi has taken this initiative and is helping many others to join and contribute to this Endowment to bring a sustained benefit to rural India.

The W. Arthur Lewis Ashoka Fellowship

Given to honor Professor Lewis's remarkably broad contributions to our understanding of development and of key areas of the world. Established in 1986. Unrestricted.

The Mack Lipkin Sr. Memorial Endowment

In memory of Dr. Mack Lipkin, a much loved friend and doctor who was also a leader of the medical profession and a founding friend to Ashoka. Dedicated to innovations in the effectiveness and humane quality of health care. Established in 1991.

The Jan Schmidt Marmor Endowment

Jan Marmor was a wise counselor to her family, friends, and patients. She was a fine poet and artist. She was a close friend to Ashoka from its launch. With commitment and love she built a family that believed that "no good idea should go unexpressed—or unheard." Established 2003.

The Francisco "Chico" Mendes Endowment

In memory of Chico Mendes, a friend and early Ashoka Fellow. Chico created an approach to grassroots organizing in the Amazon basin that Gandhi would have recognized but that was adapted to his own, very different, environment. Chico, like Gandhi, was killed pursuing peaceful change. The preferred uses of the funds are grassroots work and environmental issues, though the endowment carries no restrictions. Established in 1988.

The Helen Meresman Fellowship

In memory of Helen Meresman, the personification of breaking boundaries with determination, grace, and charm. The Helen Meresman Fellowship was established by Roger Barnett in 1997. Unrestricted.

The Jawaharlal Nehru Endowment

As the first prime minister in India, Jawaharlal Nehru was far more than a great national leader: He helped build a global community; he was a democrat; he was a historian; and he used his reflective power to hold himself to a high ethical standard. Unrestricted. Established in 2003.

The Nguyen-Phuong Family Endowment

Dedicated to supporting social entrepreneurs who operate in emerging markets; a permanent symbol of the family's keen commitment to social services in the developing world. Established 2014.

The Jacob H. Oxman Memorial Fund

In memory of Dr. Jacob H. Oxman, a devoted husband and father, and a kind, caring, generous, and principled man. This endowment is used to support an Ashoka Fellow. Any additional funds can be used either to support another Fellow or to cover operating costs. Established in 1986. Unrestricted.

Diane Pierce Phillips Ashoka Fellowship Endowment

Diane Pierce Phillips led an exemplary life of spiritual integrity and servant leadership as a U.S. Peace Corps volunteer, wife and mother, registered nurse, hospice volunteer, minister of the United Church of Christ (Congregational), and spiritual director. Established in 2003. Unrestricted.

The Eiler Ravnholt Ashoka Endowment

In memory of Eiler Ravnholt, a friend and role model to the founder of Ashoka, a man of values and hard work. He was a dedicated public servant and active citizen, generous with his time, voice and heart. He was a lover of history and defender of our collective responsibility to assist those in need—his own life was shaped by the Great Depression, World War II and the GI bill. Eiler was a fervent and loyal supporter to the vision of Ashoka throughout its existence: He will be missed by the entire Ashoka community. Established in 2012 and devoted to social justice.

The Daniel Saks Ashoka Fellowship

In memory of Dan Saks who, had he lived longer, would have changed U.S. employment policies even more profoundly than he already had. Dan was also one of Ashoka's earliest creators, beginning in 1963. This fellowship is focused on creating work opportunities for the poor or otherwise disadvantaged. Established in 1986.

The Morton Sand Memorial Endowment

Mort Sand, long a highly successful business entrepreneur, turned his energy and creativity to solving society's ills over his last decades. He helped build Ashoka's Entrepreneur-to-Entrepreneur program, created business opportunities for Brazil's street girls through three Fellows there, and was key to the launch of the Ashoka U.S.A./Canada program. The Mort Sand Endowment will be used in the U.S.A./Canada. Although it is unrestricted, the Endowment will give priority to enabling disadvantaged young people through opportunities in business. Established in 2002.

The Ibrahim Sobhan Endowment

In memory of Muhammed Ibrahim Sobhan, the first Ashoka Fellow in Bangladesh. He launched the innovative Association for School Based Education (ASBE) to improve rural primary education for Bangladeshi children attending government, non-government and community schools. Enrollment increased by 40%.

The Richard H. Ullman Endowment

Dick Ullman cared deeply about others—from the wellbeing of the world (reflected in his scholarly and journalistic work in the difficult field of international relations) to that of his students (who repeatedly rated him the best professor). As a young professor in the 1960s, he encouraged one of his undergraduate students in the early thinking that eventually led to Ashoka. Over the ensuing decades he was always with Ashoka—sharing ideas, opening doors, and serving on the North America Council.

Why was Ashoka such a close fit for Dick? One reason was that he believed in and helped develop young people of values. This belief—plus, in the words of his students, his "combination of rigor and candor," his "dry wit," and his "genuine kindness"—changed many lives and, as a result, many important foreign policy decisions. He intuitively knew why the Ashoka Fellows are so powerful, and he recognized the importance of supporting them.

These qualities also allowed him to change the country's course more directly. In addition to teaching at Princeton University for 35 years, he headed the 1980s Project of the Council on Foreign Relations, helped lead *Foreign Policy* magazine, and served on the Editorial Board of the *New York Times.*

The Father Eugene Watrin Endowment

In memory of Father Watrin, a remarkable educational founder and builder for over 50 years in Nepal and Ashoka's volunteer representative there for our first 15 years. His special commitment to the Ashoka vision and to all in its community, which he did so much to build, exemplifies why he had such a powerful impact on all around him. His greatest legacy is the model of how to live life well through service that is both highly important and performed with the modesty of true caring, love, and faith. For the support of Fellows working in Nepal. Established in 2004.

IN APPRECIATION: PHILIP B. HEYMANN

Credit: John Chapin

Philip B. Heymann
1932 – 2021

In the years before Ashoka's incorporation and launch, Phil helped with design issues, and he and Ann remained engaged co-venturers and close friends in all the years since then.

The Ashoka community will miss Phil deeply.

On the other hand, he will always be with Ashoka. The fit is very close, natural, and deep rooted.

Phil was an entrepreneur. For example, he launched and led Harvard's pioneering center devoted to thinking through how the people and institutions of the law should work. He pressed specifically to see how the field can and should best serve society and democracy.

This work has changed the framework through which lawyers, law schools, and the courts think about their roles.

Phil was not only an entrepreneur who changed his field's framework, his changes moved the field strongly, institutionally toward the good of all. He was, in other words, a social entrepreneur – very much, in this essence, a member of the Ashoka community.

His work to guide the profession was part of a larger but entirely consistent life – a life that always served principle and the good. Unwaveringly. And did so with a deep understanding of how things actually work – and how they might work.

He never let potential political advantage, discomfort, or faction cause him not to serve his best understanding of what was needed and the democratic process. He was a beacon of principle to others, and he had the power of trust.

Phil served four Presidents, chiefly in the Justice Department, where he was both an Associate (for Criminal Justice), and the Deputy Attorney General. He foresaw the risks to civil liberties from terrorist attacks and proposed defenses against overreaction – – before 9/11.

Earlier, he was one of Archibald Cox's chief deputies in the Watergate prosecution.

Once he was asked what he hoped to be remembered for. His response, "speaking truth to power."

All of us at Ashoka will remember him for those values and for being a friend one could always count on, no matter how difficult the circumstances.

We also will remember him for his breadth, for his special humor, for his being an entrepreneurial builder. The world, our community, and so many of us are stronger and wiser because of Phil Heymann.

Thank you, Phil.

ENDOWMENT, IN-KIND, AND PLANNED GIVING

Ashoka will, with deep appreciation, work with you regarding any form of special gift you wish to consider, including an endowment, the gift of securities, in-kind gifts, and planned giving.

Endowments

Ashoka now has well over 40 endowments, almost all to honor and/or create a lasting memorial for one or a few people who are dear to the donor(s). During 2022 and 2023, matching grants for new contributions or new endowments are very likely available. Please see the closely preceding section on endowments for more information and to appreciate the quality of the community represented by the endowments.

Gifts Beyond Money

Ashoka has the systems in place to reliably honor any conditions associated with non-monetary gifts, ranging from securities to physical assets. Our global staff and partners make this possible. For example, one donor gave us a complex of apartments in Poland, which required several years' work to manage through a complex transition. Itultimately had very significant impact on our work there.

Planned Giving

Ashoka is grateful for receiving many bequests and other forms of planned giving. It is experienced in working with donors and reliably following through on their wishes. Ashoka's work is forever. The need for change for the good is accelerating with the overall rate of change. Endowments, bequests, and other forms of planned giving make a tremendous difference in Ashoka's ability to continue being central to making this work possible and powerful.

Contacts

If you would like to discuss any of this with Ashoka, please contact **Bill Drayton** (wdrayton@ashoka.org) and/or **Gretchen Zucker** (gzucker@ashoka.org).

OPPORTUNITIES

Ashoka is working hard to support, accelerate and magnify the groundbreaking work of our ever-growing worldwide fellowship. We are fostering collaborations, opening doors to new partnerships, and building bridges across borders and to new sectors.

Volunteer changemakers can be found at every step of the way and during each phase of an Ashoka Fellow's trajectory. From as early as the nomination and selection process, through different levels of organizational growth, and with operational support virtually and on the ground, volunteers are crucial to maximizing scale and impact. They also lend their specific knowledge and skills to our global and country offices around the world, helping Ashoka staff and partners grow a variety of initiatives that underpin an "*everyone* a changemaker" world.

A partnership with LinkedIn has allowed us to reach a wide global audience of professionals who want to contribute their time and talents to help propel our work and that of our Fellows. Through the Ashoka-LinkedIn Volunteer Marketplace, we post current needs and provide a short application that goes directly to the staff or Fellow who posted on the Marketplace. In this way, we quickly and efficiently facilitate direct and fruitful connections between volunteers, Ashoka staff and Fellows. Almost every Ashoka office has opportunities.

Needs vary widely and change regularly. Some require assistance on-site and others can be met virtually. Recent volunteer opportunities have included:

- Developing business and strategic plans
- Creating communication and marketing strategies
- Building or improving websites and their contents
- Editing books and videos
- Filming documentaries of Fellows' work
- Helping young people and adults learn
- Project managing initiatives within a variety of organizations
- Conducting impact assessments
- Documenting conditions and needs in rural areas
- Researching markets and effective supply chains for rural areas
- Providing office, HR and branding support in Canada
- Managing crowdfunding campaigns
- Writing grants and researching potential donor support
- Writing journalistic reports for papers and newsletters
- Translating documents and transcribing Fellow interviews

There is no shortage of ways in which dedicated volunteers can join Ashoka's ecosystem of changemaking. In the words of Peggy Carr, a volunteer since 1987 who has managed Ashoka's virtual communications network from our global office:

"Working with Ashoka's Fellowship team has given me the opportunity to help Fellows in a direct and personal way. Whether researching a request for information or helping Fellows network with each other, the goal is always the same—forging strong links throughout the Ashoka community, of which I am happy to be a small part."

As an Ashoka volunteer, you can tap into your own changemaking power by using your unique talents to help scale the impact of Ashoka Fellows, Ashoka Young Changemakers, and others within the Ashoka network.

For more information, please visit"
www.ashoka.org/engage/contribute where you will find answers to frequently asked questions and a checklist for those volunteers traveling abroad. We are also available for any unanswered questions or unique ideas you may have for contributing to our work or expanding our partnerships at volunteers@ashoka.org.

Everyone a Changemaker!

YOU CAN SEE **THE FUTURE**

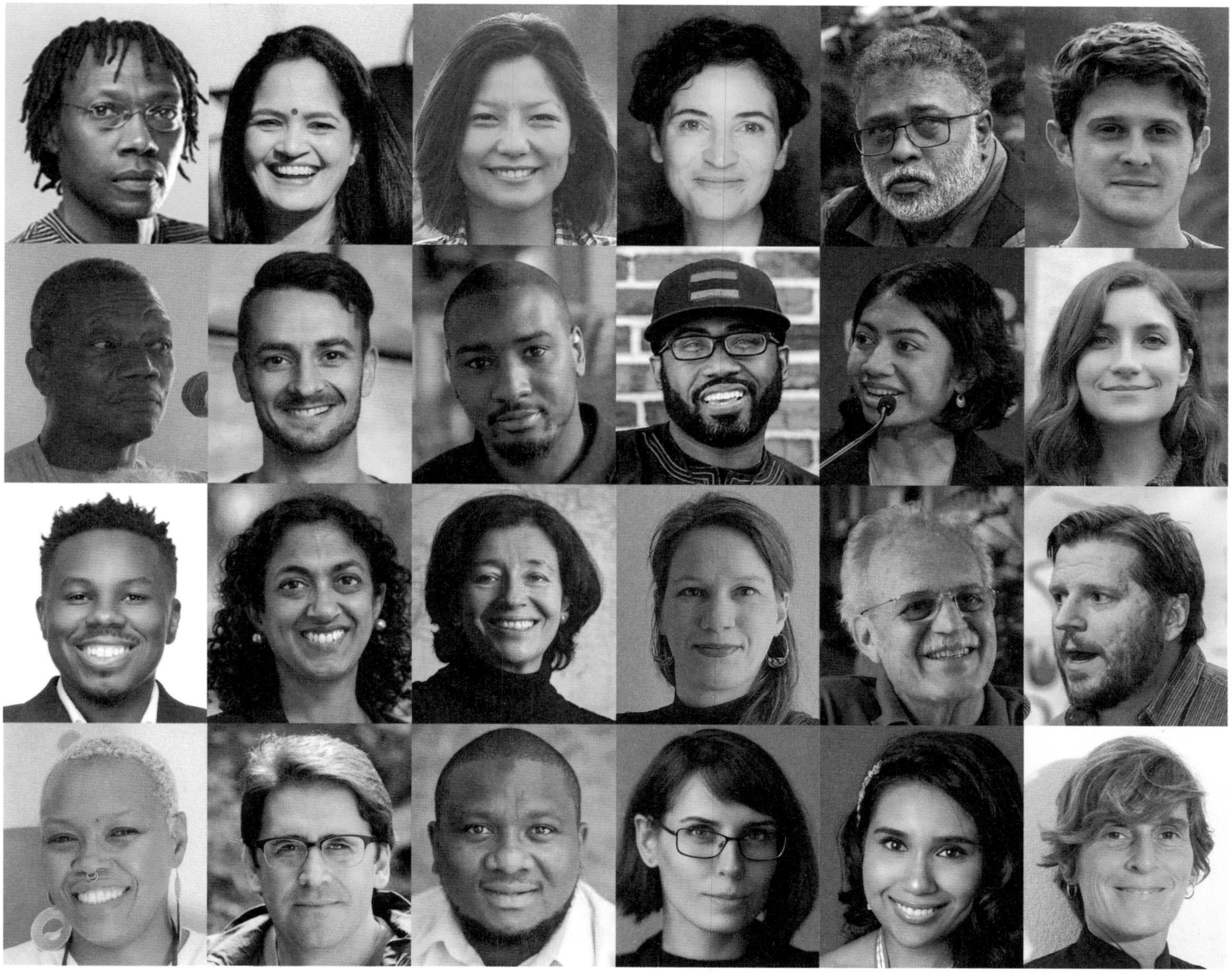

THIS BOOK IS AVAILABLE ONLINE

SCAN THE QR CODE
TO READ THE BOOK, LEADING SOCIAL ENTREPRENEURS
(PUBLISHED 2022)